SPORTS COACHING CULTURES

What do elite coaches think about coaching, players and their sport?

Why do they coach as they do?

Sports Coaching Cultures seeks to better comprehend the nature of effective coaching practice by examining the ways in which individual life and career experiences influence coaching styles and personal beliefs about effective coaching. Throughout the book, the emphasis is upon considering the *coach as a person*, and coaching practice as a complex social encounter.

Part one presents in-depth interviews with eight top-flight coaches from team and individual sports. The coaches reflect on their careers, on the value of coach education, the principles that underpin their practice, and their professional relationship with athletes. The eight coaches are Steve Harrison, Hope Powell and Graham Taylor from football, Ian McGeechan and Bob Dwyer from rugby, Di Bass from swimming, Lois Muir from netball, and Peter Stanley from athletics.

Part two presents four key themes in coaching theory, highlighting issues that emerge from a combined analysis of the eight coaches' stories:

- Coaching Pedagogy
- Coaches' Roles
- Coaches' Interactions
- Coaches' Power

Robyn Jones is a Senior Lecturer in Coach Education and Sports Development at the University of Bath, UK. **Kathleen Armour** is a Senior Lecturer in Physical Education and Sport Pedagogy at Loughborough University, UK. **Paul Potrac** is a Lecturer in Sports Coaching at the University of Otago, New Zealand.

D0144939

SPORTS COACHING CULTURES

FROM PRACTICE TO THEORY

Robyn Jones, Kathleen Armour
and Paul Potrac

Routledge
Taylor & Francis Group

LONDON AND NEW YORK

First published 2004 by Routledge
11 New Fetter Lane, London EC4P 4EE

Simultaneously published in the USA and Canada
by Routledge
29 West 35th Street, New York, NY 10001

Routledge is an imprint of the Taylor & Francis Group

© 2004 Robyn Jones, Kathleen Armour and Paul Potrac

Typeset in Bell Gothic by
Keystroke, Jacaranda Lodge, Wolverhampton
Printed and bound in Great Britain by TJ International Ltd, Padstow, Cornwall

British Library Cataloguing in Publication Data
A catalogue record for this book is available from the British Library

Library of Congress Cataloging in Publication Data
A catalog record for this book has been requested

ISBN 0–415–32851–9 (hbk)
ISBN 0–415–32852–7 (pbk)

▼ CONTENTS

▼ ACKNOWLEDGEMENTS

A book of this nature could not have been written without the efforts and support of many; indeed, a number of people throughout the world have contributed to its completion. We would like to thank Chris Cushion, Clive Brewer, Alex McKenzie and Laura Purdy, who assisted both in the interviewing process and the construction of some of the coaches' stories. Most importantly, we are indebted to the coaches who agreed to be interviewed. Their participation in this project enabled us to explore elite coaches' philosophies, practices and perceptions of 'good work' and to share them with a wider audience. We hope that we have done justice to their considerable talents.

CHAPTER 1

▼ INTRODUCTION

BACKGROUND AND PURPOSE

This book is about expert coaches and the connections between their lives, their careers, their personal philosophies on coaching and their highly individual recipes for good practice. These areas are explored, first, through the life stories of successful coaches in top-level team and individual sports and, second, in theme chapters that draw upon existing research to analyse key issues arising from the stories. Central to the book is an understanding that the coaches' stories are complex, messy, fragmented and endlessly fascinating, and that they demonstrate a need to understand the interconnections between coaches' lives and their professional practice. We argue that the coaches' stories cast doubt on the wisdom of viewing coaching, more simplistically, as a systematic, depersonalised set of standardised models and procedures; a trend which currently characterises many coach education programmes. Indeed, in bypassing the fundamental problematic and integrative elements of a coach's role, elements that have often been defined as 'intuition' or the 'art of coaching', it could be argued that previous work in the area has oversimplified a very complex process.

Perhaps similarly, a fundamental problem with coaching knowledge so far, and its accompanying 'models' approach, is that it has not taken the time to 'describe and interpret performers' "lifeworlds" ' (Strean, 1998, p. 338) before developing generalist explanations of and recommendations for 'good practice'. In order to avoid treating coaches as 'cardboard cut-outs' (Sparkes & Templin, 1992, p. 118) we must begin to embrace the personal dimensions of coaching, and the ways that coaches' previous career and life experiences shape both their views on coaching and the manner in which they set about it (Sparkes & Templin, 1992). Underpinning this book, therefore, is the belief that a professional coach is much more than a subject matter specialist and a systematic method applier (Squires, 1999), with the most important professional consideration being how the individual perceives the situation which, in turn, depends on such personal variables as values, attitudes and interests (Gouws, 1995).

The reason for telling coaches' stories in this book is to seek to demonstrate how lives, social and cultural contexts, personal experiences and philosophies, and professional practice are all interconnected in ways which challenge our traditional perceptions of the coaching process. Indeed, biographical accounts remain 'perhaps the most interesting (yet virtually untapped) potential area for performance-related description' (Strean, 1998, p. 337), particularly through their ability to highlight these connections and their effect on practice. We thus seek to paint accurate yet colourful portraits of a small group of top-level coaches to achieve what Strean (1998) describes as moving beyond the popular sports biography to 'rich accounts of excellent performers' experiences' (p. 337). The aim then, is to enable the reader to hear the coaches, understand them as individuals, relate their life stories to their philosophies on sport and coaching, and to 'see' why they coach as they do. In turn, these understandings are used to critically interrogate some key issues in coaching research and literature today. Thus, the coaches' life stories are 'contextualised and theorised within their broader social, psychological and historical contexts' (Strean, 1998, p. 337).

In borrowing from the work of Hellison (1995) in physical education, it is suggested that, while technical, tactical and physical content is important to effective coaching practice, the person of the coach is even more so. In articulating this point, Ayers (1989) contended that 'there is no clear line delineating the person and the teacher [coach]. Rather there is a seamless web between teaching [coaching] and being, between teacher [coach] and person. Teaching [coaching] is not simply what one does, it is who one is' (p. 54). Such a belief adds weight to Noddings' (1992) criticism of the developmental philosophy underpinning existing educational research and professional preparation programmes, which seemingly remain divorced from the messy reality of the pedagogical process, thus often giving an 'oddly inhuman account of this most human of jobs' (Connell, 1985, p. 4). In this respect, while 'what' and 'how' to coach are important factors, coach education, like teacher education, 'has made the error of supposing that method can be substituted for individuals' (Noddings, 1992, p. 92). In essence, 'it has removed the person from the process of knowing' (Martens, 1987, p. 29).

The argument presented here is that it is not only technical and tactical kinds of knowledge that lie at the heart of the instructional process in professional top-level sport but, also, 'the personal relationship between instructor [coach] and student [athlete], [which] develops over matters of content' (Cuban, 1993, p. 184). Consequently, in echoing the sentiments of Denton (1972) in education, it would appear necessary for future inquiry into expert coaching practice to expand upon the traditional focuses of 'what to coach' and 'how to coach' to more adequately examine the complex question of 'who is coaching'. In this way, as Martens (1987) states, we would be 'putting the person back into the study of people' (p. 41). Indeed, in seeking to understand coaches, that is, to gain real knowledge about them, we need to 'view each [coach] as a whole, as a unique being' (Martens, 1987, p. 49). Such an approach, we believe, can serve to shed greater light upon the individualities, complexities and diversities of effective coaching practice (Jones, 2000; Potrac, 2000).

STRUCTURE

This book is based on the critical analysis of the life stories of eight practising, top-level coaches, who currently operate at the very apex of their sport (the sample has won national championships, international championships, and, as coaches of national teams, world championships). The eight coaches are as follows: **Steve Harrison**, **Hope Powell** and **Graham Taylor** from football, **Ian McGeechan**, and **Bob Dwyer** from rugby, **Di Bass** from swimming, **Lois Muir** from netball and **Peter Stanley** from athletics. In many ways our coaches cover the field in terms of being involved in individual and team sports of both male and female athletes at the highest level. For the purposes of the book, they all participated in a series of interviews that were then crafted by us, as authors, into narratives. These narratives tell the stories of the coaches' lives, careers, personal philosophies on coaching and beliefs about good professional practice. The intention is to express the data in a way that will 'allow us to characterise the processes that experts use in their performances', thus helping us to 'gain a deeper understanding and description of complex interactions' (Strean, 1998, p. 336). Essentially, the coaches' stories are critical biographies that have two main functions: to represent the individual coach in as detailed and accurate a manner as possible; and to raise critical questions about that coach, about coaching and about the value and relevance of existing coaching research. These questions are then explored in detail in 'theme' chapters in the second section of the book, where the individual stories are located in the wider literature on coaching, and issues that resonate through the coaches' stories (albeit in different ways and different contexts) are critically examined. So, although each story is unique, we present them both for their uniqueness and their commonalities (Stake, 1995). Finally, in a concluding chapter, the interpreted findings are summarised and the potential of 'life-story' research into coaching, both in its practical application and its potential for further inquiry, is discussed.

WHO ARE THE COACHES?

Steve Harrison (Football)

Steve Harrison holds the highest coaching award available from the English Football Association (FA) and is presently employed as the first team coach at Middlesbrough Football Club, who compete in the FA Carling Premiership,

the highest division of professional football in England and Wales. Following successful initial spells as coach of the Watford Football Club youth and reserve teams, Steve was promoted to first team coach in 1985. Two years later, he followed his then Watford manager, Graham Taylor, to Aston Villa Football Club. In 1990, Steve moved again to coach at Millwall Football Club and it was at this time that the Football Association appointed him to the prestigious position of assistant coach to the English national team. In 1994, following a spell at Crystal Palace, he was appointed coach at Wolverhampton Wanderers Football Club. After reaching the first division promotion play-offs with 'Wolves', Steve joined Preston North End Football Club as first team coach in 1995. His three-year period at the club culminated in the winning of promotion from the third division. Following this success, Steve returned for a second spell at Aston Villa Football Club, where he coached the team to an FA Cup final appearance. In 2001, Steve moved to his current post at Middlesbrough.

Hope Powell (Football)

Hope Powell first played football for Millwall Lionesses (a leading London women's football club) at the age of eleven, before moving to Fulham and later Croydon Football Clubs. During her playing career, she won the women's FA Cup three times, including the league and cup double while captain of Croydon in 1996. She was awarded the first of her sixty-six international England caps while only sixteen, and ended up scoring thirty-five goals for her country. Hope's formative coaching experiences centred on her role as a Football Development Officer at Crystal Palace Football Club, time spent coaching in the USA and as a Community Sport Development Officer for Lewisham Council, South London. In June of 1998, Hope was appointed to her current post as the first ever full-time National Coach of the England women's team, becoming the youngest ever England coach and the first female to hold the position. Within it, Hope is responsible for the senior, under-18 and under-16 national women's teams. Since her appointment, she has taken the under-18s to the quarter finals of the UEFA Championships and the senior team to qualification for UEFA EURO 2001 competition.

Graham Taylor (Football)

Graham Taylor is recognised as one of English football's most distinguished coaches. At just twenty-three, he became the youngest coach ever to obtain the highest coaching award offered by the English Football Association. Three years later, while still a player, he was appointed to the prestigious position of Staff Coach for the Football Association. In 1972, he became head coach at Lincoln City Football Club, whom he soon led to the fourth division championship title with a record number of points. In 1978, he moved to coach Watford Football Club and guided it from the then fourth to the first division, which is now known as the FA Carling Premiership, to enjoy its highest ever league placing with the team finishing as runner-up in 1983. Graham then joined Aston Villa Football Club, whom he led to promotion to the then first division in 1988 and to yet another runner-up spot in that division in 1990. After a spell as head coach to the England national team, which saw them qualify for the European Championships in 1992, Graham returned to club football. He briefly coached at Wolverhampton before rejoining Watford and proceeded once more to lead the club to promotion to the FA Carling Premiership. Following a brief flirtation with retirement, Graham recently returned to top-level coaching at yet another of his former clubs, Aston Villa, where he currently resides. Between 1972 and 2001 Graham received a record twenty-nine prestigious 'manager of the month' awards, and has become only the third coach in the history of English soccer to preside over 1,000 professional matches.

Bob Dwyer (Rugby)

Bob's initial coaching appointment in senior Australian club rugby union was the unplanned consequence of the retirement of his club coach in 1976. During his first season as coach, he guided the Randwick club to the runners-up position in the Sydney Premiership, followed by four consecutive championship wins. As a consequence of this success, he was appointed Australian national team coach in February 1982. After two years, Bob was deposed by Alan Jones, only to win the position back again in February 1988. In 1991, he reached the pinnacle of the profession within the sport, as his Australian Wallaby team were crowned world champions after beating England at Twickenham in the Rugby World Cup final. In 1996, Bob moved to England to become Director of Rugby at Leicester Tigers, a leading English rugby union club. Although he guided them to victory in the Pilkington Cup (the premier domestic cup competition), and to the final of the 1996 European Cup, he left Leicester in the 1997–1998 season, following a dispute. After a brief spell with the 'The Barbarians', he returned to top-level English club rugby when, in the summer of 1998, he became the Director of Rugby at Bristol Rugby Club. In 2000, he returned to his native New South Wales where he remains in his current capacity as state coach to the New South Wales Warratahs in the Super 12, the world's premier club rugby competition.

Ian McGeechan (Rugby)

Ian McGeechan played international rugby both for Scotland and the British Lions, and began his coaching career at Headingly Rugby Club in Yorkshire. After three years as Headingly coach, allied to various coaching roles within the Scottish regional set-up, he was asked to coach the Scotland under-21 team. He was soon promoted to be assistant national coach and then in 1985 to Scotland head coach, a position that he held for nine years. In 1994, with the onset of professionalism in the sport, Ian accepted a new challenge, moving south to become the Director of Rugby at Northampton Saints in the English Allied Dunbar Premier League. Whilst at Franklin Gardens, the club developed on a national scale, culminating in finishing as runner-up in the League and a first ever European Cup place during the 1998–99 season. During this time, Ian was also appointed coach of the British Lions, a combined four-yearly touring side from Great Britain and Ireland. In 1989, he led the Lions to a series victory against Australia. Although the Lions lost a close encounter in New Zealand in 1993, they returned to beat the then world champion South Africans against all expectations in 1997. Towards the end of 1999 however, the lure of the Scottish national coaching position again proved too strong, as he left Northampton to return to his former role in Scotland where he currently resides.

Di Bass (Swimming)

Di Bass holds the ASA Coach certificate and has been coaching swimming for over twenty years. After a successful swimming career she moved away from the sport until she was asked by a new swimming club to help them out. In 1979 she went to Loughborough University as a mature student and undertook a degree in PE, Sports Science and Recreation Management. On finishing, she gradually became more involved with coaching the university swimmers, at times assisting with the top squad as well as coaching her own. Until recently, Di also coached the local swimming club and saw it increase its success at league and county levels. Di has, for some time, had an interest in disability sport, and in 1998 she became a coach to the GB Disability Swim Team. In this capacity, she accompanies the team to numerous training camps and competitions. In 2000, three of her swimmers were part of the very successful British Paralympic Swimming Team in Sydney where they achieved a gold, silver and bronze medal in their individual events.

Lois Muir (Netball)

At the tail end of a successful international playing career in both basketball and netball for New Zealand, Lois Muir began coaching. Having been vice-captain of the Silver Ferns (the New Zealand netball team), she was first invited to become a selector and then a coach to a New Zealand netball age-grade team on a tour of the South Pacific Islands in 1972. A year later, she became the coach of the national under-24 side and toured successfully in both Australia and the Pacific Islands. The following year she was appointed coach to the New Zealand senior side, a position she held until 1988. Following several series victories, most notably in Australia in 1986 against the Australians, the Silver Ferns were crowned joint World Champions with Trinidad and Tobago in 1979 and World Champions in 1987, which proved to be the climactic moment of Lois' coaching career. From 1988 to 1995 she became the national coaching director for Netball New Zealand and was inducted into the New Zealand Sports Hall of Fame in 1993. She is currently the Chairperson of the Boards of the New Zealand Academy of Sport (South Island) and Netball Otago. After a spell in retirement, Lois returned to coach the Wellington Capital Shakers and finally her current team, the Otago Rebels, in the New Zealand national netball league. She is generally regarded as the doyenne of New Zealand netball coaching.

Peter Stanley (Athletics)

Since gaining his Assistant Club Coach award at Elswick Harriers in 1990, Peter Stanley rapidly rose up the coaching ranks within British Athletics to gain Senior Club Coach status in both long and triple jumps five years later. During that time he became an accredited coach education facilitator and tutor, Team Manager for the North Eastern Counties Athletic team and the Jumps Coach for the Northern Regional Athletic Team. In many ways his greatest accomplishments have resulted from his partnership with the triple jumper Jonathan Edwards, for whom he became technical coach in 1994. In this respect, he helped guide Edwards to become World Record Holder, World Champion in Gothenburg in 1995, Olympic silver medallist in Atlanta in 1996, Olympic gold medallist in Sydney in 2000 and Word Champion again in Edmonton in 2001. In 2000, Peter was honoured by the British Olympic Association for his services to athletics, while a year later he was similarly awarded a Services to Sport medal by Sport England. He continues to coach many county, regional and national athletes at various ages, whilst being engaged in a host of athletics coach education programmes both nationally and internationally.

INTERVIEW FRAMEWORK AND PRESENTATION OF THE COACHES' STORIES

In-depth interviews were conducted with each of the eight coaches. The interviews were taped and transcribed verbatim for later analysis. The main purpose of the interviews was to examine the coaches' attitudes, opinions, beliefs and values in respect of their coaching in particular, and coaching effectiveness in general. Following informal introductory background queries, open-ended questions were utilised to explore the respondent coaches' perceptions about experiential, contextual and situational factors that influenced and impinged upon their practice. The interviews also probed how the coaches dealt with and used these forces to produce what they considered to be an effective learning environment for their athletes and players. Each interview covered the following areas in a flexible and conversational format:

- initial involvement in the sport and the developing desire to coach;
- significant mentors and experiences, both positive and negative;
- their preferred style of delivery;
- their knowledge sources and views of professional preparation programmes;
- the environment and climate they try to create;
- the situational factors and other constraints that affect their practice; and
- what, in essence, they are trying to achieve when they coach.

In this way, an attempt was made to obtain a deep understanding of the complex nature of dynamic coaching processes, in addition to providing an awareness of the contexts in which coaches act, and the influence that these contexts have on their instructional behaviour.

The interviews were 'reflexive' (Hammersley & Atkinson, 1983) in nature, in that each respondent was invited to explore certain themes with the interviewer (Sparkes & Templin, 1992). In this way, the coaches' perspectives remained at the heart of the interviews, with their reasons, meanings and interpretations for involving themselves in certain coaching behaviours being central. Such a perspective is of 'great importance in any attempt to explain why people act in certain ways rather than others' (Sparkes & Templin, 1992, p. 121). Consequently, although a topic guide was used to keep the interviews broadly on-track with the underlying objectives, the questions asked and the order in which they were asked flowed from the coaches' replies. In this way, they became 'conversational', with the coaches having the freedom to initiate questions and elaborate answers (Wilson, 1996). Our principal role as interviewers, therefore, was that of monitoring what was emerging and of guiding the coaches within topics that appeared interesting and important to them.

In addition to utilising the interviews as a resource to gather information from the coaches, it was also decided to use them as a topic in and of themselves. In this way, they were used as opportunities to conduct direct observations of the coaches (Seale, 1998). Such an approach was considered very appropriate to penetrate the complex and apparently intuitive world of coaches, as it demanded that we looked 'closely at the way in which they chose and used particular words or phrases to generate ideas or representations of their social world' (Seale, 1998, p. 204). By utilising such an approach, the data from the coaches' interviews could be understood as inevitably 'displaying and defending narratives of competent self-identity' (Seale, 1998, p. 215). Our job as researchers and authors was not merely to accept these self-portraits *per se*, but to generate meanings and insights from them. Thus, a conscious attempt was made to move beyond the interview transcripts into interpretations of what the coaches said. In essence, we have tried to 'step in the space' where we can understand something about the nature of the coaches who feature in this book, and how they justified their practice to us and themselves (Ely *et al.*, 1997).

Through expressing the interviews in narrative form, we have shaped or sculpted the data through our understandings of them in an attempt to 'find the subtle, blurred and often important meanings' that are their essence (Ely, *et al.*, 1997). Ely *et al.* (1997) liken it to the pearl encased in an oyster shell; the jewel being not so obvious at first. In many ways, then, we have used the method to 'tell about a culture through characters' (Richardson, 2000, p. 6), thus relating the personal to the cultural. Our aim here is not to search for universal truths with regard to coaching or to generalise these accounts into what all coaches should do, but to ensure that the reader can understand these coaches and their philosophies, and then generalise them into the context of their own practice and wider lives (Armour & Jones, 1998). Furthermore, through the use of narrative to portray the coaches, we have tried to allow our readers the opportunity to experience along with us each coach's unfolding story, not from a neutral periphery but vicariously from within. In essence, we have tried to bring to life the experiences, perceptions and stories of top coaches. Undoubtedly, these coaches have led 'storied lives' and have stories worth telling (Clandinin & Connelly, 1994). Finally, as we crafted the narratives, we were aware of Richardson's (2000) criteria for such work: 'does this piece contribute to our understanding of social life? Is the text not boring? Does it affect me emotionally and/or intellectually? Does it generate new questions in me, or move me to action? Does it seem "true" and "real"?' (pp. 15–16). If we have successfully met some of these criteria, then the first section of this book, the coaches' stories, will have fulfilled a useful purpose.

THE THEME CHAPTERS

The aim of the second section of the book, the theme chapters, is to develop further insights by analysing the coaches' stories collectively and to critically examine the issues that arise from them in the context of some key bodies of literature. Each chapter begins with a list of Key Issues, which are then addressed in specific sections. The main aim is to link theory and practice in the context of the coaches' stories, and to illustrate the multifaceted and interconnected nature of coaching as a profession. The specific areas addressed within the chapters are coaching pedagogy (Chapter 10), coaches' roles (Chapter 11), coaches' interactions (Chapter 12) and coaches' power (Chapter 13). Why these particular areas? It would be easy to say that they 'emerged' from the stories, but that is not quite accurate. Rather, it is the case that these stories could be analysed in so many ways that inevitably selection was required, thus the chapters reflect what we, as authors, consider to be important issues. We accept that others could read the stories differently and hence find other issues.

In the field of education, the term 'pedagogy' is used to describe the complex interactions that characterise teaching and learning processes. It is a useful, if somewhat ambiguous, concept and some would claim that it has merely become fashionable without offering clarity. Nonetheless, recent definitions of pedagogy are helpful when applied to the coaching process and can provide some interesting insights into a collective analysis of the coaches' stories. Chapter 10, therefore, considers the concept of pedagogy in theory and identifies four dimensions of the concept that can be used as lenses through which to view the stories. In the final section, the notion of a 'pedagogy for learning' in coaching is mooted and implications for coach professional development are discussed.

Chapter 11 addresses why the coaches interviewed in this book coach as they do, in terms of the roles they fulfil. The key questions and issues explored here include the following: What are the structural constraints on coaches' behaviours? How much do coaches choose their own behavioural pathways? How do coaches use their role? And how do they express themselves within their role? More specifically, following an introductory analysis of research regarding social roles, an examination is undertaken of the structural constraints upon the coaches interviewed in terms of the expectations of society, athletes and self on their coaching styles. The intention here is to examine the potential of elite coaches to obey, resist or use such demands in highly inventive ways. Finally, the concepts of 'strong evaluation', 'role distance' and 'self in role' are examined as useful analytical pegs that go some way towards explaining the dynamism and enthusiasm emitted by the coaches interviewed as a reflection of what Shaw (1981) has termed 'charismatic leadership'.

Chapter 12 explores coaches' interactions, principally with their athletes and players. Goffman's (1959) work on interaction provides the theoretical backdrop for the analysis within this chapter, with the concept of the 'presentation of the self' being of particular significance. Key issues examined in this respect include the relevance of Goffman's work to coaching as a framework for analysis, the strategies of impression management, the concept of possessing different coaching 'faces', and the need for situational flexibility. It is contended that through such concepts as impression management, attempts are made by coaches to present 'idealised' versions of themselves in order to maximise stated coaching goals. The chapter therefore investigates how the coaches included in this book present themselves to their athletes and why.

Chapter 13 investigates coaches' power from the basis of the refined and extended version (Raven, 1965; 1992) of French and Raven's (1959) classic typology of power. Following a definitional discussion about exactly what is meant by the 'power' of the coach, an exploration of the differing forms and varieties of power as defined by Raven (1992) is undertaken. These include those of legitimate, expert, informational, referent, reward and coercive power. Each type is examined within the coaching context, as are the potential consequences of their use, and the interaction between them. Furthermore, questions about the power of the athletes over the coach within a framework of 'empowering athletes' are debated. Finally, Chapter 14 comprises the conclusion that draws together the divergent chapters, relating them to the interconnections between coaches' lives and their professional practice. Additionally, the value of the life story/critical biography investigative genre to coaching research is discussed, and suggestions are made for some new ways in which the method could be used to inform coach education and the development of professional practice.

CHAPTER 2

▼ **STEVE HARRISON**

INTRODUCTION

Steve Harrison could be described as a 'players' coach'. He believes that a coach must respect players, value them, and support them as individuals. Driven by this philosophy, Steve strives to develop positive working relationships in his coaching sessions. His ultimate goal is to develop confident, secure players who are able to think independently and express themselves creatively. As he puts it: 'You need to treat people like adults, that's the bottom line; the days of scrapping with players are over.' Steve's coaching philosophy permeates all aspects of his work and he is wholly committed to the approach he takes.

BECOMING A COACH

Steve stumbled into coaching in more ways than one. A serious knee injury forced his early retirement from the professional game as a player. However, rather than cursing his luck on what was obviously a traumatic experience, Steve actively sought an opportunity within the club to become a coach, and he took up the new challenge with enthusiasm and determination:

> I'd signed a two-year contract at Charlton, after being given a 'free' by Watford but after the first six months of it I was injured really, my knee

wasn't right. Alan Mullary was the manager and he was going to bring in another coach, a reserve coach, and I said to him 'look I know I haven't done the business for you playing-wise and you've given me a right good contract, let me take the lads in the afternoon and let me take the midweek side while you're advertising for a reserve coach'. So he said okay. We won the midweek league and it was really good driving the minibus down to places like Exeter and places like that. So, come the end of that season, Graham Taylor at Watford asked would I like to come back as youth coach by which time I had a real feel for coaching. But I had never thought about it before that really. I just wanted to play.

Following a spell as youth coach at Watford, Steve was appointed coach of the first team. Two years later, he moved with Graham Taylor to become first-team coach at Aston Villa before, a further eighteen months on, returning to his original club as manager. It was during this time that he was appointed to a part-time coaching position with the England national team. However, Steve found the role of manager to be very different from that of coach, and he describes it as an unsuccessful and stressful period in his life. In particular, he found the administrative responsibilities of management to be irksome, and he resented the loss of personal contact with players. In a reference to the distinction between 'management' and 'workers' he explained: 'I didn't like not being on a level with the players I think. I've realised, as I realised then, that I'm a blue-collar worker not a white-collar worker. I hated the distance between me and the players.'

Consequently, Steve resigned and returned to coaching at Millwall Football Club, before settling as first team coach at Crystal Palace. This proved to be a happy and rewarding time for Steve, and he remained at the club for almost three years. In particular, he comments that he appreciated the opportunity to work with, and learn from, the then manager, Steve Coppell, a respected mentor. On the move again, Steve linked up once more with Graham Taylor at Wolverhampton Wanderers Football Club and experienced some success – albeit modest – before, via a period at Preston North End, returning to Aston Villa and finally moving on to Middlesbrough where he is currently the first team coach. As he puts it: 'Yeah, I've been around the houses a little bit really. That's how it's worked out; I've been down South, in the Midlands and up North!' What becomes clear as Steve's tale unfolds is that he has enjoyed those situations where he has been able to work closely with his players and where he has been able to learn and develop his coaching skills.

RELATING TO PLAYERS

At the core of Steve's coaching philosophy is the belief that in order to succeed, a coach needs be able to relate to players both as footballers and, more importantly, as individuals. Indeed, Steve places great store in trying to see things from the players' viewpoint, and in nurturing positive working relationships with them. It is a theme that recurs throughout Steve's story:

They [players] respond to someone who is on their wavelength. It's all about dealing with individual players. It's better to change something that's not working than give the player a bollocking because you want a certain drill to work. Pull yourself away and think how you would respond. I've been stood on a pitch with some fella saying 'that's fuckin' useless, we're back in this afternoon'. No respect. You'd do it but you'd have no respect for that coach. I think I've recognised that you've got to be on a level with the players to get a response at the coaching level. I've got to be seen to be on a par with them. I've got to be seen to be understanding their problems and be on their wavelength. If I'm on their wavelength, I'll be all right. If not, then things get harder and harder.

Steve's belief in the need to treat players as individuals is central to his coaching philosophy. He believes he should individualise feedback to players, and that it is incumbent upon him to be aware of them as different people with particular needs and traits. Hence, he sees a great deal more to coaching than training and technique; a dimension he identifies as 'psychology':

There's a lot of psychology in the game. You've got to gee some players up, others you've got to bring down because they're too fired up. Others you've got to put your arm round and give them confidence. Then there are other players that you've got to say 'hey! I don't think you're up for it today bud'. It's all psychology when you are dealing with the players. If you tell a player off in front of the other lads then you've lost him. If you 'wound' him then he won't forget it. Yeah he'll do stuff, but you'll get no receptiveness.

In addition, and linking closely with his belief in respect and individuality, Steve believes it is important to give players the confidence to make mistakes in front of him, secure in the knowledge that they will not be humiliated for so doing:

When you work with players on things that you feel they need to improve on you've got to make them comfortable to work and you can't do that sometimes in the group with everyone else. You've got to bring them away from the group, and make them work with a couple of the young apprentices so things work. So you don't give them false hope, but you give them a positive environment in which they think 'yes, things can be put right no problem'. So yes, it's very important that the player is relaxed enough to make mistakes in front of you. Like, for instance, David over there [a player] wasn't relaxed enough to make mistakes in front of me. He used to get bloody wounded. But if a player can say 'look Steve, I keep getting this wrong what am I doing?', then I can say 'look it's probably this or that and this is why'. If a player cannot say this, then there is no point doing the work because there is a barrier. It's very important that the player is willing to do it wrong in front of you in order for both of you to put it right.

Perhaps the most interesting aspect of this element of Steve's story is that, as a coach, he has to mention it at all. It might be expected that one of the key roles of a coach is to help players correct their mistakes, and yet Steve seems to hint at a culture of football and football coaching that makes it difficult for players to work collaboratively with coaches. It is a theme that will be pursued in later chapters.

A POSITIVE COACHING ENVIRONMENT

In keeping with his philosophy on players, Steve believes that developing and maintaining a positive climate in training sessions is vital for success. Thus, any corrective feedback to players must be accompanied by a positive input. This links back to his personal experience as a player: 'When I was a player, I always responded to someone who told me positive things.' At the same time, Steve is keen to point out that the coaching feedback must be credible: 'Not bullshit, you soon sort that out.' Furthermore, he prefers to take players privately to one side in order to discuss performance, particularly senior players. He is very much against the practice of berating poor performance in front of the whole group, considering this to be wholly unproductive. Rather he aims to 'make people comfortable to receive your advice'. Steve views this approach as an investment in his players, because he is aware of the potential damage that can be done to a relationship by bawling-out a player in public. As he comments: 'That's no good, you've got to get on; anyway you're going to need him tomorrow!' He believes that if problems are sorted out within a supportive framework, players are more likely to respect the advice and the coach, and be more willing to 'play' for him and, in his own words: 'believe in me and what we're trying to do'. At heart, Steve tries to encourage all players to work together, and with him, in a mutually supportive and reinforcing atmosphere:

> Your success and failure depends on everyone pointing in the same direction. If you're all not pointing in the same direction then you ain't going to be successful. But if you've got a blend of players that all believe in what you are doing then you don't need the best players. You will succeed.

LEARNING TO BE A COACH

Tracing Steve's life experiences in coaching, it is relatively easy to identify the key influences upon his personal coaching philosophy. He has been keen throughout his career to learn from others and he would argue that he is continuing to learn; even learning how not to do things has been useful. In addition, he has engaged in much trial and error along the way:

> I think you glean something from everybody. People say you learn from different people and you learn from copying what they do. If you see something going on and think 'I like that but I don't like that' then fine

14

because that is how I gleaned information and drills and stuff like that off other people. It's a copying thing. Plus the fact you learn as you go along. So you learn by experience. So yes, what I do has come from watching people I admire and people I don't admire a lot of times, but with a variation on the theme . . . you add variations of your own; I think that is how people learn. I'm going to do it this way, and you can only do that by practising and having a bit of a go at it really. Again, don't think you get it right all the time. I've learnt by mistakes and I still don't get it right all the time now. You're still learning.

In terms of coaching knowledge, Steve considers an intimate knowledge of the game vital for a top-level coach if he or she is to succeed but, of even greater importance, is how that knowledge is transmitted to players. In short, the manner and the timing of the message are all important:

So, knowledge of the game is important but it is when and how you put it over. If you start flooding a player's brain with knowledge they come off the field like that [zombie impersonation]. They've had four ecstasy tablets!! They're just pumped full of what you think they need to know. Then again from experience, again when I was a player, I used to respond to someone making two or three points to me but if someone wanted to make ten points to me in a session that lasted two and a half hours I'd start taking the piss, and I think the players would now. So I think it's knowledge of the game and the confidence that you've got knowledge of the game. You know when it's the time not to say something, it might be right what you have to say but it might be the wrong timing to say it, that's important I think . . . It's the how and when you express the knowledge that is most important.

This again reflects Steve's fundamental belief in individualising coaching input to meet the needs of both the situation and the particular player. Indeed, the links between Steve the coach and Steve the person begin to become ever clearer. For example, Steve's emphasis upon the need for positive delivery stems from his belief in establishing good relationships with the players and treating them in a manner which they can respect; as he said: 'You need to treat people like adults, that's the bottom line; the days of scrapping with players are over.'

COACH CERTIFICATION

Taking into account Steve's very personal and multidimensional view of coaching, it is unsurprising to find that he considers official coach certification programmes to be somewhat variable in quality and suitability. For example, he considers that he has gained useful information from some of his qualifications, but nothing in any great depth: 'Very useful in terms of the organisation of pitch sizes . . . and your general organisation of things such as bibs and cones. In the main,

organisation, that is what I learnt.' He gained his full FA coaching badge some years ago (until recently the highest coaching qualification in English soccer) and feels that, although acknowledging that things have changed in recent years, his experience was of a course with limited practical value:

> What I didn't learn on the Full Badge, which they have addressed now, is different styles of play. That is why in this country over the past fifteen years we've had robotic coaches being churned out playing a robotic way of football. Direct, because that is what we were taught at Lilleshall (the FA National Centre of Excellence) on the Full Badge course. A robotic, direct way of playing. So, after two weeks at Lilleshall, all the coaches came out knowing and doing the same things because that is what you passed at. I didn't agree with it. So you ended up with schoolboy teams playing it, amateur teams, professional teams and semi-professional teams all playing the four-four-two direct game. Now for me that is wrong.

Fundamentally, Steve is very critical of what he perceived to be the narrow mindedness of the British football fraternity as reflected in the coaching courses when he took them, which involved an apparent refusal to innovate and adopt new ideas from abroad: 'There really wasn't much open-mindedness on the old Full Badge course.' Such an attitude, he believes, was based on arrogance: 'This is how we do it because we're England, we're the best. That's what we do, follow tradition, and it was wrong.' However, the recent influx of top foreign players and coaches into the British game, and the success they have achieved, has given Steve great optimism that the game in England is now evolving, improving, and converging with that of the more sophisticated continental European model:

> We are changing now and just in time, otherwise we would have lost a lot of people. We're just starting to realise that what has been happening isn't right. I went to watch Portugal under-18s play England under-18s not too long ago, we beat them two-one in the last minute. We were stronger, fitter and bigger than them. We were better organised as a team but technically we were nowhere near them. I'd love to see an exchange of coaches a bit more, to find out what they do with their boys, what they work at, so we can develop our boys technically a bit more. We're a bit pigeon holed in this country. You ask a kid [in England] where they play and they'll say 'sweeper', ask a kid in Holland and he'll say 'I play football.'

What seems clear is that coach certification for Steve has been too functional and too narrow, although he acknowledges that this situation has improved considerably since the introduction of the new UEFA (European-wide) certification structure. Nevertheless, as with all the other strands of Steve's story, he appears to be yearning for a freedom of expression and a particular football culture that is hard to find in the British game. This may explain why he found the role of manager so stressful, and why he revels in the comparative freedom of being a coach.

AND WHAT OF THE PLAYERS?

Although Steve seems to be battling against what he perceives as the rigidity of the football structure in this country, he reports few problems in getting players to respond to his style of coaching. He believes that players enjoy his style because they respond to being respected and because they like to have a structured framework comprising skill tasks and game-related exercises where they must work hard:

> As you saw today it was continuous football, starting up small and progressing, so they get a lot of enjoyment and hard work out of it . . . through the week I like to think that the players enjoy the training, appreciate it, see the purpose of it and gain a lot of know-how and knowledge from that. And if I'm doing that, I'm enjoying it too.

At the core of this strategy lies Steve's unshakeable belief in the importance of concise instruction. He believes instruction has to be specific, to the point and kept simple; here again reflecting coaching behaviours that he appreciated and understood as a player. Instruction also has to be tailored to the situation and to the individual in order to be effective: 'So yeah instruction is very important, but at the right time, don't force it, let it evolve. I mean you can manufacture it, but if you force it it's false.' And underlying all that is Steve's perception that this is what the players expect and want from him as a coach: 'Players like to be worked. If you don't tell them to come in then they won't, but players generally like to be worked. They like to be in and doing quality work.' This explains his desire to give the impression that he is always in control of coaching situations, even when occurrences such as injuries and the weather conspire against his planned coaching intentions. In many ways it is a complex role that Steve plays; one that he believes his players expect of him, that they respect and that they will enjoy:

> So you have to think on your feet. It's like this morning, I was two wide players short for what I did really. But you just get on with it and give the players the impression that you are in control of it. Whereas if you start bawling or saying 'where is so and so' [using a panicky voice] you're not professional. You've got to be bullet proof, or you've got to portray that you are. You can make a joke of it and throw your notes down, 'come on let's piss off to the pub'. You make light of it but you try and show you're not bothered, you're in control and know what you are going to do. You've got to adapt, think on your feet and have things in your mind, first reserve second reserve type of thing, which isn't easy but has to be done.

Linked to all this is another of Steve's fundamental beliefs about coaching: the need to be flexible, to adapt to changing conditions and to 'coach what you see':

> The art of management and coaching is recognising the situation. If you've got players that know the game you don't need to work on pattern. If you do they'll get bored and rebel in some way. It's a fine art. I think about forty per cent of coaching is recognising situations, recognising the people and responding to the people you are working with. Coaching isn't always about this is what I'm going to do and I'm going to do it irrespective, and I'm going to make it work. You can start something, see it is not working, so what do you do? Carry on and bash away at it? Or do you say 'okay we're going to go and do this'. That is very important. There are no hard and fast lines, you've got to be pliable and recognise situations. Is it working? Yes. Can I keep it going longer than planned because you can progress further? So it's not hard and fast. You've got to bend with the wind sometimes. If it's working, can you build on it? If it's not, there is no point doing it.

In many ways, Steve's vision for coaching gives a useful insight into the complexity of the whole endeavour. It is complicated further by the focus on individuals and the imperative for the coach to address their particular needs. For example, when working with younger players, Steve believes that a coach's style must adapt accordingly. He relates a humorous story to illustrate his point:

> I think there is one thing you gain through experience when working with the apprentices and schoolboys. Terminology. They don't understand the terminology. If you are coming out with the same sort of football terms, such as 'man-on' you think it is a very simple explanatory . . . [but] I was coaching at the training ground the other day and there was a youth game on. We had an under-sixteen player who we were taking on the next year, playing on the left wing. We were winning 1–0 and Fred was the coach. There was five minutes to go and this right-winger of theirs kept going down the line. So, as the ball was going down the other side, Fred shouted to this kid 'sit there, just sit there' in order to fill the space this winger was running into. So, what did he do? He just sat down on the floor!

Here again, Steve gives some fascinating insights into aspects of a football culture that have profound impacts upon the coaching process.

EFFECTIVE COACHING

In expressing his overall view of what comprises 'effective' coaching, Steve is firm in the belief that the sessions he takes as a coach have to be enjoyable and fun for the players. Combined with his view that players 'like to be worked', Steve generally runs his coaching sessions with a firm plan in mind, driven by definite objectives,

incorporating varied but progressive activities. Consequently, they are fast moving, with the emphasis on quality work as opposed to quantity. In turn, he tries to facilitate a confident and relaxed coaching environment; something he believes emanates directly from the persona and demeanour of the coach: 'A big thing is the manner in which you put things across. I like training to be relaxed . . . You train as you play and you play as you train.' He also points out that football training has two key elements: 'one is function where you learn, where it's like a cerebral day . . . then there's the other sort of training where it's enjoyment but work'. His weekday coaching is, more often than not, directly related to the previous game: 'You coach off what you see on a Saturday'; particularly working on the weaknesses observed in that game. Thus, he would argue that he has established a varied and interesting coaching format that the players can understand and appreciate: 'At least I think they do!'

Added to this is something Steve identifies as a key ingredient of effective coaching: personal style. Although Steve openly admits to learning from watching others, he is also at pains to emphasise that to be successful, a coach needs to weave this knowledge into a personal manner. He feels that his greatest mistakes in coaching occurred when he tried to be too much like someone else:

> That's where I made my biggest mistake in management. I managed like Graham Taylor, but I'm not Graham Taylor. I wasn't like Graham, and I'll never be like him. But I thought that was the done thing. So I took my personality away and tried to do it like that and messed myself up. I didn't enjoy it at all and the players didn't either. So you work in the manner you feel comfortable with. Whether you're short and to the point and serious, whether you're jovial or whatever, the outcome has got to be the same; progress and positiveness and improvement. And whatever way you do it, you have to do it the way you are comfortable with. I've gleaned that over the years with the people I've worked with and the person that I am, I think. And I feel comfortable with that so I do it like that. Plus the fact I think you get better results!

So, for Steve, effective coaching comes from watching and learning from others, but 'with a variation on the theme'. It is this latter ingredient of coaching that, if it is as vital for success as Steve argues, makes the task of designing effective one-size-fits-all coaching courses so difficult.

SUMMARY

Steve was asked to sum-up 'what makes an effective coach' in a couple of sentences. After a long pause, he replied:

I would say that knowing your job, recognising situations, responding to players, and ensuring that whatever it may be, whether it is a lot of work or a little work, recognising that fact and doing what is required. And if those players come off the training field in the right frame of mind, tired, and happy, and feeling that it was all worthwhile, then the job is done . . . Really, it's the ability to handle men, that's the big thing, to handle people.

It is a fitting summary for Steve's story. Steve the former player, Steve the coach and Steve the person are all interwoven into a distinct and highly personal set of coaching practices. It works for him, and he would argue that it works for players. But although central to his effectiveness as a coach, Steve's approach is not suitable for everyone. As he points out: 'Now, I think that's the way I am anyway . . . I suppose it's different styles I imagine.' Even so, it is difficult to argue with some of his fundamental points; for example, on respecting players and the need to individualise coaching practice. What is fascinating, of course, is that other coaches, for their own reasons and with equally strong, persuasive arguments, just do not see things in exactly the same way.

Note: Another version of Steve Harrison's story appeared in *Sport, Education and Society* (2002), *8*(2), 213–229.

CHAPTER 3

▼ GRAHAM TAYLOR

BY PAUL POTRAC AND LAURA PURDY

INTRODUCTION

At the outset of our interview, Graham Taylor declared that had he known in advance that his career as a professional football player would be relatively short-lived, he would have remained in school to become a teacher. However, as we discussed his highly distinguished and successful coaching career, which included a period as head coach to the England national football team, Graham considered that coaching 'really is a form of teaching, so I guess, in a way, I've ended up in the same place!' Indeed, for Graham, the essence of coaching is 'knowing enough about your subject' to be able to deliver practices and information in a way that 'is of clear benefit to the players' in preparing them for the demands and rigours of competition. Hence, he believes that effective coaching is principally concerned with communicating the technical and tactical aspects of a sport in a concise and 'simple' manner to players, while striving to construct and maintain positive working relationships with them.

ENTRANCE INTO COACHING

Like most of the other coaches in this book, Graham's early career aspirations did not include becoming a coach. Instead, his principal desire was just to be a professional footballer. His passion for sport began at school, where he enjoyed extensive and varied sporting opportunities, which included representing England senior schools at football. Graham also described how his father, a sports journalist for a local newspaper, had a significant impact upon his wish to become a professional footballer as he was regularly taken to watch the local club, Scunthorpe United, play. As a consequence of his father having access to the various staff and players at the club for reporting purposes, he soon found himself totally immersed in the day-to-day life of the professional game. Indeed, when looking back upon his youth, Graham concluded that football 'was part of my life from the first day that I can remember'.

With football occupying such a central role in his life, it was perhaps unsurprising that Graham subsequently fulfilled his dream and became a professional footballer with Grimsby Town Football Club in 1962. However, this was seen by many as an uncommon and even controversial career choice for a 'grammar school boy'. In his own words:

> I was a prefect in the lower sixth form at the time that I left, and I really upset and disappointed my headmaster who gave me the biggest 'rollicking' of my life. When I left school, I had already been lined up to be the next Head Boy at the school. I was accused of letting the school down. You see, at that time, and without wanting to show any class distinctions, grammar school boys didn't go into professional football, as that was for secondary modern boys. That was the structure and culture at that time. However, I knew that I really wanted to be a footballer.

As Graham steadily adapted to the culture of professional football, it soon became apparent that he would not achieve his dream of playing at the highest level of the game. Indeed, instead of moving up from Grimsby, his career path took him to Lincoln City Football Club in the fourth division, which equated to the lowest level of professional football in England at that time.

It was at Grimsby as a twenty-year-old player that Graham first became interested in coaching, as he considered it a possible avenue to remain in professional football once his playing days were over. Consequently, he attained his preliminary coaching award the following year before becoming, in 1966, the youngest person to obtain the 'Full Badge', the highest level of coaching qualification offered by the Football Association at that time. Indeed, in what was a meteoric rise through the coaching ranks, Graham became, in 1970 at the age of twenty-six, a Staff Coach for the Football Association, which saw him deliver and assess coach education courses to candidates at all levels. Shortly after this, in December 1972, the directors of Lincoln City Football Club recognised Graham's potential and appointed him head coach.

Graham's first major coaching success came in 1976, when Lincoln was crowned champion of the fourth division. This was a feat he repeated two years later, this time as head coach to Watford Football Club. Indeed, it was at Watford, a largely unfashionable team, that Graham was to enjoy considerable success. In this respect, he guided them through the lower leagues to the first division, where they finished runners-up in 1983 and, subsequently, qualified for the UEFA Cup; an achievement

the club has not been able to equal to date. During this spell, he also led Watford to the final of the Football Association Challenge Cup, the premier knock-out cup competition in English football. As a result of such successes, Graham's services were in demand, and he subsequently joined Aston Villa Football Club. Between 1987 and 1990, he not only successfully guided the club to promotion to the first division, but he also led them to a second place finish in the championship. Following what he defines as a 'mixed spell' as head coach to the England national team, during which they qualified for the European Championships in 1992, Graham returned to club football with Wolverhampton Wanderers in 1994 before again rejoining Watford as head coach. As appears to be his trademark, he again played a key role in Watford's rise from the relative obscurity of the second division to winning promotion to the Football Association Carling Premier League, the pinnacle of contemporary English professional football. After a brief flirtation with retirement, Graham has recently returned to another of his former clubs, being again appointed head coach at Aston Villa.

LEARNING TO BE A COACH

In tracing his development as a coach, Graham described how, in many ways, he believes that he possesses a natural affinity for the role. Indeed, he has always considered himself to be 'cut out' to be a teacher or a coach, as he had, throughout his life, occupied positions of responsibility and leadership.

> I believe that somewhere along the line there are certain personalities, certain people, I would say that adapt to it and pick that kind of thing up. They are just that kind of person. So, at the risk of sounding boastful, which I certainly would not want to be, when I look back at my career, and right back to my school days, I find that when I was at infant and junior school I was a milk monitor, I was a prefect, and also head boy. At secondary school, I captained all the sports teams I played for. So, it seems pretty obvious to me now that there has been a teaching side to me. In fact, if I hadn't have been a footballer, teaching would probably have been the profession that I would have entered.

In elaborating upon his development as a coach, Graham spoke of several individuals who, at various stages of his career, made significant contributions to his coaching philosophy and practice. In particular, he spoke about the positive impact of Jimmy McGuigan, his former coach at Grimsby. McGuigan had seemingly possessed a great ability to explain certain fundamental elements of football by relating them to aspects of daily life. He thus taught Graham the necessity of emphasising 'the basics' during coaching sessions, which he continues to do to this day.

> What I liked about him was that he explained things to you. He would do it in a way that wasn't always football related; he would relate football to other aspects of normal life. He would call them 'basics' and I

GRAHAM TAYLOR

remember him saying, I know this sounds silly, but he would say, 'If you don't clean your teeth then they'll fall out, so you have to clean your teeth everyday.' Now what are the basics in the game? What are you going to do everyday? Well, you're not going to be able to hit a ball accurately over 10, 20, or 30 yards unless you practise. All simple things, but things that a lot of people forget.

McGuigan also taught him that the trials and tribulations that form part of daily life are also an inescapable part of professional football. Graham believes this message is worth getting across to his own players as he emphasises the need for a work ethic and strong mental attitude to cope with diversity. Indeed, he noted:

I've tried very, very hard to get players to understand that football is very much like life. Sometimes it's not fair, sometimes a game isn't fair to you, you've done everything that we consider to be right, everything to win the game and the referee gives a decision that is so palpably wrong that you lose 1–0. It's tough but I'm afraid that's life. Life is unfair on occasions. So you have to be strong to continue to work at what you're doing. I've always tried to work on those things with the players in terms of being mentally strong.

In recounting a final lesson he learned from McGuigan, Graham spoke of the importance of developing constructive and positive working relationships with his players, an aspect that will be examined in greater depth later in the chapter. In this respect, Graham considered McGuigan to be especially skilled at the inter-personal aspect of coaching. In illustrating this point, he depicted the relationship that developed between himself as captain and McGuigan, the coach.

I was the captain of Grimsby and on a Thursday afternoon he used to ask me to come and see him in his office. The first time he asked me to do this, I was very nervous and thought, 'What's this about?' But he was a shrewd man because he kept me onside with him as the captain. I probably became a voice for him in the dressing room. And I think most coaches and managers will tell you that the most important thing is to keep people on board if you can. And usually it's your senior players who are the people leading the dressing room. If you can get them leading it for the right reasons, because they believe in you, then that's very important. He taught me all about creating that type of situation.

In addition to learning valuable positive lessons from individuals such as McGuigan, Graham also indicated how other individuals have influenced his coaching in terms of 'what not to do'. Here, he noted how the actions of one of his former coaches led him to conclude that training should be made appropriate to the skill level and needs of the players, because asking the impossible of players only serves to damage their confidence.

He was someone from whom I learnt what not to do. Although he was the coach he was still a fantastic player. He used to score more goals than anybody in training. He was a better player than any of us and he was in his late thirties then. What it taught me was that the training sessions were for his benefit, and I thought 'that can't be right'. I remember once he was having a bit of a go at us as he thought we gave the ball away too easily at throw-ins, but we just weren't as good as him. It was a case of realising what was available. If you start asking people to do things that you can but they can't, all you end up doing is destroying their confidence because they can't do it.

In closing the discussion on the influence of other coaches and managers on his practice, Graham believes that borrowing ideas and learning from others was an integral factor in his development as a coach. In this regard, he is sceptical that 'there is anything original' in football and, as such, suggests that coaches should not feel guilty for borrowing or adapting the ideas and practices from others, as long as what is done is in the best interests of players. In his own words:

I don't think there is anything really original in football. It might be the first time you've seen things happen but everybody takes from everybody else in our game and you add it together to what suits you. I'm sure some will have taken things from me, I took things from Jim McGuigan, Jim McGuigan will have taken from someone before him. So, I don't go along with all this sort of original thinking and all that kind of thing. I think it's a big circle. So, as far as I'm concerned, everything thing goes round and round. Of course there are changes and things go on, but, in the main, you learn from watching people.

THE ATTRIBUTES OF EFFECTIVE COACHING

In discussing good coaching practice, Graham began by reiterating the need for a coach to attend 'to the basics'. He thus believes that training sessions should be carefully planned, organised, and delivered if coaches are to succeed in getting their messages across to players. Hence, for Graham, a necessary first step towards effective practice is to consider the details of the coaching environment and to react accordingly in order to lay the foundations for quality sessions:

I've learnt so many things about the basics . . . even the most silly things, but they are the right things. For example, if the sun is facing the players, you move so that they don't have to look into it. If there is somebody practising 100 yards away behind your back, you make sure that the players are not facing that way when you speak to them, as no doubt they will be distracted. If the wind is fierce and strong how do you get people into positions? So it's all those little things. But if you want to get your message across you have to be thinking about them.

GRAHAM TAYLOR **25**

Another concern that Graham voiced in relation to effective practice was the need for a coach to recognise that players learn in various ways and at different rates. Hence, he suggested that coaches should not only strive to understand how their players, as individuals, learn, but should also ensure that they tailor their feedback and instruction to these individual requirements. For example:

> You've got to recognise that those twenty people in front of you will have different ways of learning. Some can take it in straight away just by listening to what you say. However, just because I believe in a certain thing and I have pictures in my mind of how it's going to happen doesn't mean all the players do. So, I need to transfer these thoughts to the players realising that they all have different learning rates and preferences.

At the heart of Graham's coaching is his desire to ensure that the instruction and learning that takes place on the training field is directly related and transferable to situations that his players will find themselves facing in competitive matches. Indeed, Graham is highly critical of technical practices that, 'while looking good', do not adequately prepare players for the demands and rigours of winning football games. He expressed it thus:

> If you have to go up to Barrow or Workington on a shitty day and you need to actually scrap and fight for a draw, putting on five-a-side practices or small-sided games in training isn't going to give you a centre half who is prepared to get a broken nose because he has to battle for the ball. That was one of the biggest lessons I learnt. Too many coaches put on these clever, complicated and highly technical practices that, as far as I'm concerned, look good for their own benefit. At the end of the day I say, 'But what have the players got out of it?' If training is to be of benefit to the players, it is absolutely essential that they can transfer what you have worked on from Monday to Friday onto the pitch on Saturday. If they can't do this, then you really are wasting your time and energy.

In terms of the delivery of instruction and relating the technical and tactical aspects of football to his players, Graham believes that it is essential to 'keep things simple'. In this regard, he suggested that coaches should explain concepts in a straight-forward and concise manner, as he considers that players gain a great deal of self-confidence and are, subsequently, most effective when they know 'what they are doing' and 'why they are doing it'. Indeed, Graham was fiercely critical of the modern tendency to 'overcomplicate the game' and coaching in general.

> Many myths have developed about the whole game and coaching. I've listened to some people talk about the game in such a way that they appear as if they know something about the game that we don't. Now, if you look at the game it is very simple. Essentially, you say, 'Well, if goals are going to win this game, we better look into ways in which goals are actually

scored because that gives us a chance to win.' For instance, I could tell you that 90 per cent of all goals are scored from the [the goal scorer having] one touch. So why do we practise attacking moves, or allow in practice our goal scorer to have three or four touches before he shoots, why do we do that? Because that's not what happens on the Saturday. So, I would say from a coaching point of view you have got to be careful from the word go that you don't suddenly complicate matters.

In addition to the need to give straightforward and digestible instruction to players, Graham believes that a player's limitations can be considerably improved by working on his or her strengths. Indeed, while he considered this to not always be the case, he considers that increasing the self-confidence of players, through allowing them to master tasks, frequently results in a natural improvement of the weaker aspects of their performance.

You've got to be in a position where you're encouraging players during training sessions. Very rarely do I work on players' weaknesses. I always work on their strengths as, by getting their confidence to a high level, you find that their weaknesses improve as well. I'm not saying you should never work on weaknesses, but I think if you have people at a high confidence level you can then say, 'Well what about improving this?' But if you are telling someone 'you are poor' on any particular aspect then the percentage of improvement is going to be so minimal that it hardly makes any difference at all. I do believe that if you continue to work on people's strengths their weaknesses improve because their confidence is raised to another level.

Finally, like many of the other coaches in this book, Graham also emphasised that an essential feature of successful coaching in top-level sport is to ensure that each player understands his or her role within the wider team framework. He considers that players are able to make speedy and effective decisions only if they are fully aware of the responsibilities of their role and the options that are available to them. However, while he spoke with passion about the necessity for clear role definitions and an organised team structure, he also recognised the need to account for the individuality of players and, accordingly, warned against restricting or stifling creative talent at the expense of maintaining a rigid team structure. Here, he described that an effective coach is one who is capable of developing the 'right balance' between team needs and individual strengths. In illustrating this particular point, Graham spoke of his experiences when leading Watford to league and cup successes.

It's getting the balance. What I've always wanted to do is to get a team that knows the basic team functions within which the players can express their individuality. When you get that, then you're on the right track. Let me use John Barnes as a prime example. Having a John Barnes and not allowing him to express himself in the way that he can for the benefit of the team would be stupid. There was no way that I could say, 'No, you've got to play like this in my Watford team.' I had an outside right called Nigel Callaghan who was a great crosser of the ball, so he had different strengths from John. It was no good saying to John that I want early deliveries because he liked to take people on and beat them, and when he did do that the crowd loved it. Now, Callaghan could take one touch and deliver. He didn't have to beat you. You knew that Callaghan would deliver a cross almost immediately so you could make a run, so he was great for you that way. You couldn't do the same with John because John was something else, something special. But then John would create chances and score goals by dribbling past three people, what was I supposed to say? I don't want you to do that? So it was about getting a balance.

ON THE IMPORTANCE OF GAINING 'TRUST' AND 'RESPECT'

One of the most striking themes to emerge from our conversation on Graham's coaching practice was the significance he attached to the creation of positive and constructive working relationships both with individual players and with the team as a collective. Indeed, he is convinced that the interpersonal nature of coaching is the most essential feature for practitioners to consider if they wish to be successful. Here, he repeatedly emphasised the need for a coach to 'connect' with his or her athletes with the ability to gain the latter's 'trust' and 'respect' being regarded as crucial.

> Unless people are willing to listen to you, unless you're prepared to listen to them and understand them as people, the best coaching book in the world isn't going to help you. It all comes down to how well they really want to do for you. It all comes back to the relationships that you have with your players and the trust that exists between you. It can't be a relationship if it's not based on trust. That's just life.

In articulating the necessity for a coach to gain the 'confidence' of players, Graham recognised the need to create a training environment in which players feel comfortable and secure. In order to achieve this goal, he suggested that it is important for a coach to consider the requirements of players both in the immediate sporting environment and beyond, thus recognising that a coach can help to facilitate maximum performance of the athlete in many and various ways. For example, he described how he tries to remember the birthdays of his players and their respective families, as he believes such gestures serve to reinforce player respect for him not just as a competent and knowledgeable professional, but also as a person. Indeed, in echoing many of the other coaches in this book, he stated that by being seen to take an interest in each player 'you're actually showing them that you care, and whilst you show them that you think about them and the other side of life, you stand to gain a great deal in terms of your working relationship with them'. Unsurprisingly then Graham was of the opinion that, for a coach to be successful, it is important to be 'liked' by players. Here, he indicated that, while some coaches talk of the relative merits of being 'liked' and 'respected', he believes that the two are inextricably linked.

> I hear coaches say, 'I don't care whether they like me or not, as long as they respect me.' I don't go along with that. I think the best coaches will be respected but, to a great degree, they will also be liked. A coach will not be liked totally but he must be liked by the majority of the players if he is to be successful. I know very few people, if any, who are respected but not liked. For me, the two go hand in hand.

Furthermore, in recognising realistically that not every player will like his or her coach, Graham believes that some personality clashes will necessitate that a player or even the coach, in some circumstances, moves on to another team. Interestingly, he believes that such happenings should be regarded as an entirely natural feature of the coaching process in top-level sport, and not as some sort of failure on the part of either party.

> I think, as a coach, you've also got to recognise that not every player you work with is going to be happy and be able to work alongside you. There will, inevitably, be some personality clashes. Once you realise that you are not going to get the best out of one another, then most of the time the player has to move on. Sometimes it's the coach, but more often than not the player moves. There's nothing wrong with that because we don't all like one another.

When working with his players in the training environment, Graham emphasised the importance of convincing them that what they are asked to do is of real benefit to their performance. Indeed, he believes that nothing helps players to 'believe' in a coach more than when they can make connections between how the work undertaken on the training pitch is helping them to win competitive games. To assist in this process, Graham indicated that, in many ways, a coach has to be 'a good actor', as he attempts to persuade and cajole the players to 'buy into' and accept his 'way of doing things'. A necessary first step here is for him to present an 'upbeat' image of total confidence and belief in what he is prescribing for, and asking of, players: 'You need to believe in something, or show that you do, with enough conviction, as you have to translate that into your players' minds and that demands a kind of psychology.'

Central to his notion of 'psychology' is the considered use of verbal and body language, tone of voice and eye contact. Here, he believes that coaches are constantly scrutinised by their players, therefore they need to think carefully about how they act in the presence of their charges. In particular, he voiced the

GRAHAM TAYLOR

importance of hiding one's true emotions and feelings and, instead, focusing on presenting a confident, and enthusiastic 'front'. Additionally, he spoke of how he tailors his interaction in many different ways to ensure that his message is clearly received and understood by all of his players. He expressed it thus:

> There's twenty pairs of eyes on me, now we might have lost 3–0 and played badly, so they're waiting to see how I react. So, now my body language is going to be very important. Also, you learn that sometimes having quiet words with people on their own, when nobody knows you've spoken to them, helps. You have to learn about your people. Eye contact is very important if you really want your messages to get home to people. Touch is also very important, as there will be certain people that you probably don't say anything to but as they walk past you, you give 'em a pat on the back which tells them everything. So you develop different kinds of relationships with people in so many different manners to get your message across, to bring it through and I think that's all part and parcel of coaching.

A final point of interest here was the value that Graham ascribed to the use of humour within the practice environment. He suggested that humour, when utilised at the right time and place, can not only help defuse some of the tensions that are an inherent part of professional football, but can also contribute to presenting the coach in a 'human light', which he believes is widely appreciated by players.

> You can't be seen to be above a laugh, and the other thing I would say, which you have to learn, is that, while it's vital that you must take your job seriously, if you start to take yourself too seriously then you'll get found out. It's no different from any walk of life. You can't be too pompous. I know that it's very important as a coach that the players and people can see that you'll take a laugh and that you like a laugh and you like a joke, and so I think humour is very, very important.

SUMMARY

The message that emanates from Graham's 'story' is that of a coach who not only attaches great store to furthering the technical abilities and tactical understanding of players, but also of a dedicated professional who is fully aware of the need to respect the individuality of players, whilst striving to establish a strong social bond with them. In considering how he could best advise new and potential coaches, Graham believes that they should invest as much time and energy reflecting upon the relationships that they establish with their performers as they do in attempting to satisfy their thirst for various drills, activities and strategies. This encapsulates his socially aware coaching philosophy. In his own words:

> Coaching is much more than picking up a book and seeing how many cones you need for different practices and drills. They are just words and diagrams in a book, they can give you ideas, but it is how you take those pictures and words and put them into the coaching field that is important. Basically, it's all down to you as a person and of course the relationships that you have with your players.

CHAPTER 4

▼ **HOPE POWELL**

BY CHRIS CUSHION

INTRODUCTION

Hope Powell's vision as national coach is to establish England as one of the world's top eight countries in women's football. To this end, she describes herself as being concerned with developing players through facilitating learning both on and off the field, using best practice primarily from her own experiences as a player and coach. She wants to develop 'thinking players', who have the tactical 'nous' to succeed at the international level. Being critical and reflective of her own practice is central to achieving this progressive goal.

ON HER ENTRY INTO COACHING

On 1 June 1998, Hope was appointed to the Football Association (FA) as the national coach of women's football. This followed a long and successful playing career for both club and country, and a relatively short coaching one. The seeds of her interest and development in coaching, however, had been sown at an early age with her completion of the FA preliminary award at nineteen; a certification that was undertaken for no particular reason other than an underlying passion for the game. In her own words:

> it was just for the love of football really. I had a very good friend that used to take coaching courses and I think I was just swept into it, I have no

idea why. I think I went along and watched my mate coach a bit and just assisted and helped out; obviously when there was a qualification to be going on, I just went along to it to see out of interest, and that's how it happened.

Despite this almost inadvertent start, Hope followed a well-worn route into football coaching. This involved working at the Crystal Palace Football Club community scheme, 'the grass roots level' as she termed it, before doing the soccer camp circuit in the United States. These experiences gave direction to Hope's coaching as the enjoyment in working with older and more technically able players began to take shape. While still playing international football, Hope was invited by the Football Association to be part of a fledgling coach mentoring scheme, which involved working with the under-16 and under-18 national girls' squads as well as undertaking the UEFA 'B' soccer coaching licence. As a result of successfully completing this course, she was appointed coach for the national women's team. Although her potential was acknowledged and encouraged, she remains aware that her apparent meteoric rise could be viewed as somewhat fortuitous.

> I got my 'B' licence when I was still playing international football, and then there was an opportunity to be part of a mentoring strategy to work with a couple of the national squads. I took the opportunity and got my 'B' licence and then I was offered this job [national coach], which was totally brilliant as I wasn't expecting it at all!

ON HER EARLY INFLUENCES AND EXPERIENTIAL LEARNING

Hope's experiences and her reflection on them appear to be a dominant thread running through her learning process of how to be a coach. Being the recipient of coaching as a player, and working with and observing other coaches' practices are experiences that have been invaluable and influential in shaping her views on coaching. Additionally, woven throughout the initial part of Hope's story is the influence of her former coach Ted Copeland, who recognised her potential and encouraged her to gain experience and qualifications within the game:

> Ted Copeland managed or coached me 'cause he did the England (coaching) job for five years. He encouraged me to do the 'B' licence and stuff like that and so I did it to get better experience. I then worked with an older age group of players at the club I was with at the time and found that I preferred working with those players who could play a bit. I then got my 'A' (UEFA) licence and here we are.

Additionally, she considers another of her former coaches, Alan May, now ironically part of her staff, as also having been highly influential in the development of her coaching philosophy and consequent practice:

Alan May really taught me how to deal with personalities and people, if you like, the people management side of things. I think that being coached by someone you respect for a spell of time rubs off on you, and I certainly found that a lot with Alan. The sessions that he did were varied, challenging, fun, and serious when they needed to be. His coaching style or manner was very friendly but challenging, and he expected a lot which developed the players quite quickly. I actually find myself doing a lot of things in terms of the way that he did them in my own coaching now.

Experiences of course, do not have to be positive to have an effect, and Hope also learned from witnessing coaching which she feels does not have a place when dealing with players.

I won't name names but I think I've learned from negative coaches as well. I mean, I look at some of the people that have coached me and I think 'well I won't do that', often it's the mannerisms and the language used that turn players off and coaches need to be aware of that.

Hope appears very aware of her coaching delivery and the impact it can have on her players. Thus, she is at pains to consider carefully how she communicates with her players to get them to excel. Her comments in this regard illustrate some of the issues that Hope believes need to be addressed within women's football, particularly when men coach women's teams. For example:

Women's football is very different from men's football, and male coaches don't always recognise that or aren't aware of it. For example, men that have coached in the men's game sometimes tend to be quite aggressive and even verbally abusive, while in the women's game that approach just doesn't work. When they come into the women's game and find they can't do that sort of thing they get frustrated; it's not good for them or, more importantly, the players.

This is a style of coaching that Hope would not subscribe to as she feels that it is counterproductive to bully players, particularly in the long term: 'I really couldn't and wouldn't do that, I mean, even if I was coaching a group of boys I wouldn't be verbally abusive or throw tea cups and all that nonsense. You don't get the best out of players that way.' Unsurprisingly, she believes that coaches need to work with players to improve them through constructive feedback not to berate them, as this just breeds resentment and a bad working environment.

Hope is very much aware of the value and role of experiential learning in her development as a coach. Of particular significance here has been her constant and on-going observations of more experienced coaches at work. However, she is quick to distinguish between simply copying other coaches and taking ideas from them. Here she noted: 'It's important when you look at something you like that you adapt it to suit the needs of your group and deliver it in a style that is suitable to you and them.' This highlights her awareness of the necessity to synthesise observations and put them into context before implementing them into her practice. Indeed, she views her experiential learning and her adaptation of that learning as the route through which she has developed as a coach.

> This is the problem a lot of people have as they do their 'A' licence or their coaching qualification and they can't put it into [their own] practice. If you can't put it into practice, the whole process is really wasted and that's the problem. I'm convinced the way to improve is to just keep coaching, and thinking about your coaching. I know I've improved as a coach simply because I'm doing it regularly and I'm seeing things quicker and I watch other coaches and I still feel like I'm being educated.

Recognising the importance of experience, reflection and feedback in coach development has led Hope to establish a mentoring scheme for aspiring women coaches. She set up the system principally to address the problem of the lack of women coaches coming through to the top level of the game:

> I set up a mentoring strategy so that female coaches, or potential coaches could work alongside coach educators, to give them some support, to go and watch them coach, and to give them some feedback and generally help them develop. It brings coaches through and gives them the experience of international football, and talks about management and coaching in general and all those things. For some reason there just aren't enough female coaches coming through at the top end, maybe it's a case of support, developing a bit of confidence, you know, to make them believe they are good enough to pass the highest award, as, at the moment, it's an all male thing. So it's really aimed at them as much as anything.

Developing a genuine pathway for female coaches to work at the elite level is of particular importance to Hope. Indeed, she is in a unique position with regards to the other coaches interviewed in this book, not only because she possess a wider remit related to coach development in addition to coaching a national team, but also because she is one of very few women who work at a high level in a male-dominated sport and culture, complete with its inherent constraints of which she is only too aware.

ON RELATING TO PLAYERS

Hope feels that her playing experience as an international has given her an advantage when coaching at that level, principally in terms of the insights she possesses into what the players are actually feeling and experiencing whilst playing. Hence, she considers herself able to empathise with them, which helps make her a more understanding coach. She expressed it thus:

I've played against Germany and Sweden and those countries, so I know what it's like. As a coach, I think you have to recognise the speed of the game and how fast it really is. You know, when you're watching it or you're watching the video, the game looks very slow, but get on there and in five minutes your tongue's hanging out! And it's very difficult for players because sometimes coaches don't appreciate that, not that they don't try to, but they haven't had that feel, 'cause the whole thing about playing ninety minutes of international football is that it's so physically and mentally demanding. Yeah, I think I've got a definite advantage because I've played, I know what it's like.

This playing experience also appears to contribute significantly to the construction of Hope's coaching sessions. She believes that the ability to 'think like a player' gives her a feeling for the type of sessions that the players might enjoy, in addition to appropriately structuring and delivering those sessions that are less enjoyable yet still vital to team preparation. This experiential intuition or knowledge assists in ensuring a balance within her practice, as she generally tries to make her sessions fun for the players, which she believes is vital in order to get the best from them. She noted;

> In my position, I do look back to when I was a player, and ask, 'would I enjoy this?' And there are some things that you have to do that players absolutely hate and it's boring but need to be done so I do them thoroughly but quickly. I suppose I do use myself as an example, so if I didn't like something as a player then no, I don't necessarily use it.

Hence, she tries to see things from the players' viewpoint, which gives her coaching philosophy a strong element of being player centred. She tries to implement this approach through a variety of ways. An example is her selection procedure for the national squad where she attempts to ensure equality of opportunity for all potential players. For her, it is important that

> all the players are given the same coaching, the same opportunity. They all play equal amounts of games so that they are seen equally. We try to give them every opportunity and make it as fair as possible. The girls know this and I think they appreciate it.

She also believes in talking personally to those players who have come close but have not ultimately been selected for the national squad. She considers that such players need to be treated with sensitivity, lest their drive and enthusiasm be lost to the game and maybe to herself in future; an attitude which reflects her belief in caring for and supporting players in order to get the best from them. Allied to this ethic of care within Hope's philosophy, however, is a harder edge that relates to her expectation of a certain attitude and level of performance and behaviour from her players both on and off the pitch.

I'm looking for dedication, wanting to learn, open to challenges, all of those good things; these are things I expect from players. From an international standpoint it isn't just about a player being fantastic but that they recognise that they are ambassadors for the game. This is a big part in women's football, as we are trying to raise the profile, so it becomes necessary that they understand that they are ambassadors for the game. I expect them to know this and [that they] can handle that responsibility. It's all a part of being a disciplined performer.

ON BEING AN EFFECTIVE COACH

In addition to motivating and supporting her players, thus generating a positive environment, Hope believes in placing an emphasis on the technical aspects of the game within her coaching practice. She considers that this mix will encourage her players to believe in her coaching and to feel comfortable to experiment and explore the limits of their potentialities. This is important to Hope, as she strives to develop confidence in her players to express themselves and to be the best that they can be. Hence, while she believes that the establishment of a supportive climate within her sessions 'gives players the belief that they're doing things well and will encourage them to keep doing it and to keep trying', the technical aspect gives players a real sense of learning and hence improvement. What Hope perceives to be of great importance in this regard is for a coach to know players individually and to treat them accordingly. For her, 'it's important as a coach that you know your group of players and you know what particular trigger works with who'. As a result, not all players are treated the same, as she's aware that her role demands that 'different people need to be dealt with in different ways depending on where they are and what they're doing'. In further developing this point she stated:

'You really have to be aware and be able to recognise the things that are going on with individual players as you always get players that have a bad time from time to time, so it's very important as a coach to recognise that and to act accordingly.'

This, however, is not always viewed by Hope as a scientific or systematic process; rather it is the coach's 'intuition' or 'art' coming to the fore. Indeed, for Hope, her decisions on how to act in this sphere of human relations are based on her 'gut feelings', which further emphasises her reliance on her own experiences. Here, she noted that: 'working with the players on the field, I believe that you do it from the gut. I go with my gut feeling a lot. I get feelings from where I can generally tell whether we're going to have a good day or a bad day'.

Such a belief however, does not detract from what she considers perhaps the key function or role of the coach to be, namely improving players through concise technical instruction. Indeed, for her, this is the essence of her practice: 'It's really your job to identify what's going wrong, if you see a fault correct it, and then when you correct it re-do it and if necessary re-do it again'. An important part of this is relating to players individually, as, through her feedback, she tries to 'switch something on in players, to make them think a little bit more about themselves in a particular position rather than the team as a whole, so often I've got to be very specific and personal'.

Dealing with players in such an individual manner does throw up some issues for Hope, in particular a perceived notion of 'role conflict'. That is, she is conscious that on the one hand she is working with players to improve them, while at the same time selecting squads and teams, which involves judging, evaluating and selecting some players at the expense of others. As a result, she thinks that players may not be as open with her as she would like because they see her as the person who controls their international careers. Hence, she is aware of the need to develop a set of unique dynamics within her coaching staff, which results in each coach having differing but complementary roles to play within that support team. As Hope says,

> It's very difficult at times for me to reach players, as they will only tell me what they think I want to hear. That's why you need assistant coaches who are deemed the 'nice guys' that generally players will go to, as it's not easy for a player to approach the person who could give them the chop, it's very difficult for them to do that, so we, as a coaching team, have to work round it.

In further coping with this situation Hope tries to strike a balance between keeping a distance from the group whilst satisfying her desire to deal closely with the individual players within it. Here she noted:

> as a group of players, I'm very distant from them as I think I have to be to do my job right. Individually though, I collar players all the time and have a one on one with them and they find that quite easy. I'll generally pull players away and ask 'em 'how you feeling today' as well as the sport specific stuff. I think they like that individual attention but I'm careful to do it discreetly, not in front of everyone as that could take them away from the group mentally.

She believes that this approach pays dividends for her and is well received by the players; a belief that is again based on personal intuition. She rationalised the reasons why she engages in such practice as being learnt from experience, with the application of such learning again being referred to as the 'art' of coaching. Thus, she believes that 'just by watching, getting a feeling, getting information of what's going on, you become more experienced which means that you're more aware of things that are going on and better able to handle them'.

COACHING OBJECTIVES AND DEVELOPING 'THINKING' PLAYERS

What clearly emerges from Hope is that she sees her main function as being to 'develop players'. In this respect, she echoes the sentiment of many of the other coaches that are interviewed in this book. This major goal shapes her coaching practice, and is reflected in almost all of her sessions. However, although developmental work may be her natural coaching focus, it has been adopted into her current practice with the national squad for very pragmatic reasons. Here she explains:

> We're in a development stage right now with women's football. We're really in the process of developing players at the moment, so even at the international level, although the concern might be performance or winning, the actual information that the players are given, how the sessions that we put on are structured, and what we say is expected, probably won't vary a great deal. So, the preparation wouldn't necessarily be any different for games or training or whatever, as we would still incorporate the same things into the sessions. We really need to develop better players at the moment, so that's really what we focus on.

Team results or the desire to achieve results does little to dislodge this continuity, as the goal to develop players in coaching sessions remains paramount. Where Hope's coaching style, content and delivery would differ, although still operating under a developmental umbrella, is with younger or perhaps less talented players, simply because of what they are able to understand and carry out.

> For instance, if you're comparing an under-16s side to a senior side there's a big difference in what you can do. A lot of the younger kids haven't really been coached well before, so many of the things we talk about are a whole new concept to them. Getting them to understand the stuff we do at the senior level is all new to them, so you have to go slower and simpler. Senior players, on the other hand, are used to it and can move on a little bit quicker and have a greater understanding of the game so you can do more with them.

At whatever level she works, Hope contends that players need to take responsibility for their own improvement and hence she tries to build this objective into her practice. She believes that if players accept such responsibility it helps them to think independently and to solve their own problems on the pitch, a necessary attribute at the international level. Although a valued and desired quality, she acknowledges this is difficult to coach into players: 'You tell them, I want you to do this, and then regardless of what's in front of them they will still try to do it without thinking.' She considers such mechanistic reactions on behalf of players a consequence of receiving coaching that is too instructive and authoritarian in nature: 'the coaching is just too coach centred at the moment'. Hence, she laments the fact the 'players just don't think for themselves', a situation in which creativity and risk-taking is stifled through a fear of failure instilled by 'the traditional, old-school type' coaches. Hope's coaching philosophy, on the other hand, is an attempt to move away from such restrictions and to help the individual develop to his or her full potential, which inevitably necessitates the making of mistakes along the way. The sin for Hope is not in making mistakes, but in not learning from those mistakes.

In an attempt to overcome what she sees as a lack of a critical tradition in coaching and to help her own professional development and that of others, Hope engages in regular role-play and feedback sessions with fellow coaches. Hence, she considers that being critical and self-reflective are important qualities for an effective coach as, although sometimes difficult, it constantly challenges one to examine, explore and rationalise one's actions: 'I understand and I appreciate that it's hard to confront yourself and have yourself challenged, but it's so important for learning, really so important.' Equally important, according to Hope, for good coaching practice are high levels of technical knowledge, game understanding and organisation. Organisation for her reaches into every aspect of the job, from ensuring that each player understands what is expected from him or her to always being ready and on time for meetings ('9 o'clock for me is 9 o'clock not two minutes past'), which accentuates her attention to detail. However, what really differentiates the expert coach from the average in her opinion is the ability to share and convey knowledge ('Good coaches are knowledgeable *and* are able to get across their ideas in terms of player understanding, while a bad coach just isn't able to do that'); in essence, the ability to communicate well. Thus, she believes that organisation and knowledge are not enough if the delivery is not right. This involves talking, explaining and rationalising actions to players in appropriate, helpful and precise ways.

CONCLUSION

Hope's position as both elite coach and coach educator, in addition to being one of very few women operating at a high level within a male-dominated sport, has given her a unique insight into the role of the top-level coach. She acknowledges that currently there aren't enough female coaches in British football, and the fact that 'there are perhaps too many men coaching women's teams' throws up problematic issues for her if such coaches cannot adapt their practice to meet the needs of this different context. However, rather than overemphasising gender issues in this respect, she is keen to highlight the need for coaches to be responsive to their context and hence develop flexibility in their practice. Thus, she believes that coaches should develop, and be taught to develop, their own style in keeping with the needs and wants of the players and the context. Perhaps the key lesson from Hope's story is that coaches should cultivate and acquire their own style, with the needs of the players, be they men or women, at the forefront. In her own words:

> you really should coach the way it suits you. I got my coaching qualification and I will coach using those fundamentals as well as my own tactical knowledge of the game, and the experiences I've had. I've developed all of those into a general delivery style that I try to adapt to suit the players I'm with, not the women, but the players. The real difference is in them being different players, that's all.

CHAPTER 5

▼ BOB DWYER

BY PAUL POTRAC AND CLIVE BREWER

INTRODUCTION

Bob's coaching philosophy is based around the concepts of technique, role and social care. He believes that a team will not develop as a collective and coherent unit unless the coach can advance and refine the technical and tactical attributes of each and every player. Bob constantly strives not only to perfect the individual skills of his players, but also to help them develop a clear understanding of their role and function within the wider team framework. Consequently, his general outlook on coaching is one that emphasises player performance above results obtained in competitive fixtures. In order to implement effectively such a philosophy, he believes that a coach must not only possess a sound knowledge of the sport and first-class analytical and communication skills, but that he or she must also strive to generate an atmosphere of confidence both on and off the playing field. He considers that confidence can be greatly increased by a coach's ability to take a keen interest in, and care for, the sporting and wider related needs and wants of players. Indeed, Bob believes that his successes as a coach have owed a great deal to his ability to effectively combine, and juggle, the roles of teacher, social worker, psychologist and even psychiatrist.

ON BECOMING AND BEING A COACH: 'A NATURAL PROGRESSION'

Bob's entrance into the coaching profession owed as much to him being 'in the right place at the right time' as it did to any coherent or rational career planning on his behalf. His initial coaching appointment was the unplanned result of the retirement of his then club coach, Bob Outterside, in 1976. In this regard, Bob was one of several senior players at the Randwick Club in Sydney (where he made 347 senior playing appearances) who were charged with recruiting a new and suitably qualified successor. The search however proved to be fruitless, with the available candidates not being regarded as wholly appropriate. As a consequence, Bob was persuaded to apply for the post and, after a ballot that involved the entire playing squad, he was subsequently appointed to the position. Although unplanned, Bob admitted on reflection that this elevation into the coaching ranks could well be viewed as 'something of a natural progression'.

Soon after his appointment, Bob enjoyed a period of considerable success. After finishing runners-up in the Sydney Premiership during his first season, he subsequently coached the team to four consecutive championship wins. Unsurprisingly, this was noted by the Australian Rugby Board, who invited Bob to stand for the position of national team coach. Following the bi-annual election ballot traditional in Australian rugby, he replaced Bob Templeton in this role in February 1982. Following a two-year spell as national coach, Bob was deposed by Alan Jones, only to win the position back again in February 1988. Upon his return, organisation, structure and a general professional outlook were deeply ingrained facets of Bob's coaching philosophy. They were to serve him well, as his Australian Wallabies were crowned world champions in 1991, beating England at Twickenham in the Rugby World Cup final.

In 1996, Bob moved on again, this time to England to be the Director of Rugby at the Leicester Tigers, a top-level English rugby union club. Bob was attracted to the post due to its unique demands, which coincided with the professionalization of the sport. Although generally successful on the field, Bob left Leicester during the 1997–1998 season following a dispute. After a period as coach of the Barbarians, the world famous invitational touring team, he returned to top-level English club rugby when, at the beginning of the 1998–1999 season, he became Director of Rugby at Bristol Rugby Club. He stayed with the west of England club until 2000, when he returned to his native New South Wales where he remains in his current capacity, as coach to the New South Wales Warratahs in the Super 12 competition.

LEARNING TO BE A COACH

Throughout his playing career Bob expressed a keen interest in the technical and tactical aspects of the game. He considers this to be a by-product of his position as team captain during the amateur days of rugby union, when captaincy involved a 'coaching-type role'. In order to make a worthwhile contribution in this capacity, Bob seized the opportunity to attend the then newly created coaching workshops and seminars offered by the Australian Rugby Union. He found the programme to be highly rewarding, and considers it the greatest inspiration in his development as a coach.

> The major influence in how I coach was probably the Australian Coaching Programme, which came into being in the last two years of my playing career. Being interested in the game, I went along as a kind of a student coach and listened to a few things. I was very impressed by the fact that someone was telling you not what to coach, but how to coach. It got me to really think about how I structured my coaching sessions.

As a consequence of the enthusiasm and knowledge gleaned from attending these coaching courses and conferences, Bob became keen to put his newly obtained theories into practice. Thus, he combined the latter years of his playing career with a voluntary coaching position, which involved working with the local junior rugby clubs. He attributes his subsequent passion for player development to this experience. In addition to the benefits he associates with these early coach education courses, Bob also considers his prior training as an electrical engineer to be crucial in the development of his coaching style and skills. In this respect, his engineering job required him to think in an 'ordered, logical, and mathematical' manner, qualities that he believes are equally important to good coaching practice.

> I'm an electrical engineer by profession . . . So I tend to sessionalise things and see things in horizontals, verticals and cross referencing and reaching a conclusion in the bottom corner, you know, progressing things across the horizontal line, progressing things down the vertical line and everything. They all interconnect and they bring you the result at the bottom; and the bottom line is important.

As a result of such an outlook, it is perhaps unsurprising that Bob attaches a great deal of importance to the growth and management of organised, coherent coaching plans and structures, which are concerned with the production of long-term and sustained success, as opposed to short-lived overnight achievements. For example, when discussing his work at Leicester Tigers, Bob described how he had formulated a four-year plan to help the club develop successfully:

> I outlined all the things I believed to be required to create the professional environment that I thought was necessary. We had to be professional, not so much to do with money, but in terms of attitude. I said to the Chief Executive at the club that it would take us three to four years to get where we wanted to be, to have the culture in place, then we would progress quite rapidly. After the first two years, we would be able to implement programmes, have them accepted, fine tune them, and

modify them as necessary, and to a major extent, have the right people heading them.

Due to Bob's largely fast-track coaching rise, he had little experience of working with, and under, many other coaches. Indeed, he does not consider any specific individual to have shaped his development as a coach. What has influenced him however, is being on the same teams as many excellent players, a large number of whom were, or were to become, internationals. He considers that his coaching has been informed not only by watching these players in action, but also by listening to their opinions on certain techniques and tactics. Such experiences form the basis of his coaching knowledge.

> I think I'm lucky to have played with a lot of really good players. I've played with players who were much, much, better than me. But having the experience of working with them I could see what they did. I can remember the things that struck me as important at the time, and I've stored them in the back of my mind. I think the experience of playing with excellent players over a prolonged period of time has given me an ability to set very high performance targets for the players I now work with as a coach.

THE ATTRIBUTES OF A GOOD COACH AND GOOD COACHING PRACTICE

When discussing the attributes required of an effective coach, in addition to organisational ability, Bob emphasised the need for an in-depth technical and tactical understanding of the sport, or 'good rugby ability, mentally speaking'. Hence, he believes that more important than having played rugby at the highest level, although such experience is useful in helping to gain the respect of players, is the ability to critically analyse team performance and to clearly communicate that analysis to players. He noted:

> I certainly don't think you need to have good rugby ability physically, but I think you need good rugby ability mentally. It's the ability to evaluate the performance of individual players and the team, and the ability to communicate the evaluation to players, and the ability to show them how to emulate the required level. That is what the coach's role is all about. So, if he can't understand the game or communicate that knowledge, then a coach is going to have problems.

In further exploring the analytical capabilities required of a top-level coach, he considers that such practitioners need highly developed sport-specific analytical skills, which enable them to understand the origins of problems encountered on the playing field. Thus, for Bob, the ability to differentiate the source from the symptoms is a fundamental coaching quality when working with high-level performers. He noted:

An ability to distinguish cause from effect is essential. For example, a coach might say 'we've not made a good break all day; we've got to get some new centres'. But you might have the best centres and have a lousy forward pack and a lousy scrum half who are not doing anything for your centres. And you might get rid of the centres and put some new ones in, and you might have got rid have a couple of good 'uns and still not achieved what you wanted to achieve. So, good eyesight and the ability to distinguish cause from effect is essential.

In talking of good coaching practice, Bob indicated the necessity to not only improve the technical qualities of individual players, but to also ensure that they fully understand their specific roles and responsibilities on the field of play. Hence, he believes that high-quality playing performances are the natural result of highly skilled players who have a clear sense of purpose. In order to achieve this, he suggests that it is necessary for a coach to 'influence individuals'. In this respect, for Bob, the game is 'about one versus one', that is, developing each player to be better than his or her direct opponent.

Really, there is no such thing as a game, and there is no such thing as a team. There is only a collection of individuals and a collection of incidents to bring a team into performance. So, I want to influence the individuals, and I want to influence each facet of the individual incident, and to a large extent let the combination of them happen. So, I want to do the individual facets right, I don't just want to see them scoring a try, I want the try to be the by-product of individuals doing their own things right.

This viewpoint encompasses working hard with and for the individual player to give him or her both the skills and game understanding to achieve something positive for the team. To foster this philosophy of individualistic player development, Bob uses high levels of concurrent instruction during training sessions in order to create high intensity practices which encourage the players to make effective decisions as quickly as possible. He expressed it thus:

It's because I want things to be happening in a hurry. I want things to be happening quickly, I want the player to use all the visual and audible clues that he can, and make an instantaneous decision. I don't want players to make conscious decisions, I want them to accept subconscious decisions and to, just let it happen . . . So, I'm trying to give individual feedback as the drill or practice is progressing to remind players of their functions and how to execute them in a technically correct way.

At the heart of Bob's coaching then is his desire to develop the essential techniques of the players to the extent that their execution becomes an automatic, subconscious and ultimately flawless response. Bob's mission in this regard is to ingrain such technique so deeply in the players that it is able to withstand the highly pressurised environment of top-level rugby.

What I try to emphasise is that there are certain fundamental aspects of the game that have to be done right. There's a right way of doing something and there's lots of wrong ways, and although there's a little leeway, you need to stay close to doing things the right way. For example, your pass technique has to be right, because sometimes we'll be under pressure, and that right technique will stand up under pressure, while if it's wrong, it won't. It's about not being distracted by the environment or previous outcomes. In my mind, that's how you explain why some teams play really well under pressure. So I try to get each individual thinking, 'I've got to do it right, I've got to do it right.'

Allied to recognising the importance of his developmental role, is Bob's corresponding belief that a team has to be coached to win games. Consequently, he is careful 'not to lose sight of the fact that what you really want to do is to score the try and win the game'. This was a lesson he learned when his Australian Wallabies were beaten by the touring British Lions team of 1989 who, after losing the first test, used increasingly physical tactics to take the next two and hence the series in bruising encounters. In his own words:

The '89 Lions taught me a lesson in that after losing the first test they got physical and we couldn't really handle it. They intimidated us and forced us into mistakes. So that taught me that what we do is all very nice but you have still got to do what you have to do to win. You've got to win against the dirty guys too as it's no use saying after the game that those guys are illegal, 'cause the score line says that you've still lost.

Bob did not see such a viewpoint as being contradictory to his 'performance' philosophy, and was at pains to emphasise that what he was looking to develop in players here was the presence of mind to deal with the harder physical challenges while still sticking to, and executing well, the established game plan: 'It's really about developing mentally tough players who don't think they'll lose, never mind the circumstance.' This attitude, in turn, was considered to be fostered by self-belief in good technique: 'the ability to stick to the right thing to do, no matter what the odds'. In discussing how he mentally prepares his players for big matches, Bob spoke of his attempts to make them 'relish the challenge'. Such matches were actively and eagerly anticipated as they were used as an evaluation both of the team and of himself as a coach. His sentiment in this regard was very clear:

I say to them that we know it's going to be tough, but that's good for us, we want things to be tough, we want to do things that are difficult. It's what makes you good, it's what gives you an evaluation of whether you're any good or not; it's doing things that are continuously more difficult than what you have done. It's what makes you tough.

In attempting to develop his players' technical abilities and tactical appreciation, Bob believes in the need to 'speak in a language that the players can understand'.

Hence, he considers that coaches should explain concepts in as simplistic a manner as possible, as failure to do so often results in player confusion as to what is required. Furthermore, he believes that the players' understanding of a task and hence their performance of it, is greatly enhanced if a coach clearly outlines the rationale behind it. This extends to the need to understand the technical qualities required for each playing position and structuring training activities that develop these skills maximally, and to explain them as such to the players. In this respect, a coach should not only clarify 'how to do things' but also 'why we should do them', which extends into his belief in the importance of good clear communication.

> The people that know their subject best are the people who talk about it in basic terms. I distrust people who talk in a difficult language that only they can understand. Smart people can talk in common English, and explain what they want you to know. You also have to be able to describe things in a logical sequence of events. If you say to the guys, okay if we set up this way we've got this advantage, but the opposition know that, and so this is the way they'll try to cover it. Now, if they try to cover it in this way that'll give us an opportunity somewhere else, and see how it goes. And so it's that clear step-by-step thought process that seems to me to be very important, because people can understand that. A creates B, B gives C opportunity, realisation of C will give you D. It's certainly important to me, and it's important in my coaching method.

Similarly, Bob emphasises the need for a coach to carefully explain an individual's role within the wider team framework. Indeed, he considers that it is essential for every player to have an understanding of their general and sometimes particular function in the differing situations and incidents that arise during the course of a match. He believes that such an understanding results in better team performance, as individuals are not only more aware of the options that are available to them, but, subsequently, are also able to make quick and effective decisions. However, in discussing the concept of role, Bob believes that it is important for a coach not to overly control or restrict players so that they lose their ability to evaluate situations and make their own decisions. Rather, he considers that a clearly outlined team framework enables players to fully explore the dimensions of their role while preserving the degree of organisation needed in top-level competition. In further articulating this viewpoint he asserted that:

> It's absolutely vital. Some part of a coach's explanation needs to automatically include the justification of why you're asking them to do certain things in certain situations. I suppose my philosophy is to work hard for the individual so he not only has all the skills at his disposal, but he also has an understanding of what he has to do and when he has to do it. That's important to the team. A player must know what to do and be able to evaluate whether he's done it right or not. A player needs to know

what his task is if he is to give maximum difficulty to the opposition and maximum benefit to his own players.

BUILDING PLAYER CONFIDENCE THROUGH CARING

Bob believes that success on the playing field is closely related to the confidence that the players have in their coach and themselves. Consequently, he considers that it is essential for a coach to create a supportive environment in which the players feel relaxed and secure enough to 'risk failure'; a prerequisite for improvement and progress. In order to develop such a climate, he believes it necessary to act upon the needs and wants of his players both on and off the rugby field. His message here is that coaches should ensure that they facilitate the development of athletes in many and various ways.

> The coaching role is a giving role, not a taking role, so the coach needs to understand that his role is to give himself to the players. Coaches who coach simply to get results don't often succeed. What a coach has to do is help the players; he has to give himself to the players so that the players can become better players. I really think it's important to know that the role of the coach is to give, give, and give to the players.

Hence, Bob believes it necessary to establish a relationship with his players whereby they fully believe that he is working towards their best interests. He considers that players will 'believe in you' as a coach if 'you can prove to them that they are benefiting from the training programme'. He also considers that once players believe in his methods and his message, it is then possible for him to effect further and often rapid advances in their development. To get players to 'buy into your programme' is an essential part of high-performance coaching to Bob, and is an aspect in which he invests heavily.

> By and large I need the players to believe in me and what I'm saying, listen to what I'm saying and then trying to do it on the field. If you can think about players like employees, and if we can lead them into thinking that they're all part of the plans of the organisation or club, then they'll perform better, so I have to get them to believe in me. Players are like children; they love it when they're getting better. And when they think they're part of the environment, they absolutely love it. And you see it in their eyes, and in their enthusiasm, and they just know they're going in the right direction.

In further discussing this notion of player 'buy in', Bob believes that a coach must be willing to listen to the thoughts and opinions of the players, because he considers that they positively respond to a coach who is prepared to enter into dialogue with them. However, in entering into such debate, Bob ensures that such discussions are on his terms and in keeping with his agenda, thus in reality player input is limited.

He appears to believe that a coach stands to benefit from having the players think their contributions are valued, even if the reality is the opposite. Hence, although he appears willing to listen to the views of players, all parties are in no doubt as to who is 'the boss'.

In keeping with his general positive outlook on coaching, Bob emphasises the need to present players' weaknesses to them in a constructive manner. In this sense, he attempts to persuade players that they cannot fail to improve and challenges them to decide how quickly they wish to do so. In this regard, he voiced the need for a coach to engage in a partnership with players, whereby both work together to achieve performance goals.

> So we're saying to the players that we want them to do everything that they possibly can to be as good as they can possibly be. To do this, you need to convince a player that really there is no failure. Instead, it's just a matter of how quickly or slowly that he will progress. For example, I'll say to a player 'If you were bigger, fitter, stronger, and faster, do you reckon you'd be a better player?' and he'd say 'Well yeah, sure.' Then I'd say, 'Okay, well we are going to try and help you become bigger and stronger and fitter and faster.' So we know where we're going, we know what is going to happen, we know what we're going to do, we know how we're going to do it, and we'll get there together.

In addition to his commitment to 'working with the players', Bob considers a sense of humour to be an essential feature of his coaching practice. He attributes two principal benefits to its use. First, he believes that players often better remember messages that are presented with some humour, which has obvious performance benefits. Second, he considers that, through the use of humour, a coach can help to lift some of the tension that accompanies top-level sport. Here, he commented:

> I know that the players make fun of me sometimes. They get enjoyment out of being able to mimic the things I do and say, so I leave them in my repertoire because I think that's a good outlet for them. You know, some of the expressions I use, I know they think they're right funny and so they fall over laughing, but I'm happy about that because I think that, one, they remember it and, two, it gives them a laugh. It brings some comic relief to what is a pressurised job for them. I think it's all part of the psychology of coaching.

In terms of further developing the confidence of his players, Bob returned to the theme of organisation and how he attempts to establish a clear and consistent training and playing routine for his players. He considers that an organised schedule contributes to the performance and general well-being of the players as they derive a clear sense of purpose from it.

It's a bit like having a well organised child rather than a child that doesn't know what is happening. If someone doesn't know what is expected of him or when it's expected of him, he tends to be a bit all over the place, whereas the kid in the healthy environment knows you have to leave for school at 8 a.m. and you need to have made your bed by then and picked up your lunch, and that's what happens everyday. That's a very reassuring environment for anyone. So, if you can provide that type of environment, you'll get the players' confidence up. It's that environment which creates the feelings of security and self-confidence that we want in the players.

Finally, and perhaps most importantly, Bob believes that caring for his players outside the rugby setting is one of his most fundamental roles as a coach. In this respect, he believes that players only feel fully secure and confident if they consider the rugby club to be 'part of the family'. Consequently, Bob makes great efforts to involve the players' wives and children in the life of the club. Such an approach involves securing extra tickets to watch matches, organising transport for family members to and from games, helping new players and their families to find, and settle into, new accommodation, and arranging social functions. He believes that a coach should facilitate an environment in which the players feel comfortable, confident and secure, as only then can they achieve their best levels of performance. In his own words:

> A stable personal life is very important. I think that it's vital for the players to have a supportive stable environment to work in. There's a great need to ensure that the player's family support him in his role, in his job, because it's a very demanding one. So, if you want a person to realise their potential you must support them. A player needs to have confidence that everything outside his immediate control is being taken care of. Does he feel good about himself? Does he feel good about the environment? Does he feel proud of everything that surrounds him? If that's the case then he'll perform to his best. You need to be very demanding of them, in lots of ways, and in order that you can be very demanding of them you have to take a load of other things off their minds.

SUMMARY

The picture of Bob that emerges is that of a coach who is not only passionate about developing the technical and tactical abilities of his players, but one who also cares about their well-being and that of their families. He is the eternal optimistic perfectionist: 'I'm searching for the impossible, where can we get to tomorrow'. He also sees the coaching role as a creative opportunity, which is conceptualised and then built upon: 'like building a house or something'. Bob thus believes that a coach needs to continuously evolve with the game, and the related developments and expectations of players. The essence of Bob's coaching philosophy is perhaps best encapsulated in his response to a question about what advice he would give to new and potential coaches. Here, his belief in the concepts of technique, role and social care are plainly evident:

> You really have to coach in specifics as applied to each individual, whether it be tackling, catching, passing, a combination of passes, a ruck, a maul, or whatever. You have to coach all of those things, and make sure the players know their role in each of those individual situations, and then let the whole thing go together, almost by magic. Don't coach in generalities, coach in specifics. Also, the total environment is essential, and that is affected as much by what you do off the pitch as what you do on it. It's about developing a sense of confidence, self-worth, and well-being in the players, which can have a real effect on them and their performances. And that's probably the best advice I can give.

CHAPTER 6

▼ IAN McGEECHAN

BY ROBYN JONES AND CLIVE BREWER

INTRODUCTION

Ian McGeechan's coaching mission is to help players improve both tactically and technically by giving them an appreciation and insight into the workings of the game. Specifically, his philosophy centres on giving players an understanding of their roles within a team framework. Direction and structure, whilst emphasising the need to be oneself, crop up frequently in his story. These are themes that he believes in wholeheartedly and follows with conviction: 'I do what I believe in, what I believe is right, and I try and work with the players. And if people don't like it, they don't keep me. That's all, I'm just honest to myself.'

ON BECOMING A COACH

Similar to some of the other coaches in this book, Ian's entry into the coaching ranks wasn't particularly planned or intended. Being one of the leading players at the Headingly club in Yorkshire, whilst also representing Scotland, Ian accepted an invitation to become player-coach of the club, as a vacancy existed at the time. His interest in and passion for coaching grew in intensity as his involvement in the role continued. As a consequence of being successful, he was invited to join the Scottish national coaching team; an involvement, at various levels, that has continued to this day.

I got involved really by chance, it wasn't something that I said 'I'm going to coach when I finish playing.' It has just evolved with what I have been involved in and it has just taken off from there. At the start I didn't want full involvement, didn't expect to take it too seriously, but I ended up with the first team at Headingly for three years. Then Scotland asked me to do the under-21 side, then I was in as assistant coach for Scotland. I'd been involved in their districts for years, and then twelve or thirteen years ago I got involved with the Scotland job, and have been ever since really.

What Ian was really 'involved' in at the time was teaching. Being a teacher heavily influenced his views on coaching, particularly on the need to be prepared, organised and clear in his direction and communication. Ian believes that his emphasis on establishing a disciplined structure and then coaching within it is a legacy of his background as a teacher:

I'm an education man really, and a lot of what I do goes back to Carnegie where I did my teacher training. The preparation that I got there to be a teacher was second to none. They insisted on standards, discipline, it was almost like the army, that you had to be immaculate, your preparation had to be immaculate. If my notes were wrong, I had to do them again. They didn't compromise. They set a standard, and that was it. You had to meet that standard every time you prepared a lesson, every time you did a lesson, that was what they were after, standards of excellence. But it was very disciplined. Your kit had to be clean, you had to be there early, you had to have everything checked so your preparation was spot on. You knew exactly where everything was, and you went in totally in control of the whole environment.

The attention to detail and accompanying levels of preparation were principles on which Ian thrived. These principles were easily transferred from the classroom to the sports field as he was forging his personal coaching philosophy and style: 'I suppose I coached like I taught.' Although his initial entry into coaching was largely unintended, his enthusiasm for the game was never in doubt, making the transition from player to coach, on reflection, somewhat inevitable:

As a teacher, and as a player I was always looking at tactics, and was captain of teams and things, so in that way I suppose it was a natural progression to become a coach. I'd always thought about the game, and talked to players about it. I was always interested in that side of it, and just took it on at the club basically because there was no coach, and it needed some organising, so I took it on board.

ON THE IMPORTANCE OF ORGANISATION: 'GETTING RID OF THE GREY AREAS'

Ian's belief in the importance of preparation and organisation extends into what he considers to be the main role and responsibility of coaches. Specifically, he believes that players should have their roles carefully explained within the wider team framework – a case of coaching individually within a collective structure. He terms such a process 'getting rid of the grey areas in the players' minds'. Getting players to understand their respective roles will, he believes, result in better team performances. The coach's role, therefore, is viewed fundamentally as a proactive one in terms of establishing the team shape and general game plan for the season, then coaching with definitive aims in mind. Consequently, each session should have a definite purpose within the overall season plan.

> I think that a key aspect of my role here is to give direction and to plan programmes; it is to make the players better individually, so that we can then collectively and tactically be better. But it is a twofold thing. It's an individual thing, but it is also a collective thing. And the players have got to be as good as their role. By understanding their role, you get a better effective team performance. Also, I've never believed in doing practices just to make them look pretty. I think that every practice has to have a purpose, then the player builds up a better understanding of the shape of the game, because he has to see, I think that we all have to see, the same game. It's no good me coaching one [game] and the players seeing a different one . . . everything is about working towards the same game, so, in a way, that to me is the direction.

Even though he believes passionately in establishing an organised framework for his teams, Ian does not view this as restricting the players' performances in any way. On the contrary, he views such direction and role clarification as a means of allowing players to more freely express themselves: 'No matter how good the talent is in there, it can't come out if the structure which produces the stage for performance isn't there, because it hasn't got the self discipline to be used by itself.' Consequently, he considers the establishment of a 'structural stage' as a prerequisite to get the best out of players. In his own words:

> If you haven't got a structure, then I don't think that you can do anything; it all becomes too airy-fairy. I think people like structure, people like discipline, and actually the most fluid games are when you play at your most disciplined, not the other way. You get freedom of expression out of structure while you will destructure a game without discipline, not the other way around. I also relate it to if you haven't got a good control of language, then you can't be a William Shakespeare, you can't be a Wordsworth. Discipline and structure give you the opportunity to do that. Once that is in place, then you've got all of the variations that can come

through, because you have got the understanding. Everybody has to have the same framework, the same picture in their mind, and if they have that, then you have got your choices.

Getting players to take responsibility on the field and making 'good' decisions is one of Ian's principal aims as a coach. Establishing a structure through which the players can play is his means of achieving this. Thus, he considers that the more secure players are in their role-awareness, the more aware they are of the options available to them, hence the better they are at making decisions. He also believes that such security allows them the freedom to creatively explore the boundaries of their roles while maintaining a necessary degree of organisation. Consequently, he believes that the players get the best of both worlds.

Although Ian puts great store in developing his players tactically, this is not done at the expense of what he defines as the 'core skills'. Indeed, such skills are considered crucial to the successful implementation of any game plan. He considers it necessary to practise such skills until they become habitual within the players; that is, until their execution becomes 'subconscious' or 'second nature'. Hence, he is unapologetic that sometimes his coaching sessions may seem repetitive

> You ask them to do it again and again and again and again. Every time that you do it, it has got to be right. These [core skills] are personal, these are how I see the game. Because they are key to how we want to play, so in those core skills, I don't compromise. They have to be good at them. They have to practice, and be good at them. I mean I have a view of the game and how it should be played. Things that you do every time, to be able to pick the ball off the ground, to be able to move it away quickly, because if you can't do that then you can't actually develop your tactics. So we have six or eight skills which are in more or less every session, in some shape or form, sometimes in an easier way, other times just part of another drill, or a combination of drills, but they are always in there. They are the key to making it all work. The poorer we do them, the poorer we play.

ESTABLISHING A LEARNING ENVIRONMENT TO 'GROW PLAYERS'

Echoing his educational training, Ian was keen the underline the importance of establishing a 'learning environment' in his sessions: 'I'm really trying to coach individuals to understand something.' Here, ensuring the players recognised the relevancy of his coaching and related exercises was crucial, in an effort to gain what he terms a 'collective understanding'. This was often achieved through informal pre-training meetings with players, to explain and talk through what he as a coach and they as a team were trying to achieve and why: 'I feel that the players should know what we are trying to do, so I share my thoughts with them, I try and tell

them what we are doing and why. I give them reasons for the things that I do.' The importance of explaining to players why things were done in a particular way is very important to Ian, because he considers it necessary for the players to believe in what they are trying to achieve, if on-field success is to become a reality. This philosophy is perceived to be particularly evident following defeats. He believes it is vital that he gives the players direct pointers for why a game was lost; hence his immediate responses and subsequent sessions following a defeat are very analytical and explanatory in nature.

> You know, players are confused if they are losing, because they always ask 'why?' They don't understand why they lost. If you can give them reasons why, and ways of changing it, then you have given them a focus again. You don't just tell them that they played badly, or it was crap, or whatever, because it doesn't mean anything. All it does is confuse them. So, pin-point key things for them to hang on to, to work on. Give them a focus, so they know. You are giving them something to latch on to, and saying 'right, if we hang on to this, and do this, we'll win'. That refocuses them.

In further expanding upon the need for coaching sessions to be 'relevant', Ian emphasised the requirement for practices to replicate game situations wherever possible. Hence, the learning within them is contextualised – a strategy that again serves the greater goal of getting his players to understand the game. What really underlines this commitment to establishing a learning environment is his belief that he is trying to 'grow players'. Thus, he invests heavily in foundational skills and game plans and then gives players the freedom to explore their capabilities:

> There's one saying which I like, 'You give them roots to grow, and wings to fly.' That's what you try to do, you grow players. You grow the best player possible. And if the roots are not right, the flower never appears. So, sometimes you don't see the beauty of the talent that might be there, because the foundation is not right, the root is not right.

When questioned about how such a developmental philosophy co-exists with the ultimate aim of winning, the criteria by which he keeps his job, Ian gave a measured response. He acknowledged that winning was very important in his current circumstance but considered that his emphasis on developing the players tactically as well as technically was the correct one. His aim was not merely to win games but also to maximise the potentialities of his players, both individually and as a team. Coaching with such goals in mind, he believed, would result in the winning looking after itself. He expressed it thus:

> I suppose my philosophy is [pause] just to play the best rugby possible, and to challenge the players to play the best rugby that's inside them, and . . . to play a game which would stand up to scrutiny on a world stage. Tactically, I suppose that's what I am trying to do . . . You can't do

IAN McGEECHAN

everything you might want to do even with an international side, but it doesn't stop you trying to achieve, and go in that direction. Sometimes it causes problems for us, because in the environment that we are in here, winning is very important. So that has to be important, you have to be doing that. But, my philosophy is to make them play better, and by doing that, by being better at what they do, it'll make the winning easier.

ON DEALING WITH PLAYERS

In discussing the coaching climate he tries to create, Ian was aware that fractiousness or antagonisms within the 'camp' would be counterproductive to achieving good performances, thus recognising the coaching context as fundamentally a social one. Ian was also aware of his responsibility to foster an environment that 'is as helpful and as conducive to what we want to achieve'; one that the players find stimulating, comfortable and enjoyable. Hence, he was keen to stress that his 'door is always open to players', and that he needed to take the time to get to know them as people. Thus, he emphasised the importance of being accessible and approachable to his players:

> Something that they have got to be totally at ease with is talking to me about anything, whether it is rugby or non-rugby. You know, if they have fallen out with the girlfriend, or wife or whatever [laughs], mistress, you've got to take that in . . . and for some of them it's very important that you know a bit about their life, and their lifestyle, and what is happening, because if they are unhappy, they won't be playing good rugby.

He is also aware of the need to vary his motivational methods to the perceived requirements of the players: 'I mean, some players don't respond to being bawled out. Others need it. So it is totally personal, as to who is involved.' He terms it 'being flexible'. Similarly, he believes it is not productive to criticise a player in front of others, preferring to do it in private, often with video evidence to explain the shortcomings in detail to ensure understanding. The only time he considers 'laying down the law in public' is when he thinks his players have underachieved which reflects the high expectations he has of them and himself: 'The only time I have really bawled them out was after wins, when I think that we could have been better, and I think that we have got complacent, or we are accepting things.'

It is unsurprising therefore that Ian, like other coaches in this book, likes to see himself as a 'players' coach'. Having played at the highest level, he sees himself as being able to relate well to them, whilst fundamentally enjoying their company: 'I prefer it when I've got a tracksuit on and I'm out there with them.' He remains aware of the need to develop and maintain positive and empathetic relationships with players if he is to get the best out of them, while their camaraderie keeps him enthused: 'That's what I enjoy, I enjoy the rapport between them, and the chat and the conversations.'

Ian's belief in maintaining good relationships with players extends to involving them in discussions about the team direction. This relates to his aim of making sure that the players understand and 'buy in' to his game plan. However, as with the earlier point of allowing players freedom within his structure, Ian appeared acutely aware that the coach must provide the direction for such discussions. Far from being a 'free for all' therefore, such input would be limited within a fixed agenda as set by him. Consequently, although he recognises the need to listen to the players and empathise with them, he is also aware that 'there are times when you need to be dictatorial, because you need the direction to be one way'.

COACH CERTIFICATION AND LEARNING TO BE A COACH

Ian has no formal coaching qualifications and appears rather sceptical of them: 'A coaching course has never produced an international coach. I think that international coaches are different, you can't make them.' He considers that elite coaches are often unique or 'one offs'; hence he remains unconvinced of the worth of a 'coaching system' that could devalue the originality or uniqueness of coaches. However, he concedes that formal coaching courses could have a value in terms of providing a fundamental or basic knowledge about the 'specifics of rugby', or in developing communication skills. He believes that his teacher training gave him a much more solid background in this respect than any coaching certification could do, while he considers coaching courses inevitably to be dated, taking into account the speed at which the modern game is developing:

> If you are relying on coaching courses, you are relying on things that are probably about five years out of date anyway. Because once it gets on paper, it is already out of date. At this level, you are looking at new things all of the time. I mean, a lot of people are still using my stuff from the [British] Lions tour of '97 now. I was asked to do two courses for the Youth Development Officers not too long ago on the defensive things that we used there because it was such a big feature in South Africa. It's really out of date now though [laughs] as things do move on quickly. I suppose coaching courses are useful things for people who want to get involved who haven't had a teaching or an educational background though.

Concerning his continuing professional development, he laments the lack of opportunities to interact with other coaches at possible conferences or meetings to share and develop his thoughts and theories about the game and coaching in general. For coaches who work at the elite level this, he believes, is far more likely to lead to progression, rather than further attendance at systematic courses. Indeed, he believes that most of his development to date has resulted from just informally watching, talking and thinking rugby, which reflects his passion for the game: 'I suppose I'm just a total bore on rugby I think [laughs], or so my wife says [laughs].'

In contrast to some of the other coaches in this book, Ian did not have a definitive coaching mentor. As he was busy coaching from quite a young age, he reasons that he didn't have the opportunity to watch many others work. Consequently, in his own words he 'never copied anybody', although admits to 'pinching' drills from other coaches which he then integrates into his own style and philosophy. In general however, his coaching style and insights have been driven by how he analyses and perceives the game as a whole to be developing.

A recurring theme within Ian's 'story' is the need to remain 'yourself'; to be true and consistent to what you think is right as a coach. He recounts one instance from the 1980s, when he first coached the Scotland B team, in which he did not adhere to this principle and based his coaching on what he thought was required. As a result, he had a miserable experience. Nevertheless, it provided him with a conviction never to repeat the mistake again:

> I coached the way I thought they wanted me to do it, and it was awful. I didn't enjoy it, and I said to a lad who became Scotland coach a few years ago, Ritchie Dixon, who was my assistant coach then, I just said 'Ritchie, just remind me, if I ever get the opportunity to coach Scotland B again, I'm going to do it my way' and that's what I have done ever since.

Such a belief resonates with his view that a coach 'should have his own personality, a real personality'. When asked to clarify this, he spoke in terms of the need to be original, ambitious and a strong character if one is to succeed as a coach. Hence, he is firm in his own mind about the merits of his approach. His sincerity and belief in what he does and the way that he does it echoes throughout his words and provides evidence of a coach who passionately believes in his philosophy of helping players fulfil their potentialities both technically and tactically.

THE ATTRIBUTES OF A GOOD COACH AND EFFECTIVE COACHING

In order to establish a good coaching environment, Ian considers that a coach must have the respect of the players. When questioned as to why he thought his players respected him, he paused ('I don't know' [laughs]). On reflection, he returned to the theme of having empathy for players and understanding them as people as well as athletes. He considers that his own playing career as an international for Scotland and the British Lions certainly helped in this respect, both in terms of understanding the pressures on players and of giving him some immediate expert power in their eyes. However, he considers that playing at the highest standard is not a prerequisite for becoming a successful coach although some experience of high quality rugby as a player would be essential. This is based on his belief that such experience is needed to have an 'innate understanding of the game . . . you have a different understanding about what is possible because you have actually been part of it'. What is of equal, if not greater, importance to Ian

is the coach's demonstration of sound technical knowledge, which again underlines his belief in this aspect of the coach's role:

> I don't think that you can coach at this level without a reasonable technical knowledge, because a lot of the things that you do are technical . . . in that, you have to see when something is right, or wrong, you have to put something in place, or be part of a conversation or discussion which can put something in place. Now if you cannot be a full part of that, you would lose respect from the players.

In further elaborating on good practice, Ian cites the need to be a good communicator, flexible although directional, in addition to being perceptive as to the needs and wants of players. He also stresses the requirement to be patient with players, allowing them time to absorb and experiment with new information before building further upon it. He related an experience after returning from the British Lions' trip to South Africa in 1997, when he was impatient with his club players at Northampton:

> I was annoyed most of the time basically which I am generally not, as I wasn't relating to the players in any way. It wasn't their fault, it was my fault. I was confusing them, giving them too much. I was giving them too much information, giving them too much to do. I was challenging them too much. So all I was doing in fact was confusing them. In the end I had to step back, break it all down, simplify it, repeat it, and just ease off.

Hence, he appreciates the need to analyse and reflect on his own coaching practice in order to get the best out of his players. Indeed, Ian considers it a vital part of his role to sometimes just 'watch, observe and think about what's going on' both in terms of his players' performances and his own actions in contributing to them. Thus, his largely measured and thoughtful approach to coaching surfaced yet again.

In developing the discussion into his views on effective coaching, Ian was clear about the need to ensure that both the content of his sessions, and the players' involvement, were characterised by intensity. This was allied to flexibility in understanding when to demand more from players and when to be satisfied with less:

> I try to get the intensity into sessions because that is when you really force players to make decisions. But you have got to be careful to balance that, and not push them too hard, or not give them something that they can't deal with, or can't cope with. It's always monitoring what level you think that they are at, and when they are ready for something new, or when they need more pressure, or more intensity.

In his on-going search for success and excellence, Ian feels the need to constantly challenge his players, not only physically and technically but also on their understanding of the game ('I mean the intelligence of the game, tactics'). Consequently, he sets very high standards for himself and for the performance of his teams. His benchmark here is not to emulate the success of others in style or substance, but to play the 'perfect game'. Such a philosophy ties in with his absence of a role model within the game and the value he places on being original and creative as a coach. Thus, he has a clear but constantly evolving vision about how he believes the game should be played, and he coaches with this ideal in mind. In his own words:

> I just look at rugby as a world stage. I've never copied anybody; what I look at is where the game is going . . . where I want us to go. I don't compare us with England or anybody else, but what's the best game that we should be trying to play. As I said before I think, I just want my teams to play the best rugby possible, to play the best game they've got.

SUMMARY AND CONCLUSION

The picture that emerges from Ian's 'story' is of a coach who is heavily interested and involved in the game *per se*. Indeed, he appears fascinated by it. This immersion is manifest in a number of ways, such as the preparation of a definitive detailed game plan within which the players are allocated structured roles. Far from restricting them, Ian believes such clarification allows the players to better and more confidently express themselves, secure in the knowledge that support is at hand. Ian's priority is in giving players a positive learning experience, which entails working on their understanding of the game as well as techniques, thus pushing them to play to their intellectual as well as their physical capabilities. The resulting quality experience is what he wants his players to have:

> 'Sometimes you can see it, because the players will know when something has gone really well, and you know that they feel it, and part of it is that you feel it too, and if you are not aiming for the highest quality, then you will never get it.'

Although a technical element runs deeply through his philosophy and practice, Ian believes ultimately that coaching at the top level is an 'art form'; hence his conviction that systematic courses and 'coaching by numbers can only take you so far'. To excel, he believes that 'you need to get to the heart of the game. You need an understanding of it, you need an innate feel for the game, because it is emotional. The game is based on emotion, and you cannot categorise that. You cannot quantify it.'

Passion for the game and working with players to achieve excellence through a systematic game plan are the cornerstones of Ian's thinking. They have emerged from personal reflection and an educational background, and have served him well to date. Although Ian appears to highly value the control he engenders over his working environment, the essence of his coaching persona is better encapsulated in his advice to fledgling coaches. Here, his continuing enthusiasm, fervour and love of the sport are plainly evident:

Never stop learning. Understand that you never know enough. However long you have been doing it, whether it is one year or twenty years, you can still learn. You should never shut your eyes or ears to what is going on. Because as soon as you close your eyes, close your ears, you stop. You can't travel or go anywhere because you don't know which direction to go. So, the more you listen, the more you see, the better understanding you get, the more you keep moving forward.

CHAPTER 7

▼ DI BASS

BY KATHLEEN ARMOUR

INTRODUCTION

Di Bass is a swimmer, a swimming coach, a mother, a wife and a university lecturer. She is best described as a professional, knowledgeable, approachable yet firm and determined coach, and as a warm, sociable person who retains something of the fun-loving wild child of her youth. It is important to state all of these things at the outset because to understand this coach, it is necessary to grasp the complexities of a wider life. Moreover, it is worth noting that the list of Di's roles is not in some form of rank order (nor is it exhaustive). Rather, the individual roles jostle with each other, converging and foregrounding in different configurations to produce the right person at the right time in the appropriate context. Even more remarkable is the success that Di has achieved in doing so many of these roles, and the way in which she makes the junctures between them appear to be almost seamless.

WHO IS DI BASS?

Di coaches both able-bodied and disabled swimmers. She has been coaching for over twenty years and coaches both children in a local club and high-level university swimmers. More recently, she has become involved with disability swimming at the elite level and has been appointed Regional Coach for the World Class Performance Midlands swimmers. She was also one of the coaches for the GB Paralympic team

at the 2000 Olympics. Di holds the qualification of ASA Coach, one level below the highest available (Senior Coach) which is held by very few coaches. It would not be accurate to say, however, that official ASA qualifications have featured strongly in the development of Di the coach. She feels that she has learnt little from them and that they are best described as functional or as a means to an end:

> 'You just go through the process of doing the qualifications. I mean even the ASA coaches actually say this, "We don't intend to teach you anything on this course. We just want to see if you're of a high enough standard to coach at national level." '

Di identifies a primary problem with coach certification in swimming to be one of keeping both coaches and trainers up-to-date. Essentially, many involved in coaching, particularly at the lower levels, simply do not read enough:

> It's a very technical sport. And these things are developing all the time. I mean an example is, you know . . . forces in swimming, and there was a lot about lift and then lately it's been shown that perhaps this doesn't dominate and it's more drag propulsion. But I still think you'll find a lot of coaches teaching kids stuff about lift force.

In one respect, Di notes that the ASA courses should be praised – they are some of the best-known coaching courses/certificates, and other sports have copied their model. Yet, even so, the problems for Di seem to stem from the basic, unchallenging level of much of the content. As she comments about her ASA Coach course: 'I think a lot of people felt that there were much better things they could be spending their weekend doing. But I think it's sad.'

This is a good example of where Di's different life roles combine to produce a unique coach. Di is also a lecturer at a university, and this role provides both the requirement and the resources for keeping her knowledge up-to-date. Resources include the obvious access to texts and research, and the less obvious but all-important interaction with leading sports scientists who have an interest in swimmers and swimming. Thus, one of the keys to understanding Di's coaching expertise is the way in which new knowledge in swimming and sport science informs her practice. As she says, 'There is a lot to learn. I think because of the job I do I've always read a lot . . . I make sure that I spend a lot of time keeping up on swimming developments. And I read a lot around swimming and do all that.' It is unsurprising, therefore, that she has often found the more mundane aspects of coach certification in swimming to be somewhat disappointing.

WHY SWIMMING COACHING?

Like other coaches in this book, Di's entry into coaching was not planned. Previously, she was successful as a personnel officer with a major company and was earning a high salary. During this time she had no formal coaching qualifications:

I started coaching oh about twenty years ago originally without, with very few qualifications, well no qualifications really. It was interest in swimming . . . I got into coaching through somebody. I went swimming once and somebody saw me swimming and said would I go down to the local club, just to sort of demonstrate a few strokes to this club that they were setting up. And then I got involved in coaching and then carried on ever since.

Shortly after this in 1978, near her thirtieth birthday, Di was interviewed as a respondent in a research project on women in management being undertaken by Manchester University. This event changed her life:

the interviewer did Kelly's Repertory Grid with me and said 'sport is very important in your life, you should do something in sport'. And then on the radio, there was a thing about the new degree at Loughborough University in PE and Recreation Management and I thought, hmm I know a bit about management, I'm interested in sport and I applied.

The change in direction had some costs: 'It cost me rather a lot of money to come here I tell you.' However, from the outset on her degree course, Di became involved with swimming teaching and coaching, both locally and in the university. Initially, she had no official qualifications, but with her knowledge and experience, she soon found herself to be in demand.

Having her own children marked another important stage in Di's career as a coach:

I always kept very much up to date with swimming and coaching and that sort of thing. And once I got the kids and they started getting into swimming I started doing more help in there and decided that I'd do a few qualifications. And I ended up working up to an ASA Coach.

Di has been involved in swimming coaching continuously from 1979, but she has also gained lower level qualifications and some sporadic experience in coaching squash and gymnastics. She took a gymnastics coaching certificate when she was helping her children with their gymnastics 'because I thought I ought to know what I was doing' and the squash qualification because she was playing and, perhaps almost naturally, involved in some coaching at the same time. However, once the children were no longer involved in gymnastics, and she stopped playing squash, her personal interest in the activities was lost and she stopped coaching both.

In recent years Di has played a major role in young people's competitive swimming at a local club and also has involvement in a successful university swimming squad. Most recently, she encountered a swimmer at her local town club who was visually impaired. As a result, and unsurprisingly given the value she places on gaining accurate, up-to-date knowledge, Di attended an education weekend on disability swimming in order to inform her practice. From that point, Di has become

increasingly involved with disabled swimmers. Three of her swimmers were selected for the Paralympics in Sydney in 2000 and she was selected as one of the coaches to travel with the team: 'So that's how I got where I am.'

The picture that begins to emerge, therefore, is one of a coach who places a high value on acquiring the best knowledge available to inform and support her practice. Di is not willing to compromise on this, and it is a defining characteristic that can be traced throughout her career.

COACHING, SWIMMING AND WINNING

Di sees herself as a little different from some other coaches. Apart from anything else, she is a female swimming coach and although there are many female swimming teachers, there are few coaching at the top levels. Interestingly, there are more top-level female coaches in disability swimming. Di certainly believes that winning is important, but made the point several times that there is a balance to be struck between focusing on winning and 'development', especially when dealing with children. Di is very focused on development, insisting that this is the way to keep children involved in the sport, an aspiration that drives her youth coaching. She firmly believes in and practises her philosophy that 'I'd like everybody to reach their full potential.' She acknowledges that this sounds idealistic, and that not everyone can win but 'it's just making people hopefully enjoy the sport, and within the limits that we've got in terms of training time to just get everybody to do as well as they can'. At the same time, she would argue:

> it's wrong to say winning isn't important because that's what the kids want to do and if you continually go into galas and don't win then the motivation of the club is really low. At the moment at the town club, which is where I do some coaching as well, we've started winning and it's very important to the kids you know. It's like on Saturday where we actually won this trophy gala and for them to pick up the trophy at the end was great.

These sentiments, and the need for balance, would probably be shared by youth coaches in many sports. However, swimming is also unique. It is different in context and environment and Di sees the potential for problems arising from that difference. For example, given the structure of the swimming environment, it is easy for the coach to become wholly autocratic 'because you've got the swimmers in a confined space . . . you're there on the poolside, you've sorted out the training sessions, so they do pretty well what you tell them to do and it's a very controlling environment'. She has also encountered swimming coaches who are self-declared 'control freaks' who claim to be able to 'manipulate a swimmer to do what they want'. It is in this context that Di sees the potential for abuse of swimmers by coaches. The swimming environment normalises a high level of coach-dependence and this is exacerbated in the case of children 'who will do anything if the coach says 'look, I can make you win, I can make you a champion'; they'll do practically anything for that'. Indeed, given the environment, it is very difficult to structure coaching in any other way:

> Because of the environment they're in, it's really difficult to get them [swimmers] involved, you can spend ages because they've got ear plugs on, they've got hats over their ears, they've got the goggles on and sometimes if you can't see you can't hear, if you see what I mean. And really it's not placed for big conversations and lots of democracy and whatever, lots of choice. So it's quite hard and I think you'll find that some of the top swimmers are very coach dependent. And they like it that way.

This also explains why Di can be viewed as different from some – perhaps many – other swimming coaches. Her preferred style of coaching can be described as committed, thoughtful, collaborative and democratic, leading to coaching sessions that are physically and mentally demanding, and that retain a high degree of personal respect for the individual swimmer. The swimmer is expected to be a fully committed, thinking and involved participant who learns from the experience and shares the responsibility for self-improvement. This might explain why Di found herself to be in a minority on one particular ASA coaching course: 'everybody was teasing me because they said "oh we've got no time for that sort of PE philosophy". It's all sort of about winning and being autocratic – that sort of philosophy'. Di is firm in her belief, however, that there is more to coaching than this and that 'winning is not the be all and end all of everything'.

THE GOOD SWIMMING COACH

Di perceives herself to be 'softer' than other coaches with whom she works. She takes a position that is the polar opposite of being a 'control freak' yet, at the same time, she is a persistent, determined and demanding coach. For example, she is prepared to be more tolerant than other coaches when swimmers miss the occasional session; she is more likely to talk *with* them about it than to shout *at* them. She finds it difficult to identify the source of her particular approach to coaching: 'it's just a different feeling. I think it's women. Or being a mother. I don't know. Or just me!' Di also recognises that she is less willing than some other coaches to promote herself:

> 'I don't know about in other sports, but a lot of swimming coaches it's all about self promotion and I don't think I self promote either, and that maybe is good or bad, I don't know, but a lot of people have told me that and I think it's probably true.'

The reasons for this, however, are clear to Di: 'I think that's probably because swimming isn't my life.' Comparing herself with another top swimming coach, she points out, 'he says, you know, it's the most important thing in his life'. Yet for Di, once you have a family and children, and even just the fact of being a woman,

makes things 'different'. However, it is more than that: 'I have other interests, I mean, like going to the theatre or doing other stuff. So it's not the most important thing in my life. I think sometimes that's why my reactions are a bit different.'

Although Di admires several coaches, she couldn't identify a particular coach who had inspired her or who could be identified as a role model. Given that several of the coaches with whom she works are not as well qualified, and are certainly not as well informed as Di, then perhaps this is not surprising. However, of one of the coaches she commented: 'I admire him in terms of how he motivates and how he's so cheery at times . . . And I think he's great . . . so I take certain things from him.' Here again, the issue of being a woman coach arises:

> I think the best one I've come across is him. I really do, I think in terms of his commitment. I mean, I think his approach is different to mine and I could never go on the poolside and be him if you see what I mean. Because I think this is something else which is different between women and men. Men can go on and sometimes say things. But if a woman came out with it, the swimmers would look at you strangely, you know. I think it's the same in lecturing as well.

Di is referring to the joking, risqué, almost blokeish banter that some male coaching/lecturing colleagues use routinely as part of their pedagogy. She admits that this can be effective, although not for all learners, and that it can make sessions fun. Certainly there is something about its casual nature that she admires and would like to be able to emulate but she is quite certain that it would not work coming from her: 'No I can't do that. Never attempt it, it would fail so dismally.' She also feels that it is overplayed in some cases and that it can trivialise the learning activity.

THE GOOD COACHING SESSION

A good coaching session for Di is one where she gets a good reaction from the swimmers 'and sometimes you just get this feeling that it's gone well'. She suggests that it is difficult to know in advance about what will or will not be a good session. The reasons for something working – or not – are hard to pinpoint, but Di has found that it is not necessarily related to the amount of planning or preparation undertaken. Although at one level Di feels that planning and preparation are vital parts of the coaching role, sometimes she has found that spontaneous sessions work best. Importantly, these are embedded in a deep knowledge of swimming and a coherent structure – so perhaps it is just the occasional change of style that works. Ultimately, for Di, a session is judged on 'how the swimmers respond and how they react and how they come away'. Moreover, she actively seeks feedback on her sessions. At the local town club, her own children are swimmers, so she encourages them to tell her how the session went. Di also believes in setting specific targets that encourage swimmers to take some responsibility for their learning and achievements:

I think the important thing is to try and set goals in the session . . . I do try in terms of either giving target times or setting some sort of process goals or you know doing certain things like 'okay now we're going to work on streamlining' or 'now we're going to do this' or whatever.

On the other hand, sessions are bad sessions for Di when swimmers don't make enough of an effort. She recalls her frustration with one group of young swimmers at the town club who attended regularly but were not prepared to push themselves 'so it's trying to get across to them that perhaps the training occasionally has to be a bit tiring in order for it to be effective'. This lack of willingness to make an effort links with something else that irritates Di:

I do get annoyed when people regularly don't turn up for sessions. I mean I previously said that I perhaps am not tough enough on them. But like Saturday, I mean it took a lot of organising because of personal commitments and things, to actually get there for half past three for training and three people turned up. And then six people came to swim afterwards and, and I know it's exam time and I know it's difficult for a student sometimes this time of year and there's things going on like their hall balls and various other things happening. But that annoys me.

Di recognises, however, that this might be a reflection on herself and her unwillingness to be autocratic and 'hard'. She has decided that maybe she needs to be tougher with swimmers and so she is going to try to change her approach next year. For Di, being 'tougher' means that if swimmers do not turn up for sessions, then she will ask them to leave the squad. As she points out, swimming sessions require a pool but have few other environmental issues to consider – the weather is not a concern, for example. So, although characterising herself as a 'soft' coach, Di has a very low tolerance for lack of effort on the part of swimmers. She certainly would not accept it from herself and so will not accept it from them. The difficulty, perhaps, is coming to terms with the fact that some swimmers are not as highly self-motivated as she would like them to be.

DISABILITY SWIMMING

A significant recent development in Di's career has been the move to coaching disability swimming. This has posed a new set of challenges, although Di's approach to coaching has remained fundamentally the same. Perhaps the first point to be made is that Di usually works with the top-rated disabled swimmers, and many of them are in the least disabled categories, so she feels able to treat them 'just like any other swimmers'. She raises some important issues, however, about comparing the two (able bodied and disabled) swimmers and their routes to top-level swimming. In one respect, the route to the top for disabled swimmers is a little easier: 'they do work really hard, but it's a little bit easier and I think they wouldn't deny it. It is a bit easier to get to the top because there are fewer people to compete

against. So it's easier in a way'. On the other hand, Di notes that there are fewer events and the qualifying standards are a lot higher: 'to go to the Paralympics you had to be ranked third in the world. You had to have a chance of a medal'. Even so, Di would argue that the route has been a little bit easier and success has been achieved with 'not less work, but perhaps not as much work as they should have been doing'. Thus, Di identifies one of the challenges of coaching this group as

> 'getting them to realise that now the world is moving on and everybody is doing a lot more work and it's becoming a lot more professional and certainly they are now lottery funded and people are full time swimmers and you're paid to swim so they've got to do the training'.

However, there is another important way in which the routes to top-level swimming have differed for disabled swimmers, and it is located in the causes of their disability: 'They have to go through a hell of a lot you know. A lot of them are, you know, disabled because of childhood cancer and, for whatever reason, car accidents . . . you know, they've been through stuff that makes them a bit different.' That very difference is, perhaps, the reason why Di's coaching style is so well suited to disability swimming. She sees her role as obtaining the best from each of them, and her 'soft', understanding yet determined and persistent approach would appear to be highly effective. Thus, Di can appreciate the difficulties faced by disability swimmers, while harnessing the determination and persistence that they have been forced to demonstrate in order to achieve anything; indeed everything. Her reasons for finding this group rewarding to coach have nothing to do with misplaced sympathy. It is more to do with breadth and their approach to life and swimming:

> I think it was quite interesting when I went to the Paralympics and we were talking to some volunteers in the village. And they said that within the first five days of the Paralympians being there they had more fun than they've had in the two weeks at the Olympics. They are a lot less arrogant I think. Whether that will change I don't know.

Di 'gets a kick' when swimmers do well but also feels some personal responsibility when they fail to perform to their potential: 'I think some coaches don't personally take it on board. But I do feel it quite personally that I've let them down or it's something that I've done.' Nonetheless, the 'highs' make it worthwhile 'like last Saturday because you know, as I say, we won this trophy gala and everybody swam out of their skins and everybody was on a high and the atmosphere was great and the kids were great and that was nIce'.

Di still grapples with 'that slight dilemma about not wanting to have winning as the most important thing' and she is sceptical of claims made about 'development' in youth swimming: 'actually it's nothing to do with development when it comes down to it. It's to do with what do you win on a Saturday'. She is also concerned about the problems faced by young swimmers who achieve early success 'when others catch up, as they often do'. She uses her own children as examples of the success that can be gained by working on technique, persisting with training and accepting that certain phases of maturation will help or hinder progress. Her extensive knowledge of swimming, coaching, pedagogy and children is helpful in her goal of 'getting kids to stick through the tough times and not just give up'. One of the ways she attempts to do this is by encouraging swimming groups to be sociable places where social development can occur in a supportive framework. Di also sees this as one way in which isolated swimmers can compensate for the overbearing power of an autocratic coach and perhaps redress the power balance just a little. Ideally, for example, swimmers would be supportive of each other to the extent that if a coach were missing from a session, they would be willing and able to carry out a credible training set without supervision. This is entirely consistent with Di's commitment to the development of self-motivated, responsible swimmers. She acknowledges, however, 'it takes a little bit of a while to get that sort of ethos in the club'.

CONCLUSION: THE COACH AND THE FUTURE

Di has an enduring interest in swimming and in coaching. Ideally she would like to continue coaching children, university teams and disabled swimmers, although she is currently finding the load overwhelming. This is precisely because she has maintained a balance in her life, fulfilling all the roles identified in the first sentence of this chapter: swimmer, swimming coach, mother, wife and university lecturer. In looking ahead, Di stresses the point she made earlier about coaching:

> 'I do enjoy it, but it's not the most important thing in my life. But I do feel happy on the poolside. I suppose it's because, I don't know I've always been either swimming or coaching you know so I like the environment . . . I just love the feel of water myself and I just love being near water.'

Perhaps, in this final paragraph, it is time to own up to the fact that I (Armour) too have been coached by Di, so I write both as a researcher and a swimmer (of no note at all!). I also know others whom Di has coached and, in writing this chapter, I have drawn upon their knowledge and experience. A short response to the question 'what makes Di Bass an effective coach' would probably read something like this:

- Di Bass is knowledgeable, expert, empathetic, persistent, thoughtful, fun and determined.
- She is an evidence-based practitioner.
- She has a life beyond coaching.
- She wields a very persuasive kind of gentle power: she makes *you* want to succeed.

CHAPTER 8

▼ **PETER STANLEY**

BY PAUL POTRAC

INTRODUCTION

Like many of the coaches in this book, Peter Stanley considers the social bond between coach and athlete as being critical to effective coaching. It is therefore unsurprising that Peter's coaching philosophy is one that attaches great value to the notions of high-quality instruction, athlete empowerment, the creation of a supportive and challenging training environment and the social well-being of athletes. Indeed, while Peter is most obviously recognised for coaching Olympic and World Champion triple jumper Jonathan Edwards (recently retired), his story reveals his passion and energy for working with, and caring for, all the athletes under his guidance.

ENTRANCE INTO COACHING

Peter's first steps towards becoming a top-level athletics coach were somewhat serendipitous, as they owed more to family commitments than to any logical career planning on his behalf. His first passion however was, and still is, football, and while he enjoyed representing his school at the long jump, he 'really, really wanted to be a professional footballer'. Unfortunately, he was unable to realise his dreams and so, instead, settled for a non-league football career, which he enjoyed until 'old age started to creep in'. He only became reacquainted with track and field athletics as a supportive parent, and recalled how attendance at his daughter's school sports day proved to be the starting point for his career as an athletics coach. In his own words:

Like most parents, we went to watch her at school sports day. She did three events and won them all and a guy just sidled up beside me and said 'Is that your daughter?' He was Rippon Hall, a long time member and coach of Elswick Harriers the local athletics club and he invited her along to it. He would coach the group and I'd sit on a bench and watch. After the sessions had finished we would increasingly talk about various aspects of training. Looking back he just played me and reeled me in. I'd shown an interest because of my daughter, but gradually I was getting more and more into it myself and that's when he said that I ought to do a coaching course. So that's what I did, and I thoroughly enjoyed it.

After successfully completing the Level 1 coaching course, Peter took up a voluntary post as a sprints and jumps coach at the club. He found his early experiences of coaching young athletes to be hugely enjoyable and rewarding. Several months later, Peter's newly discovered enthusiasm for coaching and athletics saw him attend and pass the Level 2 coaching course. He attributes his passion for the sport to 'the purity' of athletics, which pits 'individual against individual'.

If you're on the long jump run up, no one else can interfere with you. It's not like football or rugby or most sports where you can get away with a cheap foul or have people to help you out when things aren't going well. There's no one to help you out. It's as simple as that, it's just one against one on the day. It's all about who's best physically and mentally adapted for the event. That's what really came home to me; it was the purity, as simple as that.

Peter was soon encouraged to obtain his Senior Club Coach award, which he did, and was subsequently appointed as Regional Staff Coach for both the long and triple jumps. It was in this new position that Peter first met Jonathan Edwards. At this time, Edwards was 'the flagship of the regional elite squad' and was coached by Peter's boss and then national coach, Carl Johnson. Peter soon established a good relationship with Edwards as the latter would often 'help out' with the training sessions that Peter organised for elite junior athletes within the north-east region. He believes that the nature of this bourgeoning relationship was a significant factor in Edwards' decision to ask him to replace Carl Johnson, who had elected to pursue a career in coach education. The invitation initially filled Peter with self-doubt, as his coaching experience was limited to working predominantly with junior athletes. In spite of this, he decided, after an intense period of self-reflection, to accept the role.

I was excited when Jonathan first approached me to coach him, as the best athlete I'd coached up to that date was a junior long jumper. And that was the level I thought I would be at as a coach. So, when a guy who had already won a bronze medal at the European Championships comes up to you and says, 'Would you start coaching me please', I had to say to him 'I'll have to think about this'. I had major doubts as to whether I was up to it from an experience point of view, though I thought I could offer him something technically. So, I started watching him on video for a few nights and began to pull his technique apart. In the end I phoned him and said there's certain things we need to talk about. We got together and things just went from there. I'm a very, very lucky guy, because to have an outstanding athlete approach me when I had no proven track record was wonderful. And to be honest, I think it just came from talking, just communicating. Jonathan saw the way I was working with the youngsters and he became motivated by it.

At this time, Edwards was emerging from a period of poor form as a result of a long-standing illness. However, through adhering to a philosophy centred on 'striving for technical excellence' and 'providing motivation', Peter helped Edwards to a period of outstanding success on the domestic, European, and world stages, culminating in a gold-medal performance at the 2000 Sydney Olympics.

LEARNING TO BE A COACH

In tracing his development as a coach, Peter identified several individuals whom he considered to have had a significant impact upon his coaching practice. Here, he spoke of the initial influence of Rippon Hall, noting how Hall's 'considered' and 'scientific' approach differed fundamentally from that which he had experienced in semi-professional football. This appealed to Peter.

Watching Rippon made me think back to when I was training at various football teams. It used to be if the coach said, 'Do this till it makes you sick', you'd do it. However, Rippon had a more scientific approach to things. He didn't drive them too hard, he was very technically minded and he worked on the things that would make them run faster, without a greater effort. He was a gentle trainer. He seemed to build athletes block-by-block. And, I just thought back and wished we had trained like that when we were younger and learnt the basic skills rather than just run up and down the football pitch five times or whatever it might be. So, now I place a great emphasis on teaching the skills and techniques in my own coaching, especially with young athletes.

Additionally, Peter noted how he was impressed by the way that Hall tailored his manner and interaction to meet the requirements of the athletes. Indeed, the notions of 'adapting to your surroundings' and 'knowing your athletes' form fundamental aspects of Peter's coaching philosophy. He noted:

'I'm possibly perceived as an elite coach but I like to think that I can relate to athletes of all levels. I got that from Rippon. I'd look upon myself

as a failure if I couldn't change my style to the athletes I'm dealing with and the level they're competing at.'

When discussing the advancement of his technical knowledge, Peter identified Carl Johnson as a major influence. Here, he ascribed great value to the knowledge that he was able to glean from Johnson during the completion of his coach certification courses. In his own words:

Carl came from an educational background. He was a teacher and a very good coach. He was very knowledgeable and extremely scientific. I was very lucky that when I did my Club Coach Level 2 long jump certification, there were just two of us on it. So we had Carl between the two of us for our specific event lectures. When I did my triple jump, I was one to one with Carl and he was superb, absolutely superb. He gave me a fantastic insight into the technical nature of the event.

In addition to Rippon Hall and Carl Johnson, Peter spoke of two further individuals whom he regards as key contributors to his development. First, the immense enthusiasm and support provided by Dorothy Chipchase was perceived as crucial to his evolution as a coach, as were the excellent teaching skills of Malcolm Arnold, from whose efficient and concise manner Peter learnt a great deal.

The thing that got me with Malcolm was the simplicity of the way he explained things to athletes. He tells the athletes what they are doing, what he wants them to do, and then offers corrective advice as and when necessary. But he does it all in a very simplistic manner, and never tries to blind anyone with science, which I think is a great way of doing things.

In commenting on his continuing professional development as a coach, Peter described how he continues to observe other coaches in action thus learning valuable lessons about 'what to do and what not to do' as well as 'pinching some useful drills'. For example, in recalling a recent training camp in Florida he noted:

We were all at the track at the same time but doing different things and it was great to watch other coaches and athletes. I watched what everybody else was doing and I thought to myself 'I'm going to pinch that drill' or 'I don't like that one' and so on. There's nothing wrong with that, as it helps you to further formulate your outlook on how you do things. I'm still open minded and I still want to learn, so it's great to be able to see other people at work and what they're doing.

Although he believed that a coach should not be scared to 'borrow material' from other practitioners, he or she should give careful thought as to how they would implement such activities. In this regard, he considers that it is essential for a coach to not only be fully aware of the rationale underpinning the use of a particular

drill or exercise, but also to be prepared to 'cannibalise' it so as to ensure its appropriateness for the athletes. Peter also emphasised the potential value of working with and observing other practitioners as a formal requirement of coach education programmes. Indeed, he believes that coaches stand to benefit greatly from such experiences; much more so than from simply passing written examinations:

> When I sat my exams for the senior coaching award, I knew I was prepared for them although I definitely felt I was lacking experience. I just think there should be a more structured and logical progression, as opposed to just passing examinations. Giving coaches at all levels the opportunity to work with more senior and experienced coaches would be a good way of doing things. For example, as part of the process to work with the national squads, I've been mentored by a national level coach, which I've found to be incredibly beneficial.

The notions of 'being open minded' and 'wanting to learn' are critical aspects of Peter's coaching philosophy. Throughout his 'story', he expressed a great desire to further develop and enhance his knowledge base. Here, he not only demonstrated enthusiasm for collecting books, journals, and articles related to speed, conditioning and the long and triple jumps but also articulated the many hours he then invests in synthesising such information. Indeed, Peter was eager to emphasise that while 'text books' and 'theory' provided valuable guidelines for performance, 'the art of coaching' was applying such information in a way that was of optimal benefit to each individual athlete.

> I used to go to athletics meetings and there'd be bookstalls, and I used to buy anything that looked like it might have to do with speed, conditioning and the jumps. I used to cross reference things as well, because what one person says in one book is not the same as what another person in another books says. What you've got to remember though is that each athlete is an individual experiment. So, having read the books I would have an understanding of the general mechanisms for a take-off, but it's applying that mechanism to the individual which is the hardest part. Each person is put together slightly differently and so it's not a case of moulding the person to the theory, but moulding the theory to the athlete. That's where the science of coaching changes to the art of coaching. Knowing what's in the books is okay to a point, but it's the transference of what's in the book to what's on the runway and into the pit that is most important.

In summary, Peter has been keen throughout his career to learn from a wide range of sources and he would argue that he is continuing to learn, as he firmly believes that no coach 'knows everything'. Indeed, Peter argued that for a coach to be of maximal benefit to his or her athletes, it was vital to have an unquenchable 'thirst for information'. He also emphasised the need for coaching practitioners to tailor such knowledge to meet the individual needs and constraints of their athletes, which he believes to be a skill that separates excellent coaches from the average.

DELIVERING EFFECTIVE INSTRUCTION

At the heart of Peter's instructional philosophy is his emphasis on the technical understanding and execution of a particular event, be it the triple jump, long jump, or sprints. Generally, he considers that there are two ways to help an athlete achieve success. The first involves motivating them to jump a long way, the other, to which he generally subscribes, involves 'putting everything you have been doing in training into practice, and doing it in the correct order'. This approach, combined with the nervous energy that competition produces in athletes, is Peter's recipe for improving athlete performance. Thus, it is hardly surprising that he attaches great value to the timing and delivery of quality instruction and feedback within the practice environment.

When discussing his perceptions of effective instruction, Peter initially outlined the importance of working with a relatively small number of athletes, ideally a maximum of 8–10. His reasoning for this stems from his desire to give individually tailored high quality feedback that meets the needs of each athlete within the training group. Here, he believes that his ability to give such feedback, and for athletes to subsequently implement it, is 'watered down' by having to deal with large numbers.

> I've learnt from experience that it is hard to manage more than eight athletes, because of the individual one-to-one situations that you have to get into for athletes to progress. While, they [the athletes] all have a technical model which they strive towards, they have all got their individual way of movement and associated strengths and weaknesses. For example, some are stronger at jumping up than others, some are better at taking the weight as they come down, and some have great upper body strength, while others have better lower body strength. So, the coaching becomes very much a one-to-one process within a group climate. For example, what Jonathan Edwards wants is not the same as my daughter, who is aiming for national standard. So, it's important that, as a coach, I realise this and adapt my feedback and instruction to meet their individual needs.

With regard to the timing of feedback, Peter described how he attempts to provide such information as soon as he can after an athlete has completed a particular jump, drill, or exercise. Furthermore, he firmly believes that for such feedback to be valuable, an athlete should repeat the required exercise while such information 'is still fresh in their mind'.

In further elaborating upon his outlook on the provision of feedback, Peter highlighted the need for a coach to understand the personality and traits of each

of his or her performers. Indeed, while he generally strives to provide some initial positive feedback before critiquing an athlete's performance, he suggested that a coach must 'think about who they are speaking to' before giving the feedback. In his own words,

They are all individuals when they land in the pit. Some stand up and kick sand all over the place, others look at you with frustration written all over their faces, some will show no sign of being pleased or not pleased, while one athlete actually analyses what she is doing while she is doing it. Generally, I try to think of something positive to say because an athlete knows when they have had a bad jump or a bad attempt at doing whatever they did. You have to think about your body language and pick your words very carefully in order to diffuse any anger, stress, and worry on their behalf. However, while that often seems to work, you need to get to know the individual and work out what works best with them.

To further illustrate the point, Peter described a critical incident, which led him to reflect upon his own style of feedback and the need to tailor it to the individual athlete. He noted:

It was a freezing cold night and we were working indoors. Anyway, he came down and did his jump and it was bad. It was a bad jump and he landed in the sand and looked up with a look of 'Oh God' and I said, 'You ran in well there, you just dropped your hips a bit too early.' He said, 'Pete, I don't come here to be bullshitted by you. It was crap.' He said, 'Don't bullshit me. It was crap and I'll go back and I'll do it again.' So, I thought, rather than look for positives with everybody, I'm going to base my feedback around what they want to know and what they, as individuals, want to get from each session.

In addition to espousing the benefit of understanding the personality of each individual athlete, Peter also emphasised the value of establishing a rapport with the athletes under his guidance. Here, he suggested that athletes are more likely to achieve if they think that they have a positive relationship with the coach, as they will then believe in the instruction that they are receiving. In his own words:

There's a lot to say about the relationship between a coach and athlete. You can usually get people to do something by asking them, but you tend to get more from athletes if they have got a rapport with you. I mean it's like the football analogy. You can have the best player in the world, but if he doesn't like the manager and doesn't want to play for him, then he's never gonna give of himself fully to the team. I think it's similar for athletes as well. They are never gonna give everything unless they are totally confident in, and have a rapport with, the coach.

When discussing the attributes of effective instruction, Peter underlined the importance for a coach to have an extensive knowledge of his or her sport, as he believes that athletes would expose any shortcomings in this department. Indeed, unlike many of the other coaches in this book, Peter was eager to point out that, more often than not, athletes chose to work with him and not vice versa. In order to keep on working with high-performance athletes, Peter described how it was essential for him to demonstrate a knowledgeable and credible 'front'. Consequently, he believes that the information and feedback he provides to the athletes must be seen by them to be appropriate and to contribute to improved levels of performance. In order to maintain this credible and knowledgeable image, Peter also spoke of how he refrained from actively demonstrating techniques. Given his self-confessed limited ability as an athlete, he feels that poor demonstrations would not only dilute the message that he wishes to send to his athletes, but could also result in a loss of respect for him as a coach.

> There is no way on earth that I can run down the runway and show them any technical aspect of a jump. They would just laugh their socks off. I coach three girls who can jump further than I was ever able to, so I stand well back from that. If you're going to demonstrate something you should demonstrate correctly. If I'm not demonstrating correctly, how can I expect them to execute a technique correctly when it's a case of do as I say not as I do? I regularly ask an athlete to demonstrate to others, so, I do use demonstrations but it is very rare that I will actually perform it.

CRAFTING THE TRAINING ENVIRONMENT

Perhaps one of the most unique aspects of Peter's coaching environment is the challenge of working with a group of athletes who are often rivals once the competitive season begins. Indeed, one of the most interesting issues to emerge from Peter's story is his managing of this situation to the benefit of all. Here, he outlined how he attempts to motivate and provide technical feedback that aids each athlete in their attempts to fulfil their respective potential, whilst simultaneously eliminating, or reducing as much as possible, rivalry within the training group. In order to achieve this, Peter strives to structure and deliver training sessions that he perceives not only to aid the performance of the athletes, but also to reduce competition between individuals and, ultimately, prevent the establishment of a 'pecking-order'. In his own words:

> The group generally gets on very well. However, you do get frictions because they have to compete against each other. When they join the training group, I explain this to all of them and emphasise the need for them to divorce their feelings in competition from their feelings in training. They have got to continue to train together, so it's no good having friction in training sessions. In order to do this, I don't have them compete

with each other often in training. Of course I realise that, as human beings, they [athletes] naturally gauge themselves in relation to the people around them, and I know they are going to come head-to-head in competitions. But I want them to experience excitement in competition; when they compete I want them to be up for it. So, I don't want a pecking order to be established in training, as it can drain the competitiveness and motivation out of the athletes before the actual meets themselves.

Consequently, rather than encouraging competition between athletes, Peter attempts to create a climate whereby the athletes are principally concerned with 'challenging themselves' to be the best they can, be it at the international, national, or regional level. His strategic use of weight-training sessions is particularly illustrative of how he attempts to achieve this.

The weights room session is one of mine and their [the athletes] favourites. They challenge themselves. I get them all to be quiet and composed and encourage a competitive edge against themselves. I get them to focus on doing things to their maximum ability because that is the mind set they will need to have in competition. The competition in the weights room is between themselves and the bar and the weight, not against the other athletes. It's hard for them not to compete with each other, so I play around with it. I keep certain individuals apart if, and when, I think that it's necessary to do so.

While Peter is keen to reduce rivalry and friction within his training group, he believes that the athletes can still use each other to 'spark' improved performance if the atmosphere within the training group is one characterised by mutual support. In this respect, Peter spoke enthusiastically of his recent experiences at a warm weather training camp in the USA.

I knew one of the planned sessions was going to be heavy for them [the athletes], even some of the other coaches had remarked on that. We'd been there for two weeks of solid training already and had only taken two rest days. The heat was oppressive, but not once did the athletes try and pull out of the session. They were so focused and determined. Despite their individual goals, they shared the common goal of completing the session. They just sparked off each other, and if one started to flag they were supported by the others. Plus, I believe they were all challenging themselves to get through the session as well. It was a joy to watch.

Peter clearly illustrated how he manipulates the climate of the training environment in what he believes to be the best interests of the athletes. Rather than have them focus on being 'first across the line', he strives to create a culture among the athletes that encourages them to critically reflect upon their own techniques and performances with the ultimate goal of fulfilling their individual potential. Indeed,

Peter noted that he wants athletes to 'think about how they do things, how they feel, and how their bones feel', as, ultimately, 'it's about the individual being the most ready that they can be'.

IMPLEMENTING AN EMPOWERING PHILOSOPHY

In keeping with many of the other coaches in this book, Peter strives to develop a sense of responsibility in his athletes for their own performances. His rationale for doing so is partly underpinned by the nature of track and field competitions and also by the culture of the sport itself. In this respect, unlike team sports, the members of Peter's coaching group often compete in different competitions at various locations on the same day. Consequently, he cannot watch them all, while the rules of the sport do not permit him to offer advice to athletes once a competition has started. Hence, Peter is particularly concerned to foster the ability to 'size up situations' and 'solve problems' in his athletes. He commented:

> They have to look after themselves while they're away. When they are on the track at a competition and I am not there, they have to make decisions for themselves. They have to have a feel for things if they go wrong. They have to have the awareness to perceive what is happening and make the necessary adjustments themselves. Hopefully, I educate my athletes to be able to do this.

In further articulating his desire to empower his charges, Peter described how the level of a coach's power and influence should be dictated by the developmental stage and experience of the athlete. When working with young athletes he believes that the coach should be in complete charge, as the emphasis is usually on introducing and developing basic techniques and principles. Then, as the athlete gains more experience, the power differential between the coach and performer should change so that, ultimately, the coach becomes an advisor to the athlete.

> If you start coaching a youngster, you are a 100 per cent in charge of what is happening. If you say 'put your hand in the fire', they probably will if they are committed. Initially you teach, it's as simple as that. You are the teacher and you hold all the aces. However, as the youngster gains more experience and your relationship with them grows, I think that your 100 per cent should start to reduce. Down to 80 per cent initially, 70, 60, and so on. As the relationship grows, the best feedback you can get is for them to tell you how they feel about things. If you're working on their technique and trying to change things you have to ask 'Does it feel right? Does it feel wrong? Is it just awkward?' In effect the relationship starts to get equal and stays equal until the athlete goes away on international duty. I see my role diminishing, or parts of my role diminishing, as the athlete takes more and more control. For me, coaching is ultimately about guidance rather than control.

Indeed, the ownership and control of athletes was an issue about which Peter was particularly sensitive. He was passionate in his belief that the role of the coach is to 'give something of yourself' to your athletes, while he considered coaches who use athletes to build up their own self-esteem and ego to be 'working in the wrong job and are probably doing the wrong job with their athletes'. He noted:

> The worse thing I think I've seen in athletics is when coaches perceive themselves to own their athletes. When I first got into coaching, I called the athletes 'my athletes', and it was only as I grew older that I realised that they were not 'my athletes' but that I was 'their coach'. They actually own me because they are the ones who choose to come and train with me. In effect, they decide whether to use the service I offer or not. So, I have a responsibility to give them everything that I can. It really bugs me when coaches have an almost stranglehold grip on their athletes and won't let them speak or listen to anybody else. I see it as an inadequacy on the behalf of the coach.

At the core of Peter's empowering approach is the need for mutual respect and trust between a coach and athlete. Here, he believes that both parties enter into an invisible 'contract' where the athletes trust him to 'programme the training, supervise the training, observe and tell them what they are doing', while, in return, he expects the athletes to 'adopt to a mature attitude, look after themselves' and to give serious attention 'to what should be the best advice'. With regard to communication, Peter believes that for his athletes to be able to take responsibility for their actions, it is necessary for him to always explain why he wants them to engage in a certain activity or training regime. Hence, he considers that he is responsible for educating his athletes in many facets, rather than just athletic performance. He also commented that it was important for him always to be open to questions and feedback from his athletes, as he believes that such communication not only gives the athletes a feeling of input into the coaching process, but can also serve, through subsequent reflection, to enhance his own practice.

Finally, Peter attributed his use of an empowerment strategy to the subcultural values and norms associated with track and field athletics. In particular, he indicated that the highly motivated nature and the willingness of the performers to learn and improve themselves made an empowering approach particularly appropriate.

> Generally, athletes want to be the best. They're in a cocoon of like people shall we say. They get a lot from watching each other because they can see each other's faults and they try and learn from them. If someone corrects something they will try and mimic it. Basically, they are always watching and learning from each other. And what I think that they [track and field athletes] have over other sports, and I realise that this is a bit of a generalisation, is that they are supremely motivated. With athletes,

PETER STANLEY

because the only person they have to worry about is themselves, they can continue to fool themselves, push themselves, and motivate themselves to be the best they can.

SUMMARY

The picture that emerges from Peter's story is that of a coach who is passionately committed to providing his athletes with a thorough education and understanding of their particular event. He believes that when working with high performance athletes, the role of the coach is to assist and guide rather than dominate and control. Hence, he is principally concerned with producing athletes who are not only technically proficient, but who are also able to analyse situations and solve problems for themselves. In short, Peter strives to help each athlete in his care to fulfil his or her potential, a quest which he relishes. In his own words:

> I'd like to think that I actually educate them [the athletes] to do better. I'd also like to think that I motivate them. In fact, I just love for them to improve and become better athletes. I become very satisfied as they progress and I can see progression. For me to see a technically superb jump that doesn't win a competition from an athlete that I coach is great, as I know that is the best that they can do and that really satisfies me.

CHAPTER 9

▼ LOIS MUIR

BY ROBYN JONES AND ALEX MCKENZIE

INTRODUCTION

What kind of coach is Lois Muir? On the one hand she can be considered a straightforward, uncompromising and demanding coach, whilst on the other she is obviously a very deeply caring one. She cares greatly about getting players to play to their full potential, and drives her players hard to achieve this. Hence, she constantly pressurises her players to perform: 'to cope with it all'. She expects a lot from them, and from herself.

STARTING OUT AND DEVELOPING A COACHING PHILOSOPHY

Lois began coaching as her successful international career in both basketball and netball for New Zealand was coming to an end. She decided to retire from playing whilst still an international as she did not want to 'compromise [her] standards by dropping down the levels as a player'. A strong competitive sporting streak was thus still apparent. Hence, when the chance came to be a selector for an age-grade New Zealand netball team to tour the Pacific Islands, with the support of husband Murray, she eagerly grabbed it, with no inkling of where it would soon lead.

New Zealand at the time were applying for selectors for a second, third and fourth grade [netball] side to tour the [Pacific] islands. Although our youngest, John, was only a baby, Murray said, 'You go for it. Be a selector for a week at [selection] tournament, catch up with everybody'. So that was fine. Get to tournament and the three selectors were there and then Joyce McCann, the NZ President, said, 'Oh, we made a mistake as in our constitution one of the selectors has to be the coach.' I was asked to stand as the coach. So it was then about a three-week tour in the islands, Fiji, Cooks, Samoa and we did Tonga as well. And so I rang Murray and said, 'What do you think, with all these kids at home?' sort of thing. And he said, 'Well, if you don't put your name in now, if you wait until you want to do it, they may not want you.' He said, 'We'll cope.' Mind you, he never knew it was going to be for so many years! But that's sort of how it started.

In 1973, a year following this almost chance entry into the coaching ranks, Lois was invited to coach the New Zealand under-24 team. As a result of successful tours to both Australia and the Pacific Islands, she was appointed coach to the senior New Zealand netball squad, the Silver Ferns, in 1974, a position she held until 1988. During her tenure as head coach, the Silver Ferns emerged as a dominant force in world netball. They were joint winners of the World Championship with Trinidad and Tobago in 1979, a title they won outright in the UK in 1987. From 1988 to 1995 she became the national coaching director for Netball New Zealand and was inducted into the New Zealand Sports Hall of Fame in 1993. Following a brief retirement, she returned to coach the Wellington Capital Shakers in the New Zealand national league where she again enjoyed considerable success. She currently coaches the Otago Rebels in the same league, whilst also being heavily involved with coach education within the sport.

Lois considers her basketball background as being responsible for the impact she had when she began coaching netball. Here, she was often coached by, and trained with, men in a competitive atmosphere. She credits it with 'toughening' her up ('I had to work for all I got. It made me realise that you only get what you put into it') and for her consequent introduction of a work ethic into the rather genteel world of New Zealand netball.

Most of the women that coached at that time were very nice ladies and they were saying, 'are you alright dear? You're doing well dear'. And a lot of it was wrong, you know. And I'd been coached at basketball by men who were good players. I was captain of Otago basketball and had come through learning from these people. I came through all this learning, developing and understanding in basketball, more moves, more team units, and staying connected. I got to understand all the plays, and got to be part of the deal and you've got to have your brains with you. And netball hadn't done any of that at that time. They were just nice ladies saying, 'you're alright dear, you are playing well dear'. And so I came in saying to the players, 'If you want to get better I can help you, but you have to travel the road, and you have to do it now.' And I was mean with fitness.

No doubt about it. [Suddenly] they were in a different environment altogether and it was a shock to quite a few.

In talking about the possible influence of role models and mentors who may have influenced her coaching style, Lois paid homage to Dixie Cochran, a former coach, about whom she spoke with great reverence:

When I made the first New Zealand [netball] team I came across a really good coach at that stage, Dixie Cochran. She had been a past New Zealand player and so she was the sort of person, you know, I'd sort of jump up and grab the moon if she'd have asked me. One of those coaches that you went out there and you were doing it sort of for yourself and for your country but she was an added value. I looked up to her because . . . she was a teacher. She had a great way of handling people. I think about some of the things she said even now.

Although Lois learned positive lessons from most of her coaches, from some, she also learned how not to do things. For example:

I remember there was a coach here in Dunedin when I was in school, a single woman who was an old school teacher and a real dragon. I was fortunate I was never in her classes at school but the kids who did were either very good or quivering jellies. She always used to bring out the old 'I'll show you' attitude, and you either had to take it or just fall apart. She knew her netball, but she was a bit of a bully, and it was important to stand up for yourself.

A picture thus begins to emerge of a coach who actively and continuously reflects on her experiential learning, and who possesses a high work ethic and high expectations. She believes she understands the commitment it takes to succeed, and wants to instil a similar determination in her players.

ON COMMITMENT, CARING, 'GROWING' AND COPING

Although Lois commits herself totally to her players and her profession, she is also aware that a coach usually only has a certain shelf life, precisely because of the intense nature of the job: 'I always said that a coach has only got so much energy to give. Because you've got to give everything. You make a total commitment in your energy.' She sees the role as very much a giving one; one of giving endless amounts of time and energy to players. This stretches far beyond the athletic arena to their wider well-being: 'I want to know if they're having a hard time with the boyfriend or whatever. I know [I have] to be a bit more sympathetic sometimes.' This is her commitment, and her motivation for doing so lies in her belief that the players need such support if they are to perform to the best of their abilities on court. Undoubtedly, she cares about her players; she cares that when the time arrives, they are able to cope in the high-pressure environment of elite sport, which is why she pushes them so hard. In her own words:

> I do care about players. I care about them not feeling as good and I care that they've got to lift themselves and not feel sorry for themselves with work or training. I always have to sort out some players. I have to stress them. I have to know how good they're going to be, to see if they can handle it.

At face value such a philosophy, which constantly pushes players to their physical and mental limits, does not seem to fit easily with her other general aim of empowering players to think and make their own decisions on the court. What she is really trying to do, however, is to produce battle-hardened, mentally tough players who can make decisions and succeed in difficult situations without relying on her. In emphasising this point, she referred to her aim of trying to develop and 'grow players' (a similar phrase was also used by **Ian McGeechan**) into this self-sufficient, confident and competent ideal: 'You've got to grow them [players]. You've got to feed them enough that they improve and they add value to their game and they're really doing well. Then they want more and more. Then you're coaching.'

Her commitment and caring thus are aimed at maximising the potential of her players. She believes in coaching the individual and values what the individual brings to the team. Her job is to integrate the diverse player strengths into the team framework, whilst pushing and inspiring individuals to their respective limits. To do this she has to be both sensitive and imaginative:

> Well, a lot of coaching is really about the individual. Everyone comes with skills and the coach adds value to those. We don't often let the people demonstrate what they've got. Or open their minds. We box, a lot of coaches want to box a player, and say, 'this is the only way to do it'. But the future is in the young because they are uninhibited and they do things a different way to what we've really seen. And that's the fun of it. To me, it's finding where the players' horizons are for themselves and lifting it for them.

She tries to grow the players in terms of their on-field responsibility, decision making, courage and game understanding. Consequently, although she appears to want to control much of her coaching environment, she is acutely aware of the need to let her players 'go' when on court; indeed, she insists that they do 'go', or behave independently, otherwise she considers herself to have failed as a coach:

> You're really adding knowledge to their computer (the players' thinking capacity) so that they can cope, because, as a coach, you can't go out and pull the strings for them and say 'do it now or you're off'. I've got to have

decision makers out there. We might have a game plan for this or that type of game and it just isn't working. Half way through the first quarter, if they don't change it, if they can't read the change, I'll kill them. I would absolutely kill them. I think a lot of times in coaching you see somebody come off at half time and you're 20 down and it's too late. It's because you haven't got thinkers. They're waiting on the coach to solve all the problems. I think the coach really is a facilitator that gives players their team understanding. In the game, they've got to be able to change it. They've got to have the courage to change it.

This is precisely why she pushes her players so hard, so that they can develop the courage to make game changing decisions in the heat of battle. Success in this is what she finds most rewarding about coaching: 'Sometimes you see them [players] grow before your eyes, and that's so great, so exciting.'

ON 'EFFECTIVE' COACHING PRACTICE: 'INVESTING SWEAT WELL'

Unsurprisingly, Lois runs high-intensity coaching sessions, where the players are under constant pressure to perform. This relates to her belief of always coaching with the game and game situations in mind.

> When we train, they're [the players] looking at product all the time. I'm not into lots of warm, fuzzy drills. No one should do an activity not knowing how they can use it on the court. We've got to say to players, this is where we can use it and this is why we're doing it. And I'm into quality sweat. We do it five times well. I'm not doing it ten times mediocrely. Yeah, I'm into quality sweat!

Detailed preparation is also considered crucial to Lois if success is to be achieved. This includes working hard to develop technique under pressure, to the extent of constantly revisiting it during sessions ('Under stress, you're only as good as your basics; when you're really stressed, that's all you've got left, so it's got to be good'). 'Preparation' also involves analysing the opposition both individually and collectively, before synthesising and relaying relevant information to her own players:

> I look at and analyse other players. You know, all their skills, like if they're left handed and they do this or they do that. Just minor stuff really. Or who the dominant people are on court and where they play. Where you want to be before they get there. You know, those sorts of little things that are the crumbs of the game that give you the little edge and, of course, the people thing. Like banking, you want to invest your money well don't you? Well, you've got to invest in quality sweat as well!

LOIS MUIR

Each week's preparation for Lois includes decisions on strategies and tactics to be used against the upcoming opposition, which are based upon her preceding analysis of the opposing side. This flexibility however, occurs within the boundaries of her more general philosophy of how the game should be played; thus an underlying consistent theme is maintained. Nevertheless, Lois considers it essential to brief her players on what they can expect from the opposition during the next game and how to deal with it. Her preparation consequently, whilst not being 'overkill', is thorough. Preparing her players in this way is important to Lois, as she believes it helps them be 'at peace with themselves'. When asked to elaborate on this she responded:

> It's, well, when you've done the work and you know, you're confident in your skills. You know yourself. You know what you're capable of. But you can always go higher than that. I'm not saying you box yourself. But know what you're good at and know that you can do it. I mean it's looking at an interception and thinking, 'I know I can reach that. I've done that at training. I can cover that distance.' It's about having confidence in yourself, the confidence to do it. It sounds silly, I know, but I think it's right.

Lois thus tries to develop confidence in her players, both in relation to their individual abilities and their contributory role to the team. She wants them to know 'where they fit', and what they can expect of themselves and their team-mates. She believes this knowledge brings them a degree of security and inner peace, which again, improves performance.

In further discussing 'effective' coaching practice, Lois articulated her desire to control the coaching environment as much as she is able: 'I enjoy having a group of players who I can dominate to fit me.' To achieve this, she believes in keeping a degree of social distance between herself and the players. This gives her the space to make the difficult decisions for the good of the squad, thus not allowing personal relationships to interfere with professional judgement:

> Because you've got to be beyond that. You got to be, you've got to make the decision for the group regardless who the person is. And you make that decision for the group. The total group no matter who they are, whether they're the captain, vice captain or anyone. You want to know a bit more about them but I don't want them to know too much about me. I like that little bit of respect I suppose, but they've got to believe that you're going to make the decisions for the full group. That's important.

For Lois, the maintenance of such a distance does not preclude positive working relationships with her players, or the consequent creation of an enjoyable coaching environment. Her use of humour was acknowledged as being important in generating a good atmosphere, whilst simultaneously injecting new life into potentially tedious sessions:

SPORTS COACHING CULTURES

Sometimes it just grows out of my head. I'd say something like, if they're flat on the court on defence, 'Do you want to show a play-boy full frontal or what? Give yourself an angle!' They crack up and it lifts the tension. It lightens the load and that's important sometimes. I mean it can be boring if you have a bad training night so you've got to have a bit of light relief.

ON COACH ACCREDITATION

Although Lois is supportive of coach accreditation and education in her sport, she is aware of its current limitations. Hence, she recognises certification as a yardstick and a measure of a prospective coach's commitment to learn and for 'starting coaches along the path', while being of the firm belief that 'they don't make you a good coach'. Rather, she considers that it is the 'management of people and your own philosophies' that make good coaching. What is needed within accreditation schemes in her view is a greater emphasis on the cognitive side of coaching to help coaches with problem solving and understanding game-related issues. In her own words:

> What coaches need help with is the decision making. The game plans and the counter game plans under stress. And the accreditation doesn't give you enough of that. If we spent more time, if you and I sat and watched a game and we looked at the game and you said, 'OK we made it to the break, OK how would you change that?' What would you say to those players at this break? How are you going to change what they're doing on court to that opposition? That's what should be in the accreditation and it isn't. And you see, that is really coaching. That's the true feel of it, whereas the accreditation only seems to talk about pedagogy and, you know, whole-part-whole coaching and whatever. Don't get me wrong, I'm all for that at a certain level but we've got to bring in game understanding and mentorship and stuff like that. And coaching really is individual and it should stay individual. So that needs to be sort of, one mentor coach with two others, no more than that. One-on-one. Looking at and giving that coach their full attention. Answering their questions. Looking at something and analysing those quick decisions and how to make them. Yeah. Reading the game plan; the tactical side and the counter scoring. That's what most coaches worry about and that's what they need.

For Lois, coaching is complex, cognitive and dynamically challenging, so coach education must reflect that.

ON THE ESSENCE OF COACHING: 'READING THE INDIVIDUAL' AND 'MOVING THE CHESS PIECES'

When asked what she would identify as the essence of coaching, Lois replied:

> Coaching to me is reading the individual. I think you've got to be able to read people. Read the people themselves. You know, at the world champs in 1987, I would walk behind the group [of players] just to see how they looked that morning. You know, see who was dragging their feet and who wasn't. Who I can lean on, who I have to be more careful with at that day's training and so on.

Hence, she is acutely aware of the need to be flexible and sensitive with her players, as she tries to realise every aspect of their potential. She has to be able to 'read' them correctly in order to know how hard to push them. In order to keep them on an upward spiral of progression she constantly challenges them and their perceptions, often by introducing new players into pivotal positions on court thus forcing them 'out of their comfort zones'.

> If players are at a level and they're not going to go any higher, they are predictable. Which means they're predictable to the opposition as well. So now they've got a flaw. The beauty of putting a new young player in there on court, who is unknown, is that you change the adrenalin of the experienced players because they have to look out now, because they're not quite so sure what that new player is going to do. So now we've got them out of automatic pilot, we've got them connected and looking to see how they can work with that player to lift their own game. So it actually changes the adrenalin. It makes them think, it makes people work harder.

Predictability in play is something that Lois works hard to overcome. Individual innovation and progression are what she strives for, as she constantly pushes her players to test themselves against their limits. This is central to her practice.

Although coaching at the individual level is pivotal to Lois, she also considers it very necessary to be proactive in developing detailed game plans, and letting the players react to situations within such a framework ('More proactive than reactive because the reactive comes from the game but they've got to have established plans to set people up'). When questioned about 'who owns the game plan?', she replied that the players did, before adding 'after I lead them to it'. Thus, similar to other coaches in this book, debate and democracy were apparent only within specific, tightly controlled boundaries.

In further elaborating on the macro elements of her coaching, Lois declared it the most interesting aspect of her role. Indeed, what she really enjoys is the challenge involved in the strategy and counter of the invasion game, where all the coach's preparatory, analytic and reactive skills are laid bare:

To me the greatest thing in coaching is that I love moving the chess pieces about. The art of coaching, and coaching is an art, is to use the skills of your players to the best advantage on court for that group at the time. The thing I love most is looking at the opposition bench and seeing what they could do against me. I think what we fail to do as coaches is look at our own team and say that's going well, this isn't going well; put it all in a frame see it all and say, if I was the opposition coach what would I do to me? And how would I then change my game plan? It's like the gun-fight at the OK corral – you've got to make the first move!

CONCLUSION

The portrait that emerges of Lois Muir is that of a deeply committed, thoughtful and passionate coach. She pressurises her players to cope with the demands of top-level competition through duplicating that environment in her sessions and in her expectations of them. She works players hard because she cares for their success, and believes that such training prepares them to achieve that success. We conclude her story with a brief extract from the interview where Lois discusses her continuously evolving practice and her hopes for the profession in general. It captures her infectious passion and her general philosophy:

> Alex: So, you're still learning after all your experiences?
> Lois: Oh yes, of course, I love it.
> Alex: What sort of things are you learning now then?
> Lois: People, people, people. That's what it really all boils down to in the end.

CHAPTER 10

▼ **COACHING PEDAGOGY**

BY KATHLEEN ARMOUR

INTRODUCTION

In the introductory chapter, we claim that one of the key features of this book is the way in which it demonstrates the myriad ways in which lives, social and cultural contexts, personal experiences, philosophies and professional practice are all interconnected in configurations that challenge our traditional perceptions of coaching practice. In this chapter, analysis of the concept of pedagogy in the context of the coaches' individual and collective stories provides an opportunity to illustrate that feature in some depth. Perhaps because of its connotations of being mainly about children, 'pedagogy' is not a concept that appears much in the coaching literature. Yet it is increasingly employed in the wider academic field of education and particularly in the expanding area of continuing professional development (CPD) for teachers. Pedagogy is an inclusive concept that embraces the four individual but interlinked elements of teaching (and coaching), learning, knowledge base and learning environment, but it has an overriding focus on the unifying goal of *learning*. The purpose of this chapter, therefore, is to draw upon some of the information available in the field of education, to apply it to the coaching context as expressed in the stories of the top-level coaches interviewed, and to establish a tentative case for analysing coaching from the perspective of pedagogy. The case being made is that pedagogy, as an analytical and practical tool, has much to offer an analysis of coaching practice and that it might usefully feed into debates about the effective design of coach education. Importantly, it is not claimed that there is no existing literature in coaching that addresses these issues; rather that the perspective gained from a pedagogical analysis is a little different. Thus, it is to be viewed as adding to, rather than taking the place of, related work in the coaching literature.

The chapter is organised into six sections as follows.

- In the first section, a theoretical analysis of the concept of pedagogy leads to the specific definition of pedagogy that underpins this chapter.
- In the following four sections, each of elements of coaching pedagogy is discussed drawing upon selected theorists in the field of pedagogy and linking their work to examples from the coaches' stories.
- In the final section, pedagogy is explored in the context of coach education, and it is argued that the development of a connective coaching pedagogy, fashioned on 'a pedagogy for learning' (Hargreaves, 2001), could be a useful analytical and practical tool for coaching and for coach education.

WHAT IS PEDAGOGY?

At its simplest, pedagogy is about instruction and learning, teaching and learning or 'a science of teaching'. Use of the term pedagogy in this manner has a strong tradition in mainstream Europe where the term 'didactics' is sometimes used to describe the instruction/learning process (Leach & Moon, 1999). However, in Britain, the term pedagogy has rarely been used in this general way, rather it has been used to define more specific philosophies such as, for example, 'critical pedagogy'. Currently, however, pedagogy in its broadest 'teaching and learning' sense appears to be the subject of renewed interest within education, so much so that Stone (2000) suggests its presence has almost become obligatory in education publications. However, Stone is also critical of this new trend, arguing that authors use the term loosely without making their meanings clear and that the term pedagogy is becoming so flexible that its study has become 'as rigorous as a jellyfish' (p. 94). We ought to be very clear, therefore, about the way in which the term is being used in this chapter.

In examining some of the recent attempts to define pedagogy, Watkins and Mortimore (1999, p. 3) conclude that *learning* is central. Thus, pedagogy is 'any conscious activity by one person designed to enhance learning in another'. While accepting this as a starting point, we would like to argue for a definition that more overtly signals the complexity, depth and breadth of the concept, whilst acknowledging its academic foundation and its powerful personal, professional and political components. Penney and Waring (2000, p. 6) in the field of physical education go some way towards this by describing pedagogy as a concept that

underpins 'rationale, curriculum design, teaching and learning', but still, somehow, it is not enough. We get closer to our views in the work of Leach and Moon (1999), who argue that pedagogy is about the relationships between four key elements of education: teachers, learners, learning tasks and the learning environment. Importantly, they contend that 'at the heart of this dynamic process is a personal view of the purposes of education, what constitutes good teaching and a belief in the purposes of the subject' (p. 274). Thus, the concept of pedagogy transcends the traditional concepts of teaching, coaching or instruction. Put simply, there is more to it; a theme that reverberates throughout this book both in the stories told by the coaches and the subsequent analysis of them. But perhaps we need to be clearer still.

Etymological analysis of the word 'pedagogy' provides some useful clues about its meaning and potential depth. The meaning of 'pedagogue' can be found in Ancient Greece where a pedagogue was a well-educated servant who lived with the children of a noble house and whose main purpose was to develop a child's moral integrity and take responsibility for the formation of personal and civic character. In contrast with the teacher, therefore, who was merely responsible for delivering specific instrumental knowledge, the pedagogue had a broad-ranging and holistic role in the moral development of a young person (Savater, 1997). In order to achieve this, the pedagogue lived, ate and played with his young charges. Now, although we are not claiming that a coach today is a pedagogue in the Ancient Greek sense, it is clearly the case that for many coaches, the coaching role involves rather more than mere instruction or delivery of skills. For example, **Hope Powell** believes in caring for players in order to get the best from them, particularly at low points in their career. She also wants to help players to become 'ambassadors for the game' taking responsibility for the profile of women's football: 'it's all part of being a disciplined performer'. **Bob Dwyer** identifies social care as one of the key functions of a coach. He feels that is it essential for a coach to create a supportive environment in which players feel relaxed and secure and for a coach to support a player both on and off the field: 'The coaching role is a giving role not a taking role . . . I think it's important to know that the role of the coach is to give, give and give to the players.' Off the field, this includes making the rugby club feel like 'part of the family' and involving players' families as much as possible, reflecting Bob's belief that 'a stable personal life is very important. I think it's vital for the players to have a supportive, stable environment to work in'. **Graham Taylor** and **Ian McGeechan** hold similar views. **Graham Taylor** argues that a coach must know about 'players' wives, their families . . . I took time out to get to know what their children's names were, when their birthdays were . . . because you're actually showing them that you care'. **Ian McGeechan** believes in developing players' self-discipline and personal responsibility but, at the same time, he is there to support them and to be a listener: '[you need to know] if they have fallen out with the girlfriend or wife or whatever . . . for some of them it's very important that you know a bit about their life and their lifestyle and what is happening, because if they are unhappy, they won't be playing good rugby'. **Peter Stanley** also believes that a coach must understand the personality of each player, and must know how and when to 'diffuse any anger, stress and worry on their behalf'. On the other hand, **Lois Muir** feels that it is her role to make players become tough and to develop 'stickability'. She cares about players and their personal lives/issues, but mainly because she feels they must learn to cope: 'I care about her not feeling as good and I care that she's got to lift herself and not feel sorry for herself with work or training.' Certainly then, these coaches would identify the coaching role as being rather more complex than is sometimes acknowledged and there are glimpses, in some of their comments, of the coach as a modern day pedagogue.

This takes us to the core of the discussion on the meaning of pedagogy and, more specifically, to the definition of coaching pedagogy used in this chapter. In an adaptation of Leach and Moon's (1999) definition of pedagogy in education, it is suggested here that coaching pedagogy can also be conceptualised as four individual yet interlinked elements:

- coaches
- learners
- knowledge
- learning environment.

These elements form the framework of the concept. Each is uniquely complex and in order to illustrate some of this complexity, each is discussed in turn below. However, this is only one part of the picture; it is in the combination of these elements in the midst of the unique human encounter that is coaching, that the essence of coaching pedagogy resides. This echoes Leach and Moon's (1999) second point about the personal values at the heart of education and Lyle's (1999) arguments about the personal assumptions underpinning coaching. It also points us towards the final section of this chapter where a 'coaching pedagogy' is explored in more depth.

COACHES

In the field of education, there is a growing literature on the need to understand the links between teachers' biographies, their practices and their careers (e.g., Fernández-Balboa, 1998a; Erben, 1998). Moreover, Day (1999, p. 15) tells us that any form of teacher change 'is complex, unpredictable and dependent upon past experience [i.e., life and career history]'. In the field of physical education, Armour and Jones (1998), Sparkes (1987), Dowling Naess (1996) and Schempp (1993) among others have made the same point in their analyses of the links between physical education teachers' lives, careers and pedagogies. All of this work is based on the assumption that 'The way people teach is often the way they are . . .' (Wragg *et al.*, 2000, p. 217). Similarly, Hargreaves and Fullan (1992, p. ix) suggest that: 'for teachers, what goes on inside the classroom is closely related to what goes on outside it'. Goodson (1992) also argues that an understanding of pedagogical practice is impossible without an understanding of

teachers' lives. So it is with coaching. The key to analysing and understanding coaching pedagogy resides precisely in exploring the articulations – the connections – between all the elements of the human encounter that is coaching. Coaches' lives and careers are central to their coaching philosophies that are, in turn, central to coaching pedagogy. Thus it is that the traditional 'skills and methods' approach to understanding coaching and to informing coach education must be found wanting. At some point in her or his development, the coach as pedagogue needs to put aside the usual questions of 'what should I coach?' and 'which method should I use?' to ask instead '*why* am I a coach?' and 'why do I coach as I do?' (Lyle, 1999; Fernández-Balboa, 1998b).

It is no accident that these were precisely the kinds of questions that underpinned our interviews with top-level coaches. If Wragg *et al.* (2000) are correct in claiming that the way people teach is intimately related to the way they *are*, then this will also apply to coaching. Moreover, it seems to imply that an understanding of 'the way they are' will provide helpful insights into the way that individuals coach. It also, of course, provides the essential gateway into a critically reflective analysis of practice. The coaches' stories certainly provide ample evidence about *who* they are – or would like to be. For example, right at the outset, **Steve Harrison** made it clear that he is a 'players' coach'. He describes himself as a 'blue collar worker' who wants to be close to his players to learn with them and from them. He prides himself on being a learning coach and someone who seeks to learn from any opportunities: 'If I was the coach of that England team I would have gone to the Portuguese coach and said listen, what do you do with those boys individually? What do you work at?' **Ian McGeechan** also views himself as a 'players' coach'. His background in teaching underpins his coaching philosophy, hence his belief in establishing a disciplined structure within which he can coach effectively: 'I suppose I coached like I taught.' Ian also believes that he must remain true to himself and his own style of coaching after personal experience of trying to change his style resulted in disaster. Like **Steve Harrison**, he argues that a coach should never stop learning: 'understand that you never know enough . . . you should never shut your eyes or ears to what is going on. The more you listen, the more you see, the better understanding you get, the more you keep moving forward'. **Graham Taylor** meanwhile identified a need for a certain amount of acting in coaching: 'it's no different from being in front of a class . . . acting goes into it, the best coaches would make good actors'. He is uncompromising in his view that coaches need to engage in continuous learning and also retain a certain humility: 'you can get too clever for yourself sometimes . . . be careful when it is a moment of good fortune not to say "that's my masterstroke"'. Drawing upon different life experiences, **Bob Dwyer** spoke about the influence of his engineering background: 'I'm an engineer by profession . . . So I tend to sessionalise things and see things in horizontals, verticals and cross-referencing. They all interconnect.' His coaching philosophy is underpinned by a belief in organisation, order and precision. He also feels that is essential for players to understand his decisions and that it is his job to explain it to them: 'Smart people can talk in common English and explain what they want you to know.' Ultimately, however, Bob views himself as 'the boss' and expects his players to view him likewise. **Peter Stanley** bases his coaching philosophy on 'striving for technical excellence' and 'providing motivation'. His role model was a coach described as 'a gentle trainer' who could 'build athletes block-by-block'. Thus he defines coaching as being about 'guidance rather than control . . . the worst thing I think I've seen in athletics is when coaches perceive themselves to own their athletes'. This is similar to **Di Bass** who views some swimming coaches as 'control freaks' and is at pains not to be like them. She rarely shouts at swimmers, preferring to talk *with* them about issues. As she says: 'it's just a different feeling. I think it's women. Or being a mother . . . Or just me!' She also finds it hard to self-promote in the way that other swimming coaches do and puts this down to the fact that swimming coaching is only a part of her life, which is a strong theme that runs through Di's story. For **Hope Powell**, coaching is a blend of concise technical instruction with knowing individual athletes. An influential role model was a coach who emphasised 'the people management side of things'. She identifies this as the artistic or intuitive side of coaching: 'I believe that you do it from the gut. I go with my gut feeling a lot.' **Lois Muir** is different again. She bases much of her coaching on her experiences of struggling for personal success in sport and expecting others to do the same: 'I had to work for all I got. It made me realise that you only get what you put into it.' She believes that coaching requires physical and mental endurance, that a coach must give total commitment and has to learn to cope and become a survivor. She expects nothing less from her players.

The message from these extracts is that any understanding of coaching requires an understanding of coaches that, in turn, requires an analysis of the ways in which coaches come to hold certain views about themselves and about 'good' coaching. Given the power of these views, it would be naive not to acknowledge their impact upon practice. Clearly, they are also reflected in strong views about 'good' players, valuable learning and appropriate learning environments. However, unlike Abraham and Collins (1998, p. 75), who describe this as 'perhaps the biggest problem facing the coach educator', the case made from a pedagogical perspective is that it is not an obstacle to avoid but a powerful tool to be employed in the learning process.

LEARNERS

Bruner (1999) argues that what we need to understand and analyse in any pedagogical process are the 'folk pedagogies' that drive both the instructional and learning processes. A 'folk pedagogy' is a set of beliefs about the best way for people to learn; in effect, what is 'good' for them to learn and, in particular, how and why they 'ought' to be able to learn it. Bruner (1999, p. 5) claims that these are powerful, enduring beliefs for both teachers and learners:

> theorising about the practice of education in the classroom (or any other setting, for that matter) you had better take into account the folk theories that those engaged in teaching and learning already have. For any innovations that you . . . may wish to introduce will have to compete with,

replace, or otherwise modify the folk theories that already guide both teachers and pupils.

Certainly in our earlier study of physical education teachers' lives and careers (Armour & Jones, 1998) we identified teachers' different folk pedagogies and demonstrated just how powerful they were in the teaching/learning process. This led us to question teachers' claims about being 'child-centred' and 'educating the individual child' because, as far as we could see, major decisions about 'children' had been made prior to observing individual children and establishing their 'needs'. Is this true of coaches too?

Lyle (1999) would argue that it is very much the case in coaching and an analysis of the coaches' stories in this book demonstrates that they do, indeed, abound with examples of folk pedagogy. Just as Bruner (1999) contends, we can see that coaches' pedagogies are littered with powerful assumptions about learners' minds, motivations and needs. Consider the following examples.

Di Bass believes that young swimmers must be allowed to develop, have some involvement in their programmes and take some responsibility for themselves and their training. However, she points out that the swimming environment makes any form of conversation difficult: 'they've got ear-plugs on, they've got hats over their ears, they've got goggles on . . . and really it's not placed for big conversations and lots of democracy'. Nonetheless, Di believes that personal growth is an important part of the competitive swimming experience. She also believes that swimmers learn most effectively if they have clear goals: 'I do try to think in terms of either giving target times or setting some sort of process goals.' **Ian McGeechan** talks of the need to explain players' roles carefully and of 'getting rid of the grey areas in the players' minds'. Because once players see a reason for something 'everything tends to move quicker'. He also believes that 'people like structure, people like discipline' and that they respond better when given clear pointers after, for example, losing a game: 'You know, a player is confused if he is losing . . . They don't understand why we lost . . . so pin-point key things for them to hang on to, to work on'. **Bob Dwyer** makes some similar points, arguing that players learn most effectively when they have 'a clear sense of purpose'. He tries to get each individual thinking, 'I've got to do it right, I've got to do it right', and feels they must relish the challenge. He also feels that players must be able to believe in their coach and, ultimately, do what the coach says:

> if we can lead them into thinking they're all part of the plans of the organisation or club, then they'll perform better, so I have to get them to believe in me. Players are like children; they'll love it when they're getting better. And when they think they're part of the environment, they absolutely love it.

For **Steve Harrison**, on the other hand, learners respond better 'to someone who is on their wavelength'. He feels that players must have the trust to make a mistake in front of him, so they can learn. He is firm in his belief that players respond to being respected and that they like a structured framework with concise instruction. Importantly, Steve believes that players must see a coach who is in control: 'You've got to be bullet proof, or you've got to portray that you are . . . try and show you're not bothered, you're in control.' Under those circumstances, Steve believes that 'players like to be worked' as part of their learning. From a different perspective, **Lois Muir**'s view of learners is that they need to be challenged and 'toughened'; a view that resonates throughout her story. Here again, an awareness of her personal life experiences provides the clue to her beliefs: 'it was good for me because you have your cage rattled and you look at yourself . . . I had to sort out some players . . . I had to stress them'. She also admits to being mean: 'I wanted them to be pushed by somebody mean' and she takes a dim view of those who will not rise to her challenges in the way she intends: 'women are terrible, they'll come out with a list of negatives . . . and very few positives'. Lois is aware that she should not overload players, especially the younger ones, but she has an overriding belief in pushing them to their limits for their own benefit: 'I'd like to do that to some of them [to see] if they can cope.' Good learners, for Lois, are positive, strong, striving copers. For **Hope Powell**, aggression in coaching is counterproductive: 'you don't get the best out of players that way'. She argues that male coaches in women's football can cause problems: 'men that have coached in the men's game tend to be quite aggressive and even verbally abusive, while in the women's game that approach just doesn't work'. In general, Hope bases her assumptions about her learners on her own experiences as a player, asking herself: 'would I enjoy this?' Different again is **Peter Stanley**'s view that learners should be focused on 'challenging themselves' rather than comparing themselves to others in the group and **Graham Taylor**'s belief in working on players' strengths rather than highlighting their weaknesses 'because their whole confidence level is raised' making learning more likely.

Added to this mix of assumptions about learners, are the assumptions guiding the learners themselves about 'proper' learning. This book focuses primarily on coaching from the perspective of coaches, (even though the coaches themselves are also viewed as learners). However, as Hallam and Ireson (1999) point out in the context of education, teachers cannot learn for their pupils and, of course, the same applies to coaches and athletes. Yet learners themselves are essentially complex: 'each pupil is a unique individual and has their own idiosyncratic knowledge base, preferred ways of learning, personality, motivations, interest, values, and social history. These factors contribute to the ways in which they undertake learning and need teaching' (p. 69).

The potential for conflict exists where a coach's assumptions about worthwhile learning and 'good' learners clashes with the understandings held by learners. This is demonstrated vividly in Cushion's (2001) research on soccer coaches in football youth academies where young players had to juggle the competing expectations of the coach and the counterculture of the peer group. Elements of this can also be seen in the coaches' stories in this book. For example, **Ian McGeechan** points to the need to avoid antagonisms within his group and both **Di Bass** and **Lois Muir** recall frustration with athletes who do not display the levels of commitment and responsibility that they expect. This is a good example of one area where coaches and athletes sometimes struggle to understand each other.

In a discussion on pedagogy in a school context, van Manan (1999, p. 19) defines the practice of pedagogy as 'constantly distinguishing more appropriate from less appropriate ways of being and interacting with young people'. He argues that we need to be critically aware of the ways in which learners experience our teaching and he points out: 'Strangely, this question of how the young people we teach experience their relationship with teachers is seldom asked' (p. 19). However, van Manen claims that when we do ask pupils to share their experiences of learning and of teachers, the responses can be revealing. For example, he says: 'When we ask students to describe their classroom experiences with teachers, it becomes immediately evident how students often see teaching in terms of style, personality, and qualities such as fairness, patience, commitment and kindness' (p. 19)

The central case being made, and the lesson for coaching, is that by focusing more closely on the experiences of learners, coaches might find themselves to be surprised, and to be more effective as a result. Indeed, it might be worth following the example of Brookfield (1998) who, as a professor of pedagogy with responsibility for staff development within higher education, regularly places himself in the position of a new learner in order to experience learning first-hand. From this, he is able to understand learning 'viscerally' (p. 17) and thus plan professional development more realistically. He argues, for example, that all those involved in instructional roles need to be constantly reminded that:

■ good teaching is teaching that is critically reflective
■ good teaching focuses on helping students to learn
■ the most important knowledge we need to teach well is an awareness of how our students are experiencing their own learning.

Perhaps the key point to take from all this is the imperative to place learners and learning at the heart of the coaching process, rather than coaches and coaching. It is more than semantics, and this idea will be pursued further in final section of this chapter, where the case is made for developing a 'pedagogy of learning' (Hargreaves, 2001) in coaching. Importantly, this is not an argument for prioritising athlete performance, as has been the case in much coaching literature, but rather for focusing on athlete *learning* as the basis of coaching practice.

KNOWLEDGE

Building upon the theoretical and practical evidence about coaches and learners, it is now timely to turn to that element of coaching pedagogy where the coach draws upon his or her knowledge base to, for example, select appropriate learning tasks. Clearly, the selection of a learning task reflects some prior assumptions

about what is valuable and worthwhile knowledge in a specific context. It is also intimately linked, as was noted in the previous sections, with assumptions about the nature of both learning generally and the learner in particular. But what are the characteristics of a knowledge base for coaching? And, is there a sufficient base to make claims that coaching is a profession?

In an extract from a classic paper, Shulman (1999) asks these very questions about teaching and its claims to be a profession. For example, he argues that:

> The key to distinguishing the knowledge base of teaching lies at the intersection of content and pedagogy, in the capacity of the teacher to transform the content knowledge he/she possesses into forms that are pedagogically powerful and yet adaptive to the variations in ability and background presented by the students (p. 91).

From this Shulman (1999, p. 64) defines a 'knowledge base' for teaching in the following categories:

- content knowledge;
- general pedagogical knowledge, with specific reference to those broad principles and strategies of classroom management and organisation that appear to transcend subject matter;
- curriculum knowledge, with a particular grasp of the materials and programmes that serve as 'tools of the trade' for teachers;
- pedagogical content knowledge, that special amalgam of content and pedagogy that is uniquely the province of teachers, their own special form of professional understanding;
- knowledge of learners and their characteristics;
- knowledge of educational contexts, ranging from the workings of the group or classroom, the governance and financing of school districts, to the character of communities and cultures; and
- knowledge of educational ends, purposes and values, and their philosophical and historical grounds.

Within this framework, Shulman identifies 'pedagogical content knowledge' as the key to defining and understanding teaching; as that special area of expertise that separates the pedagogue from the mere content-based instructor. The question, then, is whether coaching can claim to have a similar pedagogical content knowledge and if so, whether it is similar to that existing in teaching.

Teaching and coaching have often been viewed as distinct and separate activities. The assumption was made that teaching was, somehow, a worthier, more professional activity. This was probably borne of a need to justify a four-year teacher-training programme for what often, in practice, ended up in schools looking remarkably similar to a coaching activity. It was also an endeavour to make physical education teaching respectable within the sceptical academic environment of education (O'Conner & Macdonald, 2002). Things have changed, however, and

coaching aspires to professional status. However, Shulman (1999) sets some tough conditions about the nature of a knowledge base that is required for a profession and it is worth considering these in the context of coaching. For example, he argues that teaching is a learned profession and that a teacher is a member of a scholarly community. Thus, the teacher must have specific depth of understanding of particular content, but must also have a broad education that facilitates new understandings and that is flexible, adaptable and open to new interpretations. Similarly, he argues for the necessity of a body of formal research and scholarship in the field, particularly in the areas of schooling, teaching and learning. Within this, he includes the requirement for study of the 'normative, philosophical and ethical foundations of education' (p. 66). He also points to the need to identify the characteristics of effective teaching (without allowing those to become canonised into immutable models of good practice) and to the imperative to draw more systematically upon the 'wisdom of practice' by conducting research and collecting and storing knowledge about the practices of the most able practitioners. As he argues, 'Practitioners simply know a great deal that they have never tried to articulate' (p. 68). Perhaps the most important insight from Shulman's work, however, is his insistence that we recognise how little we know about learning, teaching and knowledge. It is a humbling insight; and one that can help coaching as it lays claims to being a profession, to avoid some of the mistakes made by the teaching profession. It may be wholly unprofitable, for example, to seek one-size-fits-all 'models' of effective coaching. Rather, as Shulman argues about teaching, we might want to seek to understand more about the complexities of coaching from expert practitioners – however we care to define 'expert'. Certainly, the coaches whose stories are told in this book can be defined as expert, and so it is interesting to see what they can tell us about coaching knowledge and, more specifically, about that aspect of knowledge that distinguishes the coach as pedagogue from other knowledge experts in relevant fields (for example, sport sciences). As Shulman argues, this is about 'the capacity of a teacher to transform the content knowledge he or she possesses into forms that are pedagogically powerful and yet adaptive to the variations in ability and background presented by the students' (p. 72). Essentially, therefore, this is about the transformation and adaptation of content knowledge or, in other words, about coaches' pedagogical content knowledge. There are numerous examples of pedagogical content knowledge in the coaches' stories.

Steve Harrison sets great store by blending his knowledge of football with his knowledge of players as individuals. He stresses the importance of providing advice in a mutually supportive and reinforcing atmosphere. As he says:

> knowledge of the game is important but it is when you put it over and how you put it over. If you start flooding a player's brain with knowledge they come off the field like [a zombie]. They've had four ecstasy tablets! . . . It's the how and when you express the knowledge that is most important'. Later he describes coaching as 'a fine art.

Bob Dwyer describes essential knowledge for coaching as follows:

'I certainly think you need to have good rugby ability physically, but I think you need good rugby knowledge mentally. It's the ability to evaluate the performance of individual players and the ability to communicate the evaluation to players, and the ability to show them how to emulate the required level'.

In order to do this successfully Bob feels that it is essential to 'speak in a language that the players can understand'. Moreover, he believes that a coach must be in partnership with players, working together to achieve performance goals. He adds to this blend the value of using humour as a learning tool – both to reinforce key messages and to lift tension. **Ian McGeechan** describes coaching knowledge as a 'twofold thing', balancing individual and collective learning:

I've never believed in doing practices just to make them pretty. I think a practice has to have a purpose, then the player builds up a better understanding of the shape of the game . . . It's no good to me coaching one [game] and the players seeing a different one . . . everything is about working towards the same game . . . everybody has to have the same framework, the same picture in their mind.

He is also aware of players' limitations and the need to pace things carefully:

I try to get the intensity into our sessions here because that is when you force players to make decisions. But you have got to be careful to balance that and not push them too hard or not give them something that they can't deal with, can't cope with.

Di Bass bases her coaching knowledge on extensive reading, research and preparation, but she also admires colleagues who can use humour and banter to motivate swimmers. She feels that this would be inappropriate for her personally, but sees that it can make sessions fun for some learners. She is very interested in seeking feedback from swimmers about her sessions, believing that it is important to learn from the learners about what works. Similarly, for **Lois Muir**, reading the individual player and encouraging them to be individuals is key: 'a lot of coaches want to box a player; say this is the only way to do it . . . but the future is in the young because they are uninhibited . . . and that's the fun of it. I like the people with a bit of the devil and a bit of spark'. In one aspect, however, Lois is uncompromising: 'I'm a bit of a technique person' thus believing that only when players have solid skills under pressure can they play effectively. In a game situation, she describes her role as one of arranging 'chess pieces on the field. It's moving them about for the best of the whole group'. She also argues that contrary to popular opinion, the time to make changes is when the team is winning. This is because she is very keen to preserve an element of surprise in her play, seeing this as crucial

to success. She also uses the wisdom of experienced players on the court to help her make appropriate coaching decisions. **Graham Taylor** raises a different issue: 'unless you can transfer what you do on the training pitch to what is required in the actual game, what are you doing?' He raised this issue at several points in the interview and was insistent that key coaching knowledge must be based on the players' needs and exactly what happens in the game: 'let's strip the game of emotion and see what happens . . . you've got to look at it with your own eyes . . . once people start to say this is *the* way to coach you should turn off'. **Hope Powell** makes a similar point and stresses the need to relate to players individually and 'make them think a little bit more about themselves in a particular position rather than the team as a whole', while **Peter Stanley** identifies technical understanding, the timing and delivery of quality instruction and feedback, and the ability to motivate athletes so they can 'put everything together' as the core of coaching knowledge.

Given the complexity of coaching knowledge as described by these coaches and, in particular, the ways in which coaches describe pedagogical content knowledge, perhaps questions could be raised about the adequacy of the knowledge base for coaching. Are the level and depth of critical scholarship in coaching sufficient to support claims that coaching is a profession? The establishment of degree courses in coaching is a promising move, and would seem to address some important issues about the professional requirement for a broad education. Still, some fundamental questions remain about the nature of the scholarship supporting such courses, the level and suitability of the content knowledge base, and the ways in which pedagogical content knowledge is conceived.

Finally, Shulman (1999) argues for a process of 'pedagogical reasoning' that includes the following stages: comprehension (the need to understand in order to teach), transformation/adaptation, evaluation, reflection and new comprehension (new learning on the part of the teacher). **Bob Dwyer** provides a good example of new comprehension: 'The '89 Lions taught me a lesson in that after losing the first test they got physical and we couldn't really handle it, they intimidated us and forced us into mistakes. So that taught me . . . you've got to win against the dirty guys too.' However, lest we are tempted to place Shulman's process and stages into a map or model for successful coaching, he makes it clear that these stages often occur in different orders, at different times, or not at all. Coaching pedagogy simply is not that straightforward.

LEARNING ENVIRONMENT

Elsewhere, we have argued that coaching is essentially a social practice created in the interaction of coaches, athletes and the club environment (Jones *et al.*, 2002; Cushion, 2001). Yet even this needs further elaboration in consideration of a coaching pedagogy. Leach and Moon (1999, p. 267) provide a useful starting point for this discussion in their use of the term 'pedagogic setting'. They define this as 'the practice that a teacher (or teachers), together with a particular group

of learners, creates, enacts and experiences'. Thus, coaching can be defined as a pedagogic setting and can be analysed as such.

Underpinning the notion of a pedagogic setting is the work of Lave and Wenger (1999) who argue that learning is 'situated' in specific 'communities of practice'. They draw upon the examples of apprentice learning to illustrate the ways in which apprentices learn from masters and, of key importance, gain legitimate access to the appropriate community of practice. In the case of learning to be a soccer coach, for example, one of the traditional 'conditions' of legitimate access is success as a player. Moreover, unofficial 'mentoring' by experienced coaches to novice coaches forms a major (but largely unregulated) form of coach education (Cushion, 2001). The value of this analysis, and its associated term 'communities of practice' is that it shifts the emphasis from teaching to 'the intricate structuring of a community's learning resources' (Lave & Wenger, 1999, p. 23). Importantly, it is not claimed that these communities of practice are homogenous, culture-sharing groups; rather it is assumed that 'members have different interests, make diverse contributions to activity and hold varied viewpoints . . . however it does imply participation in an activity system about which participants share understandings concerning what they are doing' (1999, p. 25).

Perhaps one of the most obvious ways in which this theory links to coaching is the recognition that the community of practice central to any sport has an important role in assuring that apprentices learn the 'culture of practice' appropriate to that sport. In these terms, the top-level coaches who appear in this book can be recognised as 'masters' in the sense that they create learning, together with their learners, in the appropriate sport-related community of practice. As Lave and Wenger (1999) argue, 'the practice of the community creates the potential "curriculum" in the broadest sense' (p. 22). For example, 'it offers exemplars (which are grounds and motivation for learning activity), including masters, finished products, and more advanced apprentices in the process of becoming full practitioners' (1999, p. 23).

If learning environments in coaching are considered to be pedagogic settings, then we need to look for the ways in which coaches and learners create, enact and experience their practice. If it is accepted, for example, that a community of practice is 'a set of relations among persons, activity, and world, over time and in relation with other tangential and overlapping communities of practice' (Lave & Wenger, 1999, p. 25), then the sheer complexity of the learning environment in coaching is signalled. If learning is situated, as a social practice, it needs to be understood as a dynamic and fluid process within a dynamic and fluid setting. This is precisely where Leach and Moon's (1999) notion of a 'pedagogic setting' is helpful as an analytical tool. Reflecting on the coaches' stories, a number of key factors about learning environments as pedagogic settings emerge. One of the most forceful comments in this regard was from **Bob Dwyer**:

> The total environment is essential, and the total environment is affected as much by what you do off the pitch as what you do on it. It's about

developing a sense of confidence, self-worth and well-being in players which can have a real effect on them and their performances.

The key to this, for Bob, is organisation and the assumptions he makes about stability and confidence:

> It's a bit like having a well organised child rather than a child that doesn't know what . . . is expected of him, when it's expected of him and he tends to be a bit all over the place, whereas the kid in the healthy environment . . . knows what he is doing . . . and that's a very reassuring environment.

Hope Powell uses her expertise, experience and intuition to watch players, be aware of them and learn from them so she can establish the coaching environment appropriately, while **Peter Stanley** sees the size of group as an important feature of the learning environment. He likes to work with up to eight athletes at one time 'because of all the individual, one-to-one situations that you get into for athletes to progress . . . a one-to-one process within a group climate'. He also stressed the need to be open and honest with athletes, finding that they tend to see through 'bullshit' anyway. **Graham Taylor** emphasises a learning environment centred on trust. Echoing **Peter Stanley**'s comments, he seeks to establish that trust by trying to be completely open with players: 'let them know where they stand'. **Steve Harrison** talks about establishing a confident, relaxed and flexible learning environment:

> Coaching isn't always about this is what I'm going to do and I'm going to do it irrespective, and I'm going to make it work. You start something, see it's not working, so what do you do? Carry on and bash away at it? . . . There are no hard and fast lines.

Ian McGeechan expects to have the total learning environment very much under his control, within which he wants players to 'grow': 'That's what you try to do . . . you grow players.' **Lois Muir** also emphasises flexibility. For her, it is players who must be flexible enough to change game plans mid-stream if they aren't working; the learning environment must be pressured but enabling. Here again she highlights the need to set up learning situations that put pressure on players to reflect on themselves and raise their own games. One of the ways she does this is to put new, young players on the court who are less familiar to the more experienced players: 'you change the adrenalin carrot of the experienced players because they have to look out . . . so now we've got them connected and looking at how they can work with you to lift their own game. So it actually changes the adrenalin'.

Leach and Moon (1999, p. 268) claim that pedagogy is centrally about 'the construction and practice of learning communities'. In considering the learning environment in coaching as a community of practice where learning is created, enacted and experienced, the case for the development of a coaching pedagogy is at its most persuasive.

COACHING PEDAGOGY: A PEDAGOGY FOR LEARNING

In summary, the case for developing a more explicit understanding of coaching from a pedagogical perspective rests on an understanding of the concept of pedagogy as:

- multidimensional and connective
- centrally about learning
- developed from the term 'pedagogue'.

As was noted at the outset, the concept of pedagogy has traditional links with schools, education and pupils, but it is clear that it has much to offer an analysis of coaching and that it strikes chords with some existing literature in coaching. For example, for many teachers, the need to 'care' for and about pupils in a broad sense is a central part of teaching (Day, 1999). If the coaches in this book are in any sense typical, then there are coaches who also care, in a holistic sense, about their athletes. A connective, multidimensional pedagogy of coaching, therefore, is all about the connections between coaches, learners, types of knowledge and learning environments. It establishes coaching as a community of practice within which learners (both coaches and athletes) create the learning that is central to coaching and the practice of sport. The complexity of this process is, of course, both exhilarating and daunting. Yet, in order to consider a coaching pedagogy, that complexity must be faced, and ways of grasping it must be found. To this end, the final section of this chapter is devoted to exploring two possible starting points; both drawing upon recent research on pedagogy in education: firstly, an enhanced focus on *learning* and learners in coaching and, secondly, what is possibly a logical outcome, a critical analysis of coach education.

A pedagogy for learning in coaching?

Dipping back into the world of education, Hargreaves (2001) argues that schools are largely governed by a curriculum that is, in the main, a curriculum for teaching. It is designed for teachers and determines what is to be taught. He also claims that, unfortunately, many teachers read the national curriculum as both content and method thus avoiding the need to develop a more appropriate pedagogy. As he points out:

> We must think afresh what we mean by 'curriculum' and by 'pedagogy'. We need to forge new kinds of linkage between the curriculum for teaching that guides what is done in schools, colleges and universities and the curriculum for learning by which each individual shapes an agenda for a lifelong education . . . we need to learn far more about how people learn in natural and authentic situations.

In order to achieve this, Hargreaves claims that educators will need to engage in new forms of professional learning that are more likely to enable them to develop

pedagogies that resonate with today's society and that meet the needs of today's young learners.

The implications for coaching, and particularly for coach education, are interesting. Learners in coaching situations are also part of the wider, changing society that Hargreaves (2001) identifies. Furthermore, it would appear that some existing coach education could best be described as providing a curriculum (recipe?) for teaching. For example, some of it barely acknowledges that learning is situated, that authentic learning activities are essential (Putnam & Borko, 2000) and that coaching is a community of practice that is creating coaching knowledge. Yet the charge levelled at the teaching profession is that until a more intellectualised pedagogy (Leach & Moon, 1999) can underpin education, the claims of teaching to be a profession can be challenged. Could the same be said of coaching?

In an attempt to outline some of the key features of a more intellectualised pedagogy, Leach and Moon (1999) argue that effective pedagogic settings have the following characteristics:

- 'a theory of pedagogy must encompass all the complex factors that influence the process of teaching and learning. In creating and sustaining pedagogic settings [coaches] crucially determine both the nature and quality of learning' (p. 268);
- 'within such settings a broad understanding of the human mind and cognitive science, as we understand it today, would seem a crucial aspect of [coach] knowledge . . . therefore, within any pedagogical setting, the mind must be viewed as agentive, complex and multifaceted' (p. 270);
- 'in creating pedagogic settings a conceptual distinction should be made between the curriculum as planned and enacted and the curriculum as experienced by learners' (p. 271);
- 'overt planning is required to ensure that pedagogic settings build the self-esteem and identity of learners' (p. 272);
- 'pedagogic settings should create the conditions for reflection . . . developing habits of mind that enable learners to be reflective, questioning and critical is central to pedagogy' (p. 272).

So, a good starting point for the establishment of coaching as a respected profession could be the development of a coaching pedagogy that begins with the recognition that coaching is a pedagogic setting, in Leach and Moon's (1999) terms, and that learning is at its core. Clearly this has implications for coach education.

Professional development of coaches

If coaching is to be a profession, then *professional* development is what professional coaches need. But how should this be structured? And how would it differ from existing forms of coach education/certification? The answers to these questions can be found both in the stories told by the top-level coaches in this book, and also by looking again at the world of education, where research on professional

development and pedagogy has begun to change thinking and practice. First, it is interesting to note that the coaches had strong comments to make about coach education. Their comments are thoughtful, relevant and insightful and, based as they are upon experience, we would argue that they point the way towards the kind of professional development that experienced coaches as pedagogues need and deserve. What they said is as follows.

Lois Muir:

> people can go through accreditation . . . but that doesn't mean to say that they're a good coach. And I get nervous when people think of accreditation, going through to level three or something like that makes them a great coach, where it is the management of people and your own philosophies and everything put together that hits. It's the management of the people you've got, that's coaching. It's the art of the game . . . accreditations doesn't do the right thing. What coaches need is decision making. The game plan. And the counters under stress. And the accreditation doesn't give you that. If we spent more time, if you and I sat down and watched a game [and we analysed the game] that's what should be in the accreditation and it isn't. And you see that is the art of coaching. That's the true feel of it . . . and coaching really is individual and it should stay individual. So that needs to be . . . one mentor coach with two others, no more than that . . . People, people, people. You watch people. And people management, that's the fun of it.

Bob Dwyer found some inspirational coaching courses in Australia. His comments hint at courses based on developing pedagogical content knowledge of the kind advocated by Shulman (1999):

> Being interested in the game I went along as a kind of 'student coach' and listened to a few things. I was very impressed by the fact that someone was telling you not *what* to coach but how to coach. It got me to really think about how I structured my coaching sessions.

Ian McGeechan felt that he learnt much that he values from his teacher training.

> A coaching course has never produced an international coach. I think that international coaches are different, you can't make them . . . If you are relying on coaching courses, you are relying on things that are probably about five years out of date anyway . . . but coaching courses are very useful things for people who want to get involved who haven't had a teaching or educational background because it helps you to communicate.

One element of professional development that is missing, in Ian's view, is the opportunity to interact with other coaches, possibly at conferences or meetings, to share knowledge and experience. He believes that for coaches at the top levels, this would be far more effective in developing practice than attendance at traditional courses. As he puts it: 'coaching by numbers can only take you so far'.

Steve Harrison believes that much of the most valuable knowledge in coaching comes by learning from other coaches: 'It's a copying thing, plus the fact that you learn as you go along, so you learn by experience . . . you add variations; I think that is how people learn.' He has found official coach certification to be limited: 'Very useful in terms of the organisation of pitch sizes . . . and your general organisation of things such as bibs and cones. In the main, organisation, that is what I learnt.' Of more concern is his charge that coaching courses can stifle creativity:

> That is why in this country over the past fifteen years we've had robotic coaches being churned out playing a robotic way of football . . . because that is what we were taught at Lilleshall on the Full Badge . . . So after two weeks at Lilleshall, all the coaches came out knowing and doing the same things because that is what you passed at . . . There's been no openmindedness on the Full Badge course.

Yet, for Steve, successful coaching is all about being individual, having a personal style and 'the ability to handle men, that's the big thing, to handle people'. Importantly, he would love to see 'an exchange of coaches' as a key part of professional development to enable him to learn from other talented coaches.

Di Bass feels that she has learnt relatively little from coaching courses; rather they are perceived as a means to an end. Like **Ian McGeechan**, she has found that knowledge relevant to swimming progresses more rapidly than the courses and trainers can accommodate: 'It's a very technical sport . . . and these things are developing' yet the courses are often at a very basic level. For high-level coaches who have wide experience and who are also reading extensively in the field, this kind of professional development is always likely to be unsatisfying and inappropriate.

Hope Powell can see much of value in coach certification courses in football, but is concerned that many coaches are unable to take the lessons learnt and apply/modify them to their own practice. Like others, she is very keen to see mentoring becoming more firmly established as part of coach education and, to that end, she has established a mentoring process for aspiring female football coaches: 'it's a case of support, developing a bit of confidence . . . make them believe they are good enough to pass the highest award as, at the moment, it's an all male thing'. Having broken into this male domain, she is very keen to help other women to do the same thing.

Peter Stanley recalled some excellent coach education experiences but, like **Hope Powell**, he was keen to promote the value of working with and observing other top-level coaches as a requirement of coach education programmes. He sees this as offering valuable opportunities to build upon the knowledge gained from written examinations: 'I just think there should be a more structured and logical progression, as opposed to just passing examinations. Giving coaches at all levels

the opportunity to work with more senior and experienced coaches would be a good way of doing things.'

Graham Taylor argues strongly for coaching courses to be seen as only the start of coach education: 'I think you have to show that you are prepared to qualify as such but that's only the start of it. You haven't ended the thing once you've got the qualification . . . it's just starting.' He feels that he was widely misquoted over his comments about the appointment of Sven-Goran Eriksson as coach to the England Football team:

> they completely missed the point . . . what I actually said and what I still do say is that if over the last 25–30 years the Football Association has put millions of pounds into their football coaching courses, if then we give the top job to a non-English person, surely we have to look at what the content of those courses has been.

It is important to note that these coaches' comments resonate strongly with recent research on professional development in both education and other fields. For example, Day (1999, p. 204) points out that professional development activities for teachers are unlikely to be effective if they are not 'based upon an understanding of the complexities of teachers' lives and conditions of work nor upon an understanding of how teachers learn and why they change'. In the light of the evidence presented in this book, it seems the same can be said of coaches' biographies, practices and careers. Importantly, this is also broadly reflected in some existing research within coaching (Schempp & Graber, 1992; Abraham & Collins, 1998; Cushion, 2001). Other research in education has sought to identify 'principles' for effective professional development. For example, the National Partnership for Excellence and Accountability in Teaching in the USA (NPEAT, 1998) and the National Foundation for Educational Research in the UK (NFER, 2001) have identified that the most effective professional development:

- focuses strongly on student learning;
- supports teacher autonomy in the structure and focus of the development activities;
- is closely linked to daily practice;
- is mainly organised around collaborative problem solving; and
- is continuous, coherent, progressive and supported by follow-up learning.

As Garet *et al.*, (2001) point out, if teachers are at the centre of raising educational standards, they will need to engage in professional development that extends their own learning and pedagogies whilst also learning more about how their pupils learn. From Garet *et al.*'s research, three 'core' features of effective professional development were identified as:

- a focus on content knowledge;
- opportunities for active learning; and
- coherence with other learning activities.

Active learning is described as the 'opportunity for teachers to become actively engaged in meaningful discussion, planning and practice' (Garet et al., 2001, p. 925). This could be in the form of observing and being observed, planning and implementing new material and methods, reviewing progress, and presenting or leading discussions and writing. Such research would appear to lend some support to the plea made by the coaches in this book, who are seeking opportunities to engage, critically and reflectively, with other top-level coaches in a shared professional culture (Loughran & Gunstone, 1997). Within this framework, it must also be recognised that expert help from outside the immediate community of practice can be very valuable (Stein et al., 1999). Stein et al. also point to the need to consider the context; the total learning environment in which a teacher works. Crucially, Loughran and Gunstone (1997), among others, remind us that professional development is not something that can be 'delivered', rather it should be about 'working with, not doing to [professionals] so that appropriate time, support, understanding and personal development are seen as investments in personal growth' (1997, p. 161). This, we would argue, could be an important starting point for the development of a coaching pedagogy and new forms of coach professional development. However, it also hints at one of the key barriers to changing professional development practices: the professional developers themselves and the motivation and skills they have to work in new and unfamiliar ways (Stein et al., 1999).

SUMMARY

So, in summary, what can we say about the potential of 'pedagogy' as an analytical concept in coaching and as a practical base upon which to consider professional development in coaching? Perhaps the first thing to acknowledge is that there is no suggestion that the field of education has got it somehow 'right' and that the field of coaching ought to copy it. On the contrary, although there is an increasing interest in pedagogy within education, and particularly in the key notion of 'learning', this is a relatively recent development. Second, the world-wide explosion of interest in professional development for teachers, often viewed by governments as the solution to any number of society's ills, is probably overoptimistic at best, and naive at worse. Yet, funding for professional development for teachers is now more widely available than in previous years and the level of research and scholarship has also risen. Indeed, some of the more recent research and writing in this area is noteworthy, building, as it does, upon earlier work in education and evidence from other professions. So what can coaches learn from this trend? And how can such learning advance claims for the recognition of coaching as a fully fledged profession? This chapter closes with the identification of five steps towards the development of a coaching pedagogy and the professional development associated with it.

1   Recognise that coaching is intellectual work and that the coach is a modern-day pedagogue.
2   Consider the developmental needs of experienced coaches – the comments made by the coaches in this book could be a good starting point – and then examine the implications for all coaches.
3   Explore, in more depth than has been possible here, the links between research and scholarship in pedagogy in education, and like-minded research and scholarship in coaching.
4   Analyse the ways in which professional development for coaches would have to change if it were based on the concept of pedagogy with learning at its core.
5   Consider the professional development needs of those who currently 'supply' or 'deliver' professional development in coaching.

CHAPTER 11

▼   **COACHES' ROLES**

BY ROBYN JONES

KEY ISSUES

INTRODUCTION

'Role' is an interesting concept. We generally employ the term to describe how we use or slot into different personas for different aspects of our lives. Indeed, it is a concept that is evident in many generic coach education programmes as a way of appreciating the multiple functions of a coach. Role is also a complex concept, which greatly influences how we act and behave; hence it is worthy of deeper analysis than presently afforded within such programmes. This chapter explores the notion of a 'role' within coaching, and how coaches come to know and use different roles in their practice. It seeks to identify, clarify and understand such roles, and specifically examines why the coaches interviewed in this book coach as they do, in terms of the roles they fulfil. However, rather than seeking prescriptive or normative answers about what coaches ought to do, the chapter attempts to undertake a sociological analysis of the roles coaches perform; for example, linking the performance of the coach's role to wider social influences (Shaw, 1981). Raffel's (1998) insightful analysis of 'role and the problem of the self' provides a broad framework within it for understanding the ways in which the coaching self is embedded in, and expressed through, a role. More specifically, following an introductory analysis of research on social roles, an examination is undertaken of the structural constraints upon the coaches interviewed in terms of the expectations of society, athletes and self on their coaching styles. Far from reducing individual action to the level of mere 'mechanical compliance' to social expectation (Raffel, 1998), the intention here, as the chapter progresses, is to examine the potential of elite coaches to obey, resist or use such demands in highly inventive ways (Lemert, 1997). Hence, it considers if, how and to what extent coaches are socialised into their working behaviours, whilst simultaneously acting as independent reflective agents. Finally, the concepts of 'strong evaluation', 'role distance' and 'self in role' are examined as useful analytical pegs that go some way towards explaining the dynamism and enthusiasm emitted by the coaches interviewed as a reflection of what Shaw (1981) has termed 'charismatic leadership'.

The significance of an analysis of role lies in identifying and understanding the interpersonal dimensions of coaching which are increasingly being recognised as central to effective practice (Jones, 2000). Such dimensions relate to the relationship issues of intensity, quality and trust among others (Broderick, 1999). Indeed, in all probability, a repertoire of such and similar role behaviours are implicit in the workings of many successful coaches. The objective here is to make such behavioural roles explicit through an examination of the processes that define and reproduce them, thus leaving us better able to both discern what our tasks are and to articulate the service that we perform as coaches (Ollhoff & Ollhoff, 1996). Such awareness is increasingly needed as some of the traditionally defined aspects of roles become obsolete in rapidly changing contextual circumstances (Gouws, 1995), as characterised by current progressive developments in the field of coaching. It is needed as it has the power to inform change through deliberate analysis, adjustment and accommodation (Gouws, 1995).

Additionally, it is hoped that such analysis can lead to increased understanding about the evolving roles that coaches play in their social exchanges, particularly with their athletes. That is, about how the interplay of structure and agency are manifest in elite coaching practice. This could enable the development of a useful framework for planning and managing more carefully the social, interactive dimensions of coaching, whilst also allowing better reflection on boundary definition, planning and management of role fulfilment within our coach education programmes (Broderick, 1999).

A CURRENT ANALYSIS OF SOCIAL ROLES

Social roles have traditionally been explained from a structural perspective where actions are considered to be driven by expectations, that is, 'the expectations an actor holds for herself [sic], and the expectations an actor believes others hold for her' (Troyer & Younts, 1997, p. 692). A role is thus derived from a shared expectation for behaviour (Carron, 1988); a process that has been termed 'role acquisition' (Ollhoff & Ollhoff, 1996). Hence, when an individual assumes the role of the coach they engage in a set of behaviours that they perceive to fulfil that role; behaviours that are understood by them and other group members (Mack & Gammage, 1998). An interesting question that inevitably emerges here, and is partially addressed within the chapter, is whose expectations really matter in determining action? (Jones, *et al.*, 2002). In other words do coaches act in ways they think they should, or in ways they think their athletes think they should?

This perspective on the construction of roles, which has tended to emphasise their constraining and determining features, has recently been the subject of some debate (Callero, 1994). It has been criticised for not managing to capture the complex and dynamic nature of roles (Rodham, 2000), and mirrors the emerging consensus among sociologists that 'society consists of both powerful determining structures and actors that posses a degree of efficacy, freedom and creative independence' (Callero, 1994, p. 228); in essence, an individual's behaviour consists of both uninhibited decision-making (agency) and the influence of wider social factors (structures). Consequently, it has been argued that role theory, in order to produce a more comprehensive understanding of role behaviour, should focus on the impact of (and the relationship between) structure and agency on the formation and development of social roles. This acknowledges the need to appreciate the individual's 'self hood' (Raffel, 1998) and how it is responsible for guiding action. Such an approach enables us to better appreciate the complexity of role behaviour, by taking into account not only the expectations of other role sets (e.g., audiences) but also of the role incumbent and the dynamic interaction between them (Rodham, 2000). Consequently, the analysis borrows from the tenets of social exchange theory, which emphasises not only the constraining effects 'of the social structure, but also how individual action collectively creates, reproduces and changes social structure' (O'Brien & Kollock, 1991, p. 140). Indeed, it becomes obvious that the behavioural similarities and variations observed within coaching practices can be explained by the impact of both structure and agency, as coaches act both as they choose and how they are influenced to choose (Lemert, 1997).

In recognising the dual impact of structure and agency on the construction of role, Callero (1994) agrees that both approaches need to be combined if a more complete explanation of role theory and human behaviour is to be developed. The need for such a convergence in approaches has resulted in the proposition that social roles would be better understood from a 'resource perspective' (Callero, 1994), which would lead to an improved grasp of the 'why' and 'how' of role behaviour as opposed to only the descriptive 'what' (Rodham, 2000). This perspective offers a better understanding of the interdependent relationship between individual action and the collective structure (Callero, 1994) by locating actions in the intentionality of individuals and the contexts within which they work (Rodham, 2000). Hence, it can be considered that individuals are actively involved in the process of 'role-making' as opposed to passively 'role-playing' (Callero, 1994; Raffel, 1998), which has profound implications for our understanding of the coaching process. Indeed, perhaps it is in these caveats of conscious invention, improvisation and creative independence that coaching practice becomes inspirational.

In the milieu of coaching practice then, how do structures and individual coaches come together and interact to define the coaching process? This is a practice that is described by Lemert (1997) as being what is original to oneself and at the same time common to those of a similar social kind. In his work on social practice, Bourdieu proposes the concept of *habitus* as the bridge that links structure and agency. Here, it is considered that people are endowed with a series of internalised schemes and it is through these schemes that they produce their practices (Ritzer, 1996). Bourdieu describes this as 'the internalisation of the structures' of the social world (1989, p. 18). Because habitus is acquired as a result of occupation of a social position, for example, that of the coach, those who occupy the same positions tend to have similar habitus (Ritzer, 1996).

Common lessons are thus absorbed about manners, customs and style and become so ingrained that they are forgotten in any conscious sense (Jarvie & Maguire, 1994). However, although in this respect society is 'written into the body' (Bourdieu, 1990), the individual is still empowered to act back on the social world as each person remains a unique individual within the common matrix. So, were our coaches socialised into actions dictated by external pressures?

'PLAYING THE ROLE': THE COACH AS A SOCIALISED INSTRUCTOR

Almost without exception the coaches spoke of the need to give their athletes a clear sense of direction both in terms of task and role responsibility. Hence, they openly admitted that instruction and prescription formed a predominant part of their pedagogy and their consequent coaching personas. **Ian McGeechan** and **Bob Dwyer**, in particular, emphasised the need to establish a directive structure; acknowledging the necessity to be dictatorial at times. Even **Peter Stanley**, who appeared to work very much in partnership with his athletes, recognised that on occasions, 'you really need to be the teacher'. How did they learn such strategies and roles? That is, if coaching is a matter of common 'role playing', who wrote the script, set the scene, and constructed the scenario? (Shaw, 1981). The answer appears to lie in both the wider socialisation process, and more specifically, in the perceived expectations of athletes.

The expectations of society

A partial answer to the question of role acquisition is to say that society, or the social structures that comprise it, creates the roles we fill in life; it is a process of occupational socialisation. Thus, despite the individual nature of each coaching position, coaches form a sub-society of interlocking groups, 'a community rooted in sport and what it symbolises, and hence they identify themselves collectively as a meaningful social segment' (Sage, 1989, p. 88). This creates a social network or structure which both influences and enables the expression

of similar attitudes and value orientations, and through which cultural traditions flow (Oakes, 1989; Sage, 1989). Such a notion builds on Sage's (1989) earlier, predominantly structuralist position on the impact of 'organizational socialization' upon coaching behaviour. 'Organizational socialization' has been defined as the process by which rookie coaches 'on the job acquire the skills and supporting cultural ideology necessary to participate as contributing members of an occupation' (Sage, 1989, p. 87). In addition to learning the technical aspects of the job, this social practice inculcates coaches with shared understandings regarding the ideology and critical aspects of the occupation (Sage, 1989). Such a process also enables coaches to understand and interpret everyday events related to the job by highlighting 'how we do things and what matters around here' (Sage, 1989, p. 87).

According to Gouws (1995), the socialisation process is probably best described in terms of Bandura's (1977) social learning theory, the application of which takes place at both conscious and subconscious levels. Pivotal to Bandura's hypothesis is that much of what we learn is through modelling, a notion that is widely supported by others (e.g., Ollhoff & Ollhoff, 1996; Arends, 1988), who concur that effective contact and attentive observation of a model are essential to the development of a new role. Thus, when we enter a new situation we immediately search to find our role, through picking up verbal and especially non-verbal cues to tell us what others expect of us (Ollhoff & Ollhoff, 1996). Indeed, according to Bandura (1977), 'most human behaviour is learned observationally through modeling; as from observing others, one forms an idea of how new behaviours are performed', which later serve as guides to action (p. 22). It appears that we would rather copy an old role than risk creating a new one, as the latter requires both mastery of the social situation and abundant self-belief. It is unsurprising therefore that most of the coaches interviewed cited role models whom they considered to have influenced their early development as they 'felt' their way into their new positions, as such models provided 'an initial road map into an uncertain future' (Kekale, 1998, p. 240). The influence of role models over the coaches however varied greatly, from **Lois Muir**'s reverence for her former coach Dixie Cochran ('I'd have jumped up and grabbed the moon for her') to **Bob Dwyer**, **Di Bass** and **Ian McGeechan** who did not think that they had had any. However, when pushed, even they acknowledged some influences over their coaching development, be they former players, teachers or coaches. The general consensus in this regard was expressed by **Steve Harrison**: 'I think you learn something from everybody; you learn by copying what people you admire do, and then you add variations of your own.' However, although mentors were cited, their influence past the first years of the coaches' careers was limited, displaying an independent strand in the latter which will be explored a little later in the chapter.

It appears that the practitioners interviewed here were socialised into an instructional style of coaching because, fuelled by the initial influence of role models, this was what the culture of the occupation demanded. Ulrich and Walker

(1982) provide an explanation for the predominance of instruction within this socialisation process, related to society's narrow yet widely held definition of the coach, who is obliged by both the task and the nature of sport to act in certain ways. In this respect, society has limited the coach's role to the selection, organisation and deployment of talent in an efficient time-saving manner in order to win (Lombardo, 1987). Thus, the coaching role has come to reflect society's emphasis on product values rather than process concerns (Hellison, 1973), which has resulted in many coaches holding an authoritarian orientation (Potrac *et al.*, 2002; Gensemer, 1980). This prescriptive predominance could also reflect coaches' needs to operate within an unambiguous occupational comfort zone in which they clearly understand what their socially well-defined traditional role is to be. Thus, tradition and societal values can be seen as major forces, which tend to suppress the initiation and implementation of any coaching programme that deviates from the prescriptive norm (Danziger, 1982).

According to Carron (1980), another possible explanation for the directive pedagogy adopted by the coaches interviewed may lie in the perceived nature of the athletic situation itself. Here, coaches, in a manner similar to members of other groups, are socialised into certain role prescriptions and behaviour patterns often through functional expediency; that is, 'the coach must efficiently direct the performance of a large number of individuals, often with only a fixed, minimal amount of time available' (Carron, 1980, p. 62). Consequently, the need for control, organisation and unquestioned athlete response, as manifest in high instructional levels, would appear to be a result of the requirements of the situation. Indeed, many of the coaches spoke about situational constraints and their influence on their pedagogy. For example, **Di Bass** was only too aware that the swimming environment normalises a high level of coach dependence, as the hats, earplugs and goggles that are worn by swimmers often mitigate against in-depth collaboration and exploration at the pool side. Other coaches meanwhile cited constraints in terms of time ('the amount of time that you have at your disposal to change things is often not long enough' – **Bob Dwyer**), and the weather ('when you've got the elements against you, you've just got to keep the players hard at it, on the move' – **Steve Harrison**) as having an influence on their respective coaching styles. Allied to their awareness of the 'bottom line' of outcome, many believed such constraints necessitated a high level of control and direction on their part.

The expectations of athletes

When examining the role of the coach, because it is a social one, an explanation of it cannot be limited to one person's behaviour. Hence, it must also 'include the behaviour of others which provides the rights enabling the actions of the individual' (Lopata, 1991, p. 1). As Znaniecki (1954, p. 521) points out,

> Every social role is performed within a social circle of people who accept a particular individual as a person presumably *fit* for the performance of

this role. His [*sic*] circle cooperates with him by granting him and actively supporting those rights which he needs in order to perform effectively his functions.

Consequently, as all members of a central actor's role 'set' (those within an immediate circle of interaction) depend on his or her performance in some way, they develop beliefs about what he or she should or should not do as part of his or her role; these are role expectations (Rodham, 2000). In this context, the athletes, as part of the coach's role set, press behavioural expectations on the coach, thus defining his or her expectations about how he or she should act (Troyer *et al.*, 2000).

According to Broderick (1999), in such a 'service' encounter as coaching, each party has learned a set of behaviours that are appropriate to that situation. These behaviours or role scripts define the boundaries within which social interactions occur. Parties within such encounters have clear role expectations of each other and will evaluate the service given on the basis of the perceived role performance of the service provider. Thus, the degree to which the service provider engages in the role script that is perceived as being appropriate may determine the overall benefits of the encounter as perceived by the client. It is argued that if the focal actor, the coach in this regard, meets the role expectations of the client, that is the athlete, and encourages appropriate role involvement on the part of the latter, positive outcomes should result. However, when the perceived requirements associated with a particular role are unclear or are not met, role ambiguity develops, which leads to dissatisfaction and feelings of inter-member tension (Carron, 1988). For example, when a coach is not acting in a way athletes perceive he or she should, a counterproductive atmosphere is created (Mack & Gammage, 1998), as 'it is always demanded that the actor be what he [*sic*] is playing' (Shaw, 1981, p. 52). Indeed, from the athletes' point of view, the key evaluation criterion of a coach is the effectiveness or 'satisfactoriness' of role performance (Gouws, 1995). Similarly, if the differing parties (coach and athletes) 'have congruent expectations, judgments of effectiveness may become complicated with one participant proclaiming effective performance and the other seeing only ineffective performance' (Gouws, 1995, p. 32). The outcome, defined as role dissensus, is unfavourable to all (Pajak *et al.*, 1984).

According to Lombardo (1987), it appears that the athletes themselves exert great pressure on the coach to direct their activities. In this respect, they expect him or her to improve and refine their skills by intensive practice sessions and the employment of expertise, and would rather not participate in 'laborious and esoteric self-discovery techniques' (Ulrich & Walker, 1982, p. 72). Similarly, when an athlete's principal concern is the final outcome, he or she loses interest in the opportunity for pertinent, personal and novel insights and discoveries inherent in the learning process (Lombardo, 1987). The result is the creation and nurturance of dependent athletes who come to rely on the coach and his or her 'infallible' system (Lombardo, 1987). The athletes, in turn, often resist and reject efforts to give them decision-making opportunities. Hence, according to Kossek *et al.*,

(1999), it is the social expectations of athletes that define the boundaries of coach role embracement and create perceived sanctions if behaviour is otherwise.

Research by Shaw (1981) in education appears to support this notion, with pupils defining teachers' role in a limited way, stressing strongly the instructional and formal aspect of it. Any other pedagogy, for example critical questioning, was likely to be rejected and viewed as evidence of weakness or incompetence and despised as such. Likewise, a major criticism that is levelled by students at teacher training courses is that they rarely received advice of a straightforward and prescriptive nature, which led to feelings of frustration (Shaw, 1981). Similar conclusions were also drawn by Pajak *et al.*, (1984), who found that teachers' perceptions of their own behaviour reflected the perceived needs and expectations of others in their role set. Hence, appropriate role behaviour was viewed as a salient ideal for retaining status (Leifer, 1988). In addition to being socialised into instructional behaviours by peers and role models, athletes could also be bringing coaches 'into line' with regard to their practice. It was evident that some of the coaches interviewed felt similar pressures in relation to appropriately fulfilling their perceived roles through the use of directive behaviour. Here, they believed that their athletes expected a degree of prescription from them, manifested within high intensity sessions, which they delivered accordingly. **Steve Harrison** expressed it as such: 'players like to have a structured framework comprising fast past sessions of skill tasks and games; they like to be worked, so that's what I do'. Similarly, **Di Bass**, in commenting generally on coaching styles rather than her own pedagogy, agreed that 'a lot of the top swimmers are very coach dependent. And like it that way'.

Indeed, the coaches perceived that any failure on their behalf to establish clear expectations for their athletes generated confusion and frustration among the latter. They believed that athletes like to be told and be clear as to what is expected of them, as when lucid priorities are established, respondents have little difficulty in deciding on the appropriate behaviour (Secord & Backman, 1974). In this way, both coach and athlete are playing complementary roles, where the emphasis is on matching the interactive behaviours of people playing interdependent roles (Gouws, 1995). Such a notion concurs with Shaw's (1981) belief that much of human behaviour is influenced by the desire to fulfil and satisfy the expectations of others. This seems most particularly to be the case when 'others' are perceived to be in some position of authority, which has implications for understanding the traditional nature of power in the coach–athlete relationship. This is a concept that is more fully explored in a later chapter.

Unsurprisingly, Carron (1988; Carron & Widmeyer, 1996) has asserted that a circular relationship exists between role behaviour and cohesion, which ultimately impacts on team performance. Hence, having clearly defined and accepted roles leads to increased cohesion among 'team' members. In extending the earlier work of Hendry (1969) who examined swimmers' assessments of an 'ideal coach' stereotype, he found strong agreement between coaches and athletes concerning the characteristic role behaviours of coaches (Carron, 1980). Here, there was

complete agreement that coaches are 'the initiators of control behaviour, athletes the recipients' (p. 62). Coaches were also perceived as needing to dominate the athletic environment by 'exhibiting a high degree of power, influence and control over athletes, while permitting the athletes little opportunity to express such behaviour' (p. 61). Ollhoff and Ollhoff (1996) term such a phenomenon as role consensus, which occurs when one has acquired the role and everyone agrees that he or she is acting appropriately in that role. The coaches interviewed here seemed to strive for such a consensus, not always through the adoption of a hierarchical structure, but from the necessity of having 'everybody pointing in the same direction'. This understanding of a common directive and the individual's role within it was considered crucial to team success. **Ian McGeechan** defined it as such: 'we all have to be aware of what we can expect from each other; we all have to see the same game otherwise we won't be successful'.

On the importance of athletes knowing their roles

A further clear theme to emerge from the interviews, particularly from those coaches of team sports, was the commonly held belief that athletes need to know their roles well in order to be successful within them. Thus, the coaches believed that team members need to know who occupies which role and what is expected of each individual within those roles, leading to a firm understanding of how he or she and other athletes contribute to the team (Mumma, 1994). This was something particularly emphasised by **Bob Dwyer**, **Graham Taylor** and **Ian McGeechan** who believed that in order to have a clear sense of purpose, players need to fully understand their roles and responsibilities within the team framework. **McGeechan** referred to it as 'getting rid of the grey areas', and highlighted it as a fundamental aim of his coaching practice. In order to carry out their jobs properly, it was believed that every player should have a good understanding of the role associated with every other position as well as their own and hence would know what everyone else was likely to do in a given situation. In this respect, 'they must be able to take the role of the others' (Lee, 1993, p. 102). Such role clarity gives a sense of direction, purpose and value and equates to team role theory, which relies on the notion that there are various well and widely understood team roles which complement one another to make up an effective team (McCrimmon, 1995). The emphasis on role clarity within team development also echoes the work of Belbin (1981), who suggested that 'super-teams' comprise individuals who play different but mutually well-defined complementary and supplementary roles.

However, far from restricting the players in their charge, the coaches believed that such role adherence gave players the freedom to express themselves within the established structure. It was considered that role definition gave the players the security of having somewhere to anchor their understandings of how they should contribute to the team's performance. It was also believed that it gave them a platform upon which to play, without which they would become uncertain, confused and frustrated about exactly what was expected of them. Hence, rigid role adherence was consciously often considered a necessary first step in good team development, with players being allowed to explore the boundaries of their given roles only after this was achieved satisfactorily.

In the words of **Ian McGeechan**,

> No matter how good the talent is, it can't come out (if) the structure which produces the stage for performance is not there . . . If you haven't got a structure you're too airy-fairy. You get freedom of expression out of structure, not the other way around . . . If you haven't got control of language you can't be a William Shakespeare . . . (once) you all have the same framework, then you've got choices.

Graham Taylor took this notion of achieving a balance between team structure and individual expression a step further by linking it to player self-discipline, particularly with reference to them taking responsibility for their own actions. He noted that

> A group of players are definitely far better for having discipline in knowing what's right and wrong in terms of what's expected of them, while also having the complete freedom to do whatever they want, knowing that if they get it wrong there are consequences. You need the balance, because if you're too rigid with what you ask of players they won't try anything, but then if they try things in the wrong situations and we lose the ball, they have to accept there will be consequences. You have to balance the expectations here.

'MAKING THE ROLE': THE COACH AS A COMMITTED IMPROVISER

According to Goffman (1959), socialisation may not so much involve a learning of the many specific details of a single concrete part; but rather that the 'individual learns enough pieces of expression to be able to "fill in" and manage, more or less, any part that he [*sic*] is likely to be given' (p. 73). Hence, while the structure may be fixed before hand, 'the details of the expression and movements used do not come from a script but from command of an idiom, a command that is exercised from moment to moment with little calculation or forethought' (p. 74). Within such a philosophy, the individual self is given the will to act independently albeit within the larger structural confines, echoing the earlier work of Zimmerman (1970) on 'role-following'. Here, the actor is considered to be not only filling a set role but is also appreciative 'that there is room and even the need for much active, interpretive work in order to produce adequate role performance' (Raffel, 1998, 4.1). It is based on the premise that fixed role expectations could never be sufficiently detailed for actors to adequately fulfil their social roles, as the actual events of everyday life are too dynamic and complex. An adequate role follower thus, is not 'just a passive recipient of society's rules but an actively

COACHES' ROLES

engaged actor, with creative, negotiating and interpretive skills' (Raffel, 1998, 4.4). Such an individual is viewed as being resourceful and even 'masterly in his use and expression of convention' (Blum & McHugh, 1984, pp. 114–115). The following section seeks to explore whether the coaches interviewed demonstrated such traits.

The conscious evaluative self and role distance

In developing the concept of the self further, Mead (1952) defined it not as a matter of being utterly unique, but that it is 'an object to itself' (p. 136). Hence, the self is socially influenced but acts with consciousness. Mead further explains the process of becoming a self as being able to take the attitude of others. This entails more than seeing others' viewpoint, as it involves the awareness and adoption of others' expectations into his or her role behaviour (Raffel, 1998). It also consists of more than just merely competently following the rules, because if an actor is truly conscious in this regard, he or she should be considering whether the action is right and worth doing in the first place as opposed to merely thinking about doing the action well (Raffel, 1998). In this respect, Raffel (1998) draws a distinction between the 'principled' and the 'rule-guided' actor. The principled actor believes in the rightness of his or her actions, with his or her practice actively reflecting his or her values. Thus, 'unlike the rule-guided actor, their self is available in their actions; their actions say something about, affirm and represent what they believe' (Raffel, 1998, 6.3).

Support for this notion also comes from the work of Taylor (1989) who believes that the essence of selfhood lies not in phenomena like uniqueness but in the capacity for 'strong evaluation'. Hence, the self is able to make one's perceptions, desires, motivations and actions objects of evaluation. For Taylor, a self is a being that can work out what to do by reflexively applying standards of worth; thus 'it affirms its self in the sense of its identity, that is, what it really cares about, what matters to it' (Raffel, 1998, 7.2). Such an individual would have a personal commitment to the worth and worthiness of their behaviours and strategies, which leads us to query the depth of our coaches' self-reflection regarding their motivations and actions. Had they theorised the 'rightness' of their practice, as opposed to just consciously acting on the expectations of self and others?

Certainly the coaches interviewed seemed able to rationalise their behaviours and strategies, particularly in respect of the content of the sessions as well as the environment they tried to create within them. As **Lois Muir** stated: 'Of course I need to evaluate my performance all the time, both in what we do sport wise and how I treat the players, and what the consequences of those actions are.' **Peter Stanley** was also conscious of the need to evaluate both himself and his athletes in the quest for improvement. In his own words: 'you analyse the performance of your athletes in competition, but I think you should also analyse your own performance in support of your athletes. "How could I have done that better?" Now that's a good question.' Similarly, **Steve Harrison** was keen not to 'wound' his players unnecessarily, thus constantly taking stock of his actions, while **Hope Powell** also considered self-examination and challenge as crucial to continued learning and hence personal progression. Indeed, many of the coaches appeared especially aware of the need to nurture the fragile nature of the coach–athlete relationship, as they remained ever vigilant of the potential consequences of their actions in relation to their athletes' performances. It appears then that they exhibited a substantial measure of consciousness and role choice, which relates to the perceived opportunity structure regarding choice within the role (Gouws, 1995). The coaches demonstrated a degree of latitude in shaping their roles to better suit their preferences and capabilities, and those of their athletes. Hence, they displayed a sense of autonomy and self-efficacy as they chose, through reflection, how to play the role of coach.

An additional field of investigation in relation to examining coach behaviour within role theory is linked to Goffman's (1969a) concept of role distance. This refers to the individual distancing himself or herself from the seriousness of the role, possibly through the use of humour. Given that humour is often a major aspect of the coaching environment (Brewer & Jones, 2002), through its use, the personality and individuality of the coach are seen to emerge. In this respect, a need appears to draw on individual informality to meet role responsibilities. Indeed, this apparent gap between role obligation and actual role performance allows for individual expression, which could mark the inventive practitioner from the mechanistic average. However, a question arises: why would a coach, or anyone in such a position of authority, feel the need to act in such an informal way? Goffman (1969a, p. 75), in using an example of a surgeon, offers an explanation:

> In order to ensure that the members of his team keep their heads during the operation, the chief surgeon finds himself under pressure to modulate his [sic] own demands and his own expectations of what is due him. In short, the chief surgeon is likely to find himself with a situated role function of anxiety management and may find that he must draw on his own dignity, on what is owed his station, in order to fulfil this function. A kind of bargaining or bribery occurs, whereby the surgeon receives a guarantee of equability from his team in return for being a 'nice guy' – someone who does not press his rightful claims too far.

Steve Harrison, **Graham Taylor**, **Lois Muir** and **Bob Dwyer** all told similar stories from within their own practice, again linked to the use of humour. For example:

> The players, I think, get enjoyment out of being able to mimic the things I do and say, so I leave them in my repertoire. I know they think some of the expressions I use are right funny, but I'm happy about that because I think they'll remember it and it gives them a laugh. I think it's all a part of the psychology of coaching.

> (**Bob Dwyer**)

I'd say something like, if they're flat on the court on defence, 'do you want to show a play-boy full frontal or what, give yourself an angle!' They crack up and it lifts the tension, although it doesn't mean mediocrity is OK from then on!

(**Lois Muir**)

However, **Di Bass** sounded a more cautious note. Although acknowledging the potential effectiveness of humour, she did not use such banter as a part of her pedagogy because she didn't think it would work for her. Although she has seen it work very effectively with some of her male colleagues, she felt that as a female, she could not emulate that style successfully. In this regard, **Di Bass** is in a unique situation, one where gender sensibilities kick in. Her response mirrors her reflective, thoughtful and socially aware coaching style, and her appreciation that coaching is, at heart, a socially context bound activity.

Nevertheless, in returning to the interactive point at hand, Goffman (1959) described such jokey behaviour on the part of the leader as establishing the 'working consensus' of a group. Such a consensus, which relates to agreed upon situational roles, is considered critical because, without it, both individual and collective goals could be undermined (Troyer & Younts, 1997). Role distance only seems to appear however when one reaches a stage of competency and confidence, with the individual keen to show that he or she is not fully involved in the activity. Hence, it is again possible for a person to both perform a role and maintain something like the self, with the latter appearing in the form of one's distance from the role; that is, in this instance that one is not *just* a coach. A similar strategy according to Goffman (1969b) is that of the 'spotty alibi'. This is where the individual intentionally presents an incomplete alibi, doing so even when he or she is well able to present a better one. The subject is thus engineering a discrediting of his or her own image within the role. As indicated above, such role distance was repeatedly evident in the coaches' willingness to 'play the fool' on occasions, thus using humour to develop the desired coaching climate. Such action was undertaken by the coaches not to show that they were any less expert but to display their 'human side', thus increasing their perceived ability to relate to their athletes whilst still in (the coach's) costume. The behaviour of the coaches in this respect can be interpreted as striking 'bargains' with their athletes in order to achieve positive working relationships, which in turn were perceived as necessary for success.

Role as resource: how do coaches use their role?

In giving added credence to the individuality of human action, coaching behaviour can also be explained in terms of Callero's (1994) definition of role as a 'cultural object'. Specifically, in drawing upon the work of Heise (1977; 1979) and Schwalbe (1987), he suggested that roles serve as 'performance images' that, at the cognitive level, help to guide action. Such 'performance images' are not consistent across social structures but reflect existing cultural beliefs about appropriate role behaviour. In this respect, the prior socialisation experiences of coaches, the nature of coach education programmes, and traditional societal beliefs regarding effective coaching behaviour, could all influence the 'performance images' of coaches, and their resulting practice. Such an analysis is further concerned with how established or accepted roles become a vehicle for agency (Callero, 1994); that is, how coaches use their role to best effect in their dealings with athletes and others.

The 'role as resource' concept examines how roles are used to gain access to other resources, for example, cultural capital (Bourdieu, 1993), which could refer to a coach's ideas and reputation. Indeed, many of these forms of capital are accessible only *through* roles (Callero, 1994). Roles thus are regarded as tools in a struggle to control other resources like status which, consequently, can be viewed as the product of role use. In this way, roles can become a vehicle for agency and be viewed as making action possible rather than simply limiting or controlling choice. Indeed, according to Callero (1994, p. 237), 'power is less a quality of the role than a consequence or dynamic of role use'. Hence, the concepts of role playing and role making are, to an extent, extended into the notion of 'role using' (Callero, 1994). With respect to the coaches interviewed in this book, many of them appeared to use their roles in situations where they perceived that clear and strong leadership was needed. Thus, they were often at pains to emphasise that, although they valued athlete involvement and contributions, it was their responsibility to take the 'big' decisions. **Lois Muir** expressed it as such: 'You've got to go beyond the players, and they've got to know that you can'; a sentiment that was echoed by **Bob Dwyer**'s reference to 'you've always got to be the boss'. Hence, evidence existed that the coaches were not averse to using the power invested in their role to push through their own agendas when they perceived it necessary to do so. In essence, there were times when they used their roles to assert their authority.

Self in role, caring and charismatic leadership

Raffel (1998) borrows from the work of Blum (1994) in furthering the notion of agency within structure through developing the concept of 'self in role'. Here, the role becomes something that is intrinsically worth doing for the individual and not something that is simply expected. The role becomes more than just a set of prescriptions that the actor feels obligated to comply with because of the position he or she occupies, and becomes something that invokes social meanings and traditions and is 'endowed with rightness' for him or her (Raffel, 1998).

In this context, it refers to someone who sees coaching as an embodiment of values, something to actively further and not merely to comply with. It is a principled commitment that helps provide for doing more than is expected within the role; for example, for a coach, it could mean extra sessions with athletes who need them, taking time to know athletes' wider lives, and giving extra time through thoughtful feedback and discussion about performances and the factors that affect

them. In essence, it is a philosophy of caring; caring about athletes and the coaching process in general.

According to Raffel (1998), if a role is to become all this for someone it implies that something of the self is invested and displayed in how they fulfil that role. The self we see here however is not some socially autonomous individual, but one

> that is an object to himself [sic] in that he is reflecting on the possible significance of what he does. He is principled in that only some sense that it is right or worthwhile rather than expected can account for the level of commitment that he displays (8.6).

Here is someone who is *simultaneously* fulfilling social needs and realising personal values, that is, performing a role and realising the self. Indeed, this self consists of an awareness of identity which transcends specific roles, and is able to manage the transactions between personal motives and role (Williams, 1998). Hence, there is no reason to believe that coaches have to give up their selves to fulfil their roles. Identity and principles can be invested and expressed in the doing of the role, not only in the distance from it, as the self can appear at the same time as playing a role. This is the difference between being competent and being *committed*; that is, 'someone who is not just resourceful, even masterful in representing the conventions of their role, but additionally seems willing to do things that could never quite be expected of anyone in the role in question' (Raffel, 1998, 8.9). It is a conscious, reflective self who is expressing, through his or her actions, what is important to them, at the same time as playing a role. Consequently, we can see the self of the coach emerge in a caring, helpful and committed response. Indeed, perhaps such individuals should say that they have no real choice in their actions, not because they lack unreflectively the full awareness of all possibilities, but because they are fully aware of what they believe a coach ought to do and are totally committed to delivering it (Raffel, 1998).

This concept of the committed, caring and conscientious individual is positively related to one who has intense involvement, as expressed through the investment of high levels of energy and time in work roles (Kossek *et al.*, 1999). It also corresponds to the concept of 'extra-role' behaviour, which is defined as discretionary action that benefits the organisation, and goes beyond existing role expectations (Van Dyne *et al.*, 1995). Many of the coaches interviewed exhibited such traits, which are perhaps best summed up by **Bob Dwyer** ('It's important to know that the role of the coach is to give, give and give to the players'), **Graham Taylor** ('You've got to show the players that you care; that you think about the other side of their lives') and **Lois Muir** ('You've got to give everything you've got; a total commitment of your energy'). This benevolence appeared to stretch far beyond the sporting realm into that of the holistic well-being of athletes as many spoke of the necessity to value, respect and care in order to get the best out of athletes. Hence, they believed in the need to develop and establish a positive, relaxed (although intense) working climate, one where athletes feel relaxed enough to 'make mistakes in front of you' (**Hope Powell**) as they constantly and consciously strive for improvement. However, **Lois Mulr** in particular was at pains to point out that the caring climate was not an end in itself, rather it was considered beneficial for event or game outcome to which the players still had an over-riding responsibility: 'I can be a bit more sympathetic if they're having trouble with their boyfriends or something, but when the game comes around, that baggage has to be left outside, they've still got a job to do.' The sentiment was also echoed by **Di Bass**, who, although in many ways she thought herself a 'soft' coach, considered the 'caring' approach as the best way to elicit determination, best effort and responsibility from her swimmers.

The coaches' behaviour in this regard also appeared to be characterised by originality, intensity, and strength of purpose. Hence, many unashamedly saw themselves as perfectionists, searching for the 'impossible' (**Bob Dwyer**) or for the 'perfect game' (**Ian McGeechan**). Others meanwhile emphasised their intense work ethic of 'quality sweat' (**Lois Muir**) which they also expected from their athletes, as well as experiencing a sense of personal failure when their athletes underperformed (**Di Bass**). Through such drive, desire and care they invested much of themselves in their coaching personas, hence they appeared able to transcend the limits of their coaching role through a realisation of the self in attempts to gain the respect and affection of their charges, which they considered necessary to push the latter to ever improving performances. It could also be said that they challenged their athletes to excel by virtue of their own personal qualities thus displaying a degree of 'charismatic leadership' (Shaw, 1981). Indeed, according to Shaw (1981), such leaders are those who create a following by force of their personality and teaching, and thus engage the interest of others by their integrity and convictions. This concept relates to that of referent power, discussed in a later chapter, where it is the individual as opposed to the role that is respected. Research on this stems from the widely accepted theory of charismatic leadership (Fiol *et al.*, 1999), which postulates that the behaviour and corresponding performance of such leaders and their followers tends to exceed that of their non-charismatic counterparts. Although it is accepted that such leaders can be powerful agents of social change (Fiol *et al.*, 1999), the question remains of what the actual behaviours of charismatic leaders are, and were they evident in the practice of the coaches interviewed?

According to Fiol *et al.* (1999), charismatic leaders tend to employ consistent communication strategies for breaking down, moving and realigning the norms of their followers. Similarly, they offer innovative non-conventional solutions to problems, and persuade their followers to embrace them, which appears consistent with a role-making strategy. However, they also ensure 'frame alignment' occurs, which refers to the linkage and congruence between leader orientations and followers' interests and beliefs. The general ideology thus becomes unified and complimentary; similar to that of role consensus discussed earlier. To achieve such alignment, charismatic leaders take the time to articulate an ideology clearly, thus providing, as a first step, a 'vivid and positive image of the future' (Fiol *et al.*, 1999, p. 453). In this respect, they explain and rationalise the value of the change or strategy to their followers, while implementing it with sensitivity.

The coaches that were interviewed also displayed signs of innovation, inventiveness and frame alignment in their practice; hence experimentation was prominent. In the words of **Steve Harrison**: 'I think that people learn by experimenting on a theme, adding variations of your own that make sense to you; by practising that and having a bit of a go really.' They were also aware that innovation cannot simply replace convention, as sudden change is liable to lead to tension, which can undermine the intended alteration. Hence, they were largely content to take a developmental longer-term view as they appeared more concerned with the process rather than the product of coaching, even though their livelihoods often hinged on win–loss records. Indeed, their primary aim related to the potential maximisation of their athletes and teams, as they believed that if the preparatory work was done well the competitive result would look after itself. This was illustrated in **Lois Muir** and **Ian McGeechan**'s notion of patiently 'growing' players, **Hope Powell** and **Di Bass**'s developmental philosophies and **Bob Dwyer**'s long term coherent strategy for success. Such concepts echo the widely held belief that a task mastery orientation equates with 'good' coaching practice (e.g., Roberts & Treasure, 1993).

This philosophy of progressive evolution was accompanied by recognition that any change would have to be accepted and embraced by the athletes in order for it to work. The coaches were aware that, in order to get athletes to buy into and embrace their philosophies, aims and practices, they first needed to convince them of their worth and relevancy, then react to local dynamics regarding the method and speed of their implementation. Consequently, sessions were explained and rationalised to players, reflecting a belief that good coaching practice not only consisted of telling players 'how to do things' but also 'why they are done' (**Bob Dwyer** and **Graham Taylor**).

In addition to getting athletes to accept their methods, the coaches also pointed to a need for athletes to believe in them as coaches if the 'team' was to succeed. Hence, the view existed that a coach needs to acquire and hold the respect of the players (see Chapter 13 on 'Coaches' power' for a fuller discussion). As **Steve Harrison** said: 'at the end of the day, players don't play for clubs, they play for you'; a sentiment that was strongly echoed by **Graham Taylor**: 'It all comes down to how well they really want to do for you.' Much of coaching would thus appear to concern obtaining and maintaining the admiration of athletes and getting them to believe in you (the coach) as a coach (Potrac, *et al.*, 2002).

Finally, charismatic leaders attempt to increase self and collective efficacy by positive evaluations, and by emphasising followers' ties to the collective (Shamir *et al.*, 1993). Certainly, as discussed earlier, the coaches interviewed placed a premium on maintaining a positive climate in the working environment, because they believed it promoted learning and improved performance. With regard to emphasising the collective, things appear to be less straightforward. In this case,

almost all the coaches emphasised their beliefs in working with the individual athlete to improve their technique and skill levels as a fundamental aspect of their work. Unsurprisingly this was a recurring theme from both **Peter Stanley** and **Di Bass** as coaches of largely individual sports. However, individual athlete improvement was also heavily emphasised by the team sport coaches, who not only considered it an end in itself, but also as a means that was beneficial to the team. Hence, although coaching often took place at the micro level, it existed within, and was directed towards, a collective responsibility, shape and structure. Even **Lois Muir**, who considered that coaching is 'really individual', admitted that what she really enjoyed about the job was the macro in terms of 'moving the chess pieces'. As **Ian McGeechan** expressed it: 'I want to make players better individually so that we can then be collectively, tactically better as a team'; a sentiment echoed by **Bob Dwyer**: 'I want to influence the individual, to make sure that combinations then happen.'

CONCLUSION

This discussion has attempted to demonstrate the potential of role theory, through concepts such as role following, role choice and self in role, for an analysis of coaching behaviour. Hence, it aimed to 'order experiences through analysis of the self in considering future courses of conduct' (Gouws, 1995, p. 45). Undoubtedly, there are considerable constraints on a coach's freedom. These chains, or the links within them, have many origins, including those of social and psychological dispositions (Shaw, 1981). To a degree therefore, the initial picture created is of a person 'influenced by external social forces who has a tendency to internalise the social order' (Shaw, 1981, p. 71). Indeed, coaching as an activity may be readily interpreted as a form of role playing, with the training ground or gym being the theatre.

However, as we have seen, it is difficult to assess and compartmentalise the role of the coach so neatly, as such a complex job cannot realistically be broken down in a clinical way. This appears particularly so at the elite level. Indeed, according to Shaw (1981), roles are lived from the inside as well as viewed from the outside, and although there may be limits within which we carry out our roles, such roles may be performed in a seemingly infinite variety of ways. From the analysis of the coaches interviewed in this book, it becomes obvious that they played, made and presented roles they felt to be situationally necessary, albeit within an established value framework. In this respect they 'chose' their role, or rather they chose how to manifest it, which displayed some influence over their role behaviour (Rodham, 2000).

How far did our coaches see their work as a performance? Although the notion of the coach as one who puts on a performance has not been formally studied to any extent, evidence certainly emerged from this work that they were consciously aware of the need to uphold a certain image that was congruent with their position (see also Chapter 12). However, it was apparent that the coaches did not only learn to cope with the expectations that surrounded the positions they occupied, but that they were also conscious 'conspirators' in the construction of these expectations. In effect, they upheld existing roles while developing new ones (Troyer, *et al*., 2000). Strong evaluation and reflection on the content of their coaching and of their relationships with their athletes appeared significant here. They were thus involved in role making in addition to role playing which corresponds to 'job autonomy' (Troyer, *et al*., 2000). Job autonomy reflects discretion over work routines, including the ability to make decisions about how to accomplish tasks, and may be particularly important in occupations characterised by uncertain situational events, such as coaching. It appears that the elite coaches that are interviewed here had already learned how to handle such autonomy, which relates to the conscious freedom of the actor to mould the role to suit the needs of the self, the athletes and situation to maximum effect.

In conclusion, the coaches seemed to be aware of social norms and expectations regarding appropriate conduct in their position, as well as being consciously influenced to varying degrees by role models. However, they transcended both to become their own coaches, their own people; to become themselves within the role. Indeed, the need to 'become yourself' was often heard in the interviews. In the words of **Ian McGeechan**: 'You've got to be true to yourself, do what you believe in, what you think is right.' This was a self that was confident, reflective, progressive, highly enthusiastic, organised and supportive of athletes as well as being very committed to the coaching process. To achieve such selves, it is suggested that coach education programmes include components that reflect on the influences of structure and agency on role fulfilment and coaching identity, with the aim of developing directed, committed yet adaptable and caring coaches.

CHAPTER 12

▼ **COACHES' INTERACTIONS**

BY ROBYN JONES

INTRODUCTION

Interaction could be viewed as the essence of coaching; with coach–athlete relation-ships being at the heart of the coaching process. However, although both coaches and to a lesser extent athletes have recently been the subject of considerable research, little attention has been paid to the nature of the interaction between them. It is this interaction that generates athlete learning and relates to how coach and athlete connect, correlate, bond and generally 'get on' with each other. The theoretical backdrop for the analysis within this chapter is provided by Erving Goffman (1959; 1969a; 1969b), who viewed the nature of interaction as being shaped by both the environment and audience. Goffman's work examined the expectations that people hold of what is normal and acceptable behaviour, and was based on the notion that in everyday life individuals 'play roles, negotiate situations and to a certain extent are forced to be "actors"' (Marsh *et al.*, 1996, p. 73). In this way, this chapter has close links with the examination of the 'coach's role' undertaken earlier. Where this chapter principally differs from the previous one however, is in its study of interaction as a social relationship comprising a constant and dynamic 'two-way street' between engaged parties, and the strategies that individuals use to 'get their way' within it. It is concerned with how individuals present themselves and their activities to others, the ways in which they guide and control the impressions audiences form of them, and the kinds of things that they may or may not do to sustain this performance (Goffman, 1969b). Hence, the

perspective employed to analyse coaching here could be described as a theatrical one, with the principles derived being dramaturgical in nature.

Within this framework the chapter addresses broad questions about the selves, motivations and strategies that coaches bring to the interaction they have with their athletes, how these affect the interaction itself, and how they are reinforced or altered by the interaction (Pope, 1998). An understanding of such issues appears fundamental if the nature of coach–athlete relationships and the process of maximising athlete potential within an appropriate team climate are to be grasped adequately. More specifically, the chapter seeks to identify whether the coaches interviewed for this book self-consciously tried to construct and maintain an idealised image of themselves, as coaches, in the eyes of their athletes in order to generate the desired relationships and interactions with them. Through this framework, an attempt is made to analyse and explain elite coaches' actions and rhetoric as they seek to cajole, threaten and tease out their athletes' capabilities, often through semi-theatrical performances. Thus, following an introduction to Goffman's work and what it brings to coaching, the concepts of the 'presentation of the self' and 'front' are examined in the context of the coaches' justifications for their actions. This is followed by an analysis of the strategies of impression management, and of the apparent need for situational flexibility within coaching in reacting to contextual dynamics.

WHAT DOES GOFFMAN BRING TO AN UNDERSTANDING OF COACHING?

Although for Goffman, the term 'interaction' referred mainly to events that occur whenever two or more people are in each other's presence (Williams, 1998), and are engaged in 'face-to-face interaction' as he called it (Goffman, 1969b), of particular relevance to this chapter is the notion of the 'presentation of the self' in everyday life. Here, Goffman provides a detailed description and examination of process and meaning in everyday action using micro-sociological analysis to explore the details of individual identity, group relations, the impact of environment, and the interactive meaning of information (Branhart, 1994). Hence, he embarked on a detailed and close analysis of what people do when they are in the company of others, and how those doings or actions are understood (Williams, 1998). He concluded that the importance of giving a convincing impression to others, and the obligation to live up to that impression, forces people to behave in certain ways. In this regard, his findings built upon Mead's early 'social behaviourist' theories, which stated that the development of the 'self' is dependant on the existence of social groups. The key concept here is the self, and how individuals see themselves.

Central to Goffman's argument was the belief that individuals are not able to freely choose the images of self that they would have others accept, 'but rather are constrained to define themselves in congruence with the statuses, roles, and relationships that they are accorded by the social order' (Branaman, 2000, p. xlvii).

Conversely, he also considered that individuals are not entirely determined by society, because they are able to strategically manipulate social situations and others' impressions of themselves (Goffman, 1959). They were thus seen as being able to 'affect the surrounding environment in a manner congruent with their own actions' (1969b, p. 4). The self was considered a social construction; constructed by the individual within a given framework. Furthermore, he believed that individuals affected their environment through their expressions, with the meaning of the expression being very much context bound. Indeed, according to Goffman (1969b, p. 14), 'face-to-face interaction has a special place in this context because when an individual can be observed directly, a multitude of good sources of expressed information become available'. These include appearance, manner and style, which can provide a wealth of data for the audience on matters concerning the central actor's intent and competency. Communication, or verbal communication, was considered to be only one facet of these 'expression games' which, for Goffman, also involved concealment or cover and misrepresentation. He considered that certain occupations (e.g., surgeons) were ideally suited for such an analysis of communication, because they possessed the 'means of vividly conveying the qualities and attributes claimed by the performer' (1959, p. 31). We claim similar status for coaches, whose activities allow much scope for dramatic self-expression as they attempt to consistently inspire best performance from others. Indeed within coaching, as the 'behavioural and technical process through which information is communicated will naturally exude expression' (Goffman, 1969b, p. 7), individuals can, to a degree, be considered to be able to create their own reality through the strategic control and use of such expression. The particular questions for us to address within this chapter therefore are as follows. How did the coaches interviewed express themselves? What kind of expression games were they involved in? What kind of techniques of impression management did they use?

PRESENTING THE SELF AND A COACHING FRONT

In considering the 'presentation of self', Goffman (1959) utilised a dramaturgical approach to not only examine the mode of presentation employed by the social actor, but also to explain its meaning in the broader social context (Branaman, 2000; Branhart, 1994). Hence, he makes us think about how people produce recognisable and convincing performances for others (Williams, 1998), because when others sense things are 'normal' they will act or respond in a normal manner, or in the manner expected. In short, he viewed interaction 'as a performance constructed to provide others with impressions that are consonant with the desired goals of the actor' (Branhart, 1994, p. 2).

This process of establishing and maintaining a desirable (coaching) identity or impression can also be linked to Goffman's (1959) concept of 'front', which provides a further analytical peg on which to hang interpretations of the coaches' stories. 'Front' refers to 'that part of the individual's performance which regularly functions in a general and fixed fashion to define the social situation for those who

observe performance' (Goffman, 1959, p. 22). Such a 'front' serves as the means of standardisation that allows others to understand the individual on the basis of projected character traits that have normative meanings (Branhart, 1994). In constructing a front, information about the actor is provided by a variety of communicative sources, all of which must be controlled effectively to convince the audience of the appropriateness of behaviour and its compatibility with the role assumed (Branhart, 1994). In fact, the performer may well be required to repeatedly and instantaneously demonstrate the capacities he or she claims for the front during the interaction in order to uphold it. Goffman's (1959, p. 30) example of the behaviour of a baseball umpire is illustrative of the point: 'If a baseball umpire is to give the impression that he is sure of his judgment, he must forgo the moment of thought which might make him sure of his judgment; he must give an instantaneous decision so that the audience will be sure that he is sure of his judgement.'

The important point here concerns the image or the impression portrayed above all else. Hence, through the process of 'dramatic realization' (Goffman, 1959) the actor, in order to present a compelling front, is forced to both fill the duties of the position and communicate the activities and characteristics of the job to other people in a consistent manner (Branhart, 1994). A coach, therefore, would appear obliged to behave consistently 'like a coach' in the eyes of the athletes, because to maintain established power relationships he or she must uphold the standards of conduct and appearance expected of someone within the position (Goffman, 1959). Here, according to Goffman, a 'certain bureaucratization of the spirit is expected so that we can be relied upon to give a perfectly homogeneous performance at every appointed time' (1959, p. 56). Indeed, the expectations of the athletes may be the crucial issue in determining the performance or style of the coach, which supports the view that the individual puts on a show for the benefit of his or her audience irrespective of its sincerity to achieve desired goals. Goffman (1959, p. 18) described such demands as follows: 'We know that in service organizations practitioners who may otherwise be sincere are sometimes forced to delude their customers because their customers show a heartfelt demand for it . . . these are cynical performances whose audiences will not allow them to be sincere.'

This notion overlaps with the earlier discussion on social roles and implies a deterministic dynamic behind individuals' actions. The issue to investigate here however, is not whether the coaches interviewed merely complied with others' expectations, which has already been examined, but how conscious they were in doing so, in presenting the 'right front', to further their own ends. In this respect, Goffman (1969b) believed that it was in the individual's interest, particularly if he or she held a leadership type role, to control the conduct and perceptions of others, and hence their responsive treatment of him or her. This could be influenced by expressing himself or herself 'in such a way as to give them (the audience) the kind of impression that will lead them to act voluntarily in accordance with his [sic] own plan' (1969b, p. 3). Consequently, he considered that, sometimes, the individual needs to act 'in a thoroughly calculating manner, expressing himself in

SPORTS COACHING CULTURES

a given way solely in order to give the kind of impression to others that is likely to evoke from them the specific response he is concerned to obtain' (1969b, p. 6).

Many of the coaches interviewed were aware of the need sometimes to use manipulative behaviour to achieve their desired ends. For example, **Bob Dwyer** felt it necessary 'to do what you have to, to impart a certain confidence, a sense of self-worth . . . which has an effect on everything', while **Peter Stanley** was conscious 'to exude an aura of authority or total calm, as if it was always in the plan, even though I'm knotted in my stomach' at a big meet. **Lois Muir** agreed on the necessity of trying to control the coaching environment through 'put on' responses, for example, depicting a 'mean' persona in an attempt to drive her athletes to excel. Similarly, **Graham Taylor**, not only recognised the importance of 'expressing yourself in a manner that's confident so the players have confidence that you know what you're talking about', but more significantly that 'the best coaches would make good actors'. This was echoed by **Hope Powell** who was aware that she had to present a convincing confident 'front' in order to sometimes 'fool' her players, thus allowing her 'to get away with stuff'. Finally, in perhaps the clearest example of such practice, **Steve Harrison** considered it imperative that he always give the impression to his players that he was in control of the situation, even though he sometimes felt he was not. To have the players sense that he was not in total command of events or sure of his judgement was, for Steve, tantamount to losing their respect and hence any influence he might have over them. This image of control was to be protected at all costs. In his own words:

> Sometimes you just have to get on with it, and give the players the impression that you are in control of it. Just get on with it, without missing a beat, as if it's part of the plan. You've got to be bullet proof, or you've got to portray that you are.

Goffman (1969b) also considered that it was much easier for an individual to control the course of interaction and hence a relationship from the beginning of an encounter rather than 'altering a line of treatment being pursued once interaction is underway' (p. 11). This echoes the popular understanding that first impressions are important, and that with 'success', as defined by influence in social relationships, hinges the capacity to seize and hold the initiative. This can require individuals to engage in a form of subtle aggression (Goffman, 1969b). The importance of the first impression and of 'getting off on the right foot' emerged in many of the coaches' stories. **Bob Dwyer** in particular believed that 'first impressions are rarely wrong' giving support to his 'instincts'. There was also a consensus that in a first encounter, the coach has to be authoritative because, according to **Peter Stanley**, 'it is then that you hold all the aces'. This was echoed by **Ian McGeechan** who believed in being initially imposing with players: 'I think when you're introducing something for the first time, the players have to understand what it is that you're trying to do; they have to understand the ground rules.' The opportunity to dominate initial meetings and influence subsequent interactions was not lost on the coaches therefore, although both **Hope Powell** and particularly

Bob Dwyer among others did question the authenticity and effectiveness of a more forceful approach as a long term strategy: 'even when something like that works, I think it only works for a limited period of time'(**Dwyer**). Such an admission suggests that aggressive coaching tactics, which can be relatively successful in the short term, were not considered to be a recipe for sustained achievements.

The 'presentation of the self' however is not without its perils, because if the 'front' or the situation, which embraces the relationship with others involved in the inter-action is 'read' incorrectly, the coach may be discredited. Hence, if the performance is not convincing enough, or is disrupted, doubts may be thrown on the coach's projected image, with the interaction coming to a confused and embarrassed halt (Goffman, 1959). Here, the social system of face-to-face interaction breaks down, a situation that Goffman (1959, p. 13) describes as a 'definitial disruption'. Such a disruption could relate to the players not 'buying in' to the coach's persona. Coaches, consequently, have to be careful not to present a transparent, 'phoney' or false front, as they could easily lose credibility in the eyes of their athletes. The key point here however, does not concern whether the image presented is false but that the performer should include in his or her performances appropriate assertions 'and exclude from the performances expressions that might discredit the impression being fostered' (Goffman, 1959, p. 66). Such an awareness was evidenced among many of the coaches interviewed; for example, **Bob Dwyer** emphasised that 'you have to be consistently accurate in your level of expectation, and consistent in what you do', while **Steve Harrison** took pains to ensure not to 'force' his delivery lest it appear 'false'. To safeguard their image projections, individuals are involved in many 'defensive' and 'protective' practices, which are discussed in-depth in the later section on impression management.

It is widely held that the maintenance of social distance as preserved through restrictions on contact, provide a way in which a sense of awe about the focal actor can be generated and sustained in the audience. Hence, a state of 'mystifi-cation' can be developed about the performer (Goffman, 1959). Here, the performer generates some 'elbow room' or leeway to build up an impression of his or her choice. This space needs to be maintained in order to protect the image presented from too close an inspection by followers, which could discredit and destroy it. Although all the coaches spoke of the need to maintain the respect of the athletes, **Lois Muir** clearly recognised the value of social distance in achieving this: 'You want to know a bit more about them, but I don't want them to know too much about me. I like that little bit of respect, as it makes them believe that you're going to make decisions for the whole group.' Similarly, **Graham Taylor** was aware of the need to 'be one of the boys, but also apart from the boys'. Like **Taylor**, **Hope Powell** tried to juggle both perspectives, in that she acknowledged the need to keep distant while also discreetly and sensitively establishing individual rapport with her players, hence not losing the touch of personal attention. She appeared particularly aware of this issue and also sought to overcome it by assigning her assistant coaches to 'play the nice guys', while she herself kept a degree of social distance.

In this regard, Goffman (1959) argues it is important that we only act in certain ways for certain audiences. Such an awareness was reflected by most of the coaches interviewed who, when engaged in other perhaps more informal contexts didn't wish to be with their players, as it would be incompatible with the distance and the respect required in the coaching environment. Hence, the performer, in this instance the coach, segregates his or her audience and himself or herself into what Goffman describes as the 'front region' and the 'backstage'. The latter is where the performance is prepared while it is presented in the former. Unsurprisingly, the backstage is private with access to certain aspects of behaviour being controlled to prevent outsiders seeing a performance that is not intended for them (Marsh et al., 1996). It is not intended, because what people think of one another is dependant on the impression given and this impression is disrupted if they acquire (backstage) information that they are not meant to have.

A definitive exception among the coaches interviewed in this regard was **Peter Stanley**. Far from consciously and consistently maintaining a social distance, he considered himself to be a friend as well as a coach to his athletes, especially those with whom he had worked for some time. Indeed, he regularly socialised with them. An explanation for this seemingly digressive behaviour could lie in the nature of the context in this case, with athletics being a very individualised sport whilst only providing him with part-time employment. Due to financial restrictions and other work commitments, he often could not accompany his athletes to major events, so he believed that they had to be independent and self-sufficient; attributes that would serve them well in competition. Hence, he tried to build a relationship based on trust, comprising much sharing and discussion, which naturally negated against the maintenance of a social distance between the parties. **Di Bass** adhered to a similar philosophy, describing her style as 'collaborative' and 'democratic'. In addition to personal preference, her social circumstances could also have led to such a strategy. She openly admits that coaching is just one facet of her life (and not her main occupation) and hence she is aware of the need for a balanced approach.

Far from considering that the focal actor should always remain aloof and detached from his audience, Goffman also believed that 'communication out of character' sometimes stimulated interaction. He considered that 'there are occasions when it serves the higher team [coach] to lower barriers and admit the lower team [players] to greater intimacy and equality within it' (1959, p. 199). Thus, it would be in the long-term interest of the leader to grant access and extend 'backstage' familiarity to the followers. Goffman's example of such a practice in mental hospitals where milieu therapy is practised, illustrates the point.

> By bringing the nurse and even attendants into what are usually sacrosanct staff conferences, these non-medical staff persons can feel that the distance between themselves and the doctors is decreasing and may show more readiness to [accept] the doctors' point of view. By sacrificing the

exclusiveness at the top it is felt that the morale of those at the bottom can be increased.

Such inclusive strategies, with varying degrees of sincerity, were practised by all our coaches. Perhaps resulting from the unique context of athletics, **Peter Stanley** spoke most strongly in support of them:

> When I first got into coaching I called my athletes, *my* athletes. It was only as I grew older that I realised that they are not my athletes. I am their coach, and they actually own me. I need them to take control, and I'm just there as a guide really. They have to look after themselves on the track and while they're away anyway, so I need them to take control.

The team coaches also recognised the value of involving their players in wider decision making. For example, **Lois Muir** considered it important that her players 'owned the game plan and their own performances'. This ownership stretched to team meetings where issues were aired 'in front of everyone. There are no secrets, because that's part of the team thing . . . you've got to make them own it enough'. **Di Bass** also expected her swimmers to be fully involved participants in the learning process, and to share the responsibility for self-improvement. Similarly, **Steve Harrison** actively encouraged his players to ask about and discuss tactics, while **Graham Taylor** concluded that it was unfeasible to have a healthy player–coach relationship without the coach 'taking a bit on board of what the players are sometimes thinking'. **Taylor** further added that he thought it important that coaches not only be respected by their athletes, but also liked, resulting in a 'trust between you and the players' for the optimal learning environment to be created. Lastly, **Bob Dwyer** considered himself open to 'to be convinced' by player ideas, although adding that he 'was nearly always hard to convince', implying that he still maintained a firm control over strategic and tactical team decision making. This was confirmed by his reference to 'leading players to believe that they are part of the plans'. For **Dwyer**, it appears that the value of including athletes may lie in the illusion of inclusion, not the reality.

The relaxation of front, as suggested by inclusive strategies, provides a basis for barter, with the superordinate (coach) receiving a service of some kind, while the subordinate (athlete) receives an indulgent grant of intimacy (Goffman, 1959). This notion is related to that of role distance where a working consensus is established between leaders and followers. However, from the evidence of the coaches interviewed in this book, although such a relaxation of distance often takes place, both parties must continue to exist within given (role) limits, lest there be a threat to the security of the relationship and the interaction between them. In other words, the coaches, in effect, remained the ultimate decision makers and were aware of their role and responsibilities in this regard.

Finally, in this context, Goffman (1959) emphasised that in order for the front to have maximum effect, performances need to be kept enthusiastic and fresh. Indeed, his observations led him to conclude that 'often, it seems that whatever enthusiasm and lively interest we have at our disposal we reserve for those we are putting on a show' (p. 132). Thus, audiences need to be made to perceive themselves as 'special', that while they feel 'there may be other audiences for the same routine, none is getting so desirable a presentation' (p. 138). Hence, performers need to foster the impression that both routine performances and relationships to an audience have something special and unique about them. In this way, the routine character of the performance is obscured and the spontaneous aspects of the situation are stressed.

The need for a freshness of delivery was an accepted theme amongst the coaches interviewed even though many believed passionately in the development and refinement of core skills, which implies a certain repetitiveness of content. Nevertheless, the undoubted enthusiasm expressed by the coaches about their role certainly ensured that the coaching environment was kept bright and upbeat; as **Peter Stanley** said, 'I get such a buzz back from the athletes and I think I feed off that. I think I was just born to be a coach.' **Ian McGeechan** cultivated such a climate through maintaining a good lively rapport and banter with the players, while **Lois Muir** expressed it as 'trying to keep me and them (the players) out of automatic pilot'. Indeed, this was something that **Graham Taylor** felt particularly strongly about as he articulated the need 'not to lose the basics through producing variety' but was very aware that 'once players can read you totally they'll get bored because we all have a boredom threshold. So we've got to keep people alive, we've got to keep people alert, and we've got to keep challenging them'. Hence, it was considered necessary to constantly test the athletes, not through a vast array of drills, but on varying practices on a given theme. In this way, 'core skills' were refined while a respect for the dynamic ever-changing coaching context kept the delivery and interaction relatively novel.

THE STRATEGIES OF IMPRESSION MANAGEMENT

Before embarking on an examination of the techniques of impression management, and whether the coaches interviewed within this book used them, it is worth noting that the primary function of impression management is to avoid performance disruptions (Goffman, 1959). The aim is to preserve the image or front presented by the coach, as any sudden deviance away from it puts the credibility of the actor and performance at risk, and hence the respect in which he or she is held is inevitably weakened. In order to prevent such incidents from spoiling the show, performers have to possess and be able to express certain attributes to save the show (Goffman, 1959). The techniques employed to do this include numerous ploys or stratagems classified by Scheibe (1979) as involving selective feedback, pretence, deception and withholding information, with the social actor consciously 'inventing or modifying them in the course of interacting with others' (Sarbin, 1995, p. 217).

Although more positive 'tactics' could also be added to this list, a dynamic picture emerges of a coach simultaneously using and juggling a number of social strategies to achieve desired ends in the coaching process. Through such impression management, attempts are made to present an idealised version of the front or the self. Indeed, as Goffman (1959, pp. 252–253) eloquently stated:

> The self, then, as a performed character, is not an organic thing that has a specific location, whose fundamental fate is to be born, mature, and to die; it is a dramatic effect rising from a scene that is presented, and the characteristic issue, the crucial concern, is whether it will be credited or discredited.

To further illustrate the point he cited the example of executives who often 'project an air of competency and general grasp of the situation, blinding others to the fact that they hold their jobs partly because they look like executives, not because they can work like executives' (1959, p. 47). What precisely then are these strategies of impression management, and did the coaches interviewed in this book use them?

A principal defensive practice at the individual's disposal against performance or image disruption is adherence to a 'dramaturgical discipline' (Goffman, 1959). Here, the actor needs to be immersed and engrossed in the role he or she is performing, whilst being also conscious of it. They must consequently show a degree of intellectual and emotional involvement in the activity but must keep themselves from being actually carried away, so that they 'do not commit unmeant gestures in performing it'(Goffman, 1959, p. 217). This individual therefore is someone with 'presence of mind' who can instantaneously cover up any inappropriate behaviour or performance disruption on the spur of the moment, whilst still maintaining the impression that he or she is playing a part, that is, they are still in control. Alternatively, if the disruption cannot be concealed, the disciplined performer will be prepared to offer a plausible reason for discounting the disruptive event to remove its importance. Whilst many of the coaches spoke about the need to always give the impression that 'you know what you are doing', **Steve Harrison** gave a perfect example of such an instantaneous cover up strategy:

> You've got to think on your feet. Whereas if you start bawling or saying, 'Where is so and so?' [using a panicky voice], you're not being professional. You can make a joke of it and throw your notes down, 'Come on let's piss off to the pub'. You make light of it but you try and show you're not bothered, you're in control and know what you are going to do. You've got to adapt, think on your feet and have things in your mind, first reserve, second reserve type of thing, which isn't easy but has to be done.

Hence, similar to Goffman's dramaturgically disciplined performer, the coaches were aware of the need to suppress and productively channel their spontaneous feelings resulting from disruptive events in order to give the appearance of sticking to the expressive status quo. To do otherwise would be to risk the working consensus established with their athletes.

A second defensive attribute utilised to protect an individual's constructed front is that of 'dramaturgical circumspection' (Goffman, 1959). Here, Goffman was at pains to emphasise that if no care and honesty are exercised, then disruptions are likely to occur, whilst if these qualities are exercised rigidly, performers may be misunderstood, insufficiently understood or greatly limited in exploiting further dramaturgical opportunities (Goffman, 1959). This strategy involves the personification of sincerity within the performance, particularly if interactions will take place over a long period of time, as would tend to be the case with the coaches interviewed. On the other hand, a 'brief performance is a relatively safe one in which one can maintain something of a false front' (Goffman, 1959, p. 222). Hence, in general, we can expect individuals to relax the strict maintenance of front when they are with those they have known for a longer period, and to tighten their front when among persons who are new to them (Goffman, 1959). It also suggests that when we are in the company of those we have known and worked with for a long time, we are more apt to allow the self to emerge from behind the front.

In developing the theme of the need for perceptions of a sincere performance to be forthcoming for the front to be successful, Goffman also examined the individual's own belief in the part he or she was playing. This alerts us to questions about sincerity and coaches' 'performances'. However, it should not be assumed that all cynical performances are interested in deluding the audiences for purposes of self or 'private' gain, as an individual may engage in such action for what he or she considers the good of the 'team'. Here, Goffman (1959) gave the example of the many 'white lies' told by doctors to protect the feelings of their patients. The coaches interviewed in this book demonstrated a similar circumspection in recognising the need to tell their athletes 'white lies' on occasions. This extended from glossing over a poor performance, to not always telling athletes how good they are. Such utterances were always justified in relation to protecting fragile egos, through building them up or perhaps deflating them as considered necessary. The telling of such untruths was not deemed insincere or misleading, but, on the contrary, was always perceived to be undertaken in the athletes' best interests. **Ian McGeechan** provided a good example of such practice: 'Sometimes I won't tell players how good I think they are. I need to keep their feet on the ground, so I'll just tell them how to get better.'

In order to construct and maintain a successful front then, 'performers are required to exercise prudence and circumspection in staging the show, preparing in advance for likely contingencies, and exploiting opportunities that remain' (p. 218). Such circumspection can assume many forms, including taking great care to ensure that the 'right' impression is given, whilst also surrounding oneself with 'loyal and disciplined members' (p. 218). Goffman (1959, p. 219) expressed this latter tactic as follows: 'Given the fact that husband and wife are required to express marital solidarity by jointly showing regard for those whom they entertain, it is necessary to exclude from their guests those persons about whom they feel differently.' In this way they select the kind of audience that will give them the minimal amount of trouble and hence considerably lessen the prospect of disruption. The coaches interviewed here generally concurred with this strategy for success. Hence, although there was a consensus that all athletes are to varying degrees coachable, there was also agreement with **Bob Dwyer**'s belief that 'you can't make a silk purse out a sow's ear'. Similarly, **Lois Muir** spoke about the need to get players that you could influence, whilst denying that coaches 'have the Midas touch' with all players. Hence, they tended to echo **Steve Harrison**'s belief that, although success in coaching entails many factors, 'I suppose the bottom line is, if you've got high quality players, you will succeed.'

A third defensive strategy in this regard surrounds detailed advanced preparation for 'all possible expressive contingencies' (Goffman, 1959, p. 227). This involves settling on a complete agenda with regard to the interaction, down to role specifications and responsibilities for those involved in the performance, hence lessening the possibility of confusion. Similarly, almost all the coaches interviewed here emphasised that meticulous preparation and planning were a very necessary part of their practice. Indeed, as discussed earlier in the role chapter, they were very circumspect and evaluative both of their own actions and those of their athletes, particularly with regard to role specifications and expectation. For example:

> I have to show how tiny movements give clues to the man in possession. You see, a difference of only 3 inches can be significant, as it's that much closer or further away from the defender, and I have to make sure that the players know how much difference that really makes to the execution of a move. I also have to know exactly how I'm going to present that.
>
> (**Bob Dwyer**)

> Preparation is a big part of it. I do mine early ready for the next game. Really, I'm just looking at minor things. Who are the dominant people on the court and where they want to play and how I'll weave it into the next session. You know, those little sorts of things that are the crumbs of the game that give you the little edge on the opposition.
>
> (**Lois Muir**)

> I don't compromise in the sense that I work hard at the preparation. I think you have got to be right in your own mind and put that to the players, you've got to be well prepared.
>
> (**Ian McGeechan**)

Although precautions such as circumspection and detailed preparation can be taken against disruptions of projected desired images, one way of handling disturbances when they do happen is to laugh at them as a sign that their implications are not taken seriously (Goffman, 1959). Such action overlaps with the concept

of 'role distance' discussed in the previous chapter, although, in this context, it is viewed as a reactive strategy to uphold a performance as opposed to a definitive one to obtain a 'working consensus'. The result however appears to be similar. Whether intended or not, such social games, which often come to form an important part of the shared life of the group, are used as a catharsis for anxieties, which also lessen the expectation of leader infallibility by locating such *faux pas* within the realm of normative behaviour. Such a presentation of imperfection aims both to cover the disruption while also displaying the 'human side' of the leader thus establishing better relations with followers. The strategy was not lost on many of the coaches within this book; for example, **Peter Stanley** considered it to be a good thing that both he and the athletes could 'laugh at my mistakes', while **Graham Taylor** believed that 'sometimes you've got to let the players have a laugh at your expense'. Similarly, **Bob Dwyer** and **Lois Muir** considered that such episodes, in addition to developing positive interaction, bring necessary light relief to what is often a stressful occupation.

'READING THE GAME' AND THE NEED FOR SITUATIONAL FLEXIBILITY

Despite his emphasis on the social dramaturgical role of the individual, Goffman was still keen to remind readers that 'competent human subjects were expected to be capable of rule interpretation and manipulation' (Williams, 1998, p. 154). Order was thus considered as not simply the result of people following rules, but rather rules permitting people to enact and make order. Such a behavioural configuration inevitably leads to opportunities for flexibility and interpretation. Without exception, the coaches interviewed for this book emphasised the need to be adaptable and flexible in their work. **Steve Harrison** even went so far as to pronounce such practices as the 'art of coaching'; a declaration which was expressed as 'recognising the situation, recognising the people and responding to the people you are working with'. **Graham Taylor** provided a good example of such practice:

> Sometimes, I'll stop a session and say, 'This is useless, do it again' or 'Go home and come back in this afternoon', depending on what the mood of myself and the players is. I think we all have good days and bad days and some days we have to fight our way through the bad days and other days you're just as well saying leave it alone because we're just going to make it worse. You've got to have a feel for people though to make it work.

Indeed, many of the coaches interpreted flexibility as acknowledging and responding to the perceived needs of the athletes at a particular moment. For example, **Ian McGeechan** spoke of 'reacting to the environment and how the players are going', while **Lois Muir** emphasised the need to 'be able to read the people, and go from there'. **Graham Taylor** commented that such practices were indeed the essence of coaching itself: 'What exactly is coaching? It's getting the best out of what you've got available and how you do it. Sometimes, by not coaching you're

a good coach.' Hence, the ability to correctly 'read' the situation and react appropriately to local dynamics was considered vital for success.

In this respect, the coaches echoed Goffman's (1959) belief that rigidly scripted performers 'can get themselves in a worse position than is possible for those who perform a less organised show' (p. 228). Such rigidity leads one to be incapable of dealing with the inevitable sudden disruptions that might occur, resulting in the performance itself being endangered with the portrayed character being seen to crumble. A degree of flexibility, as reflected in an element of deception, is often required to maintain the front. The 'implication here is that an honest, sincere, serious performance is less firmly connected with the solid world than one might first assume' (Goffman, 1959, p. 71). This is not to suggest that such individuals are devious in their dealings, but that they recognise the need to meet changing circumstances with equally dynamic responses albeit operating within an established framework. As far as the coaches interviewed within this book were concerned, as stated above, they felt that adaptability was a requisite ingredient to be successful. Indeed, **Peter Stanley** considered that 'one of the most important things in coaching is to be flexible, 'cause the relationship between you and your athletes is always changing direction'. He would view himself a failure if he could not change his style 'to the athletes and to the level of athletics, as demanded'.

CONCLUSION

This chapter has been concerned with some of the techniques that the coaches in this book employed to sustain the impressions that they wanted their athletes to have of them. Within it, the analysis has been based on Goffman's theory on interaction and, in particular, his dramaturgical notion of the 'presentation of the self'. However, before summing up, it is worth recognising that many criticisms and critics of Goffman's work exist. These include accusations that his characters are ahistorical and disengaged from social structures, and that the concept of power is inadequately addressed (see Ditton, 1980). Whilst a full discussion of the merits of Goffman's thesis has been undertaken elsewhere which negates the need for repetition here (see Ditton, 1980; Lemert & Branaman, 2000, among others), the dramaturgical perspective seems particularly apt for analysis in this coaching context because, even his critics agree, Goffman has an extremely sensitive and acute lens through which to observe human interaction (Hepworth, 1980). It also provides an 'exhilarating sense of possibilities for personal freedom as it provides a vision of the social order as constructed and, therefore, an awareness that it can be dealt with like other constructions' (Lofland, 1980, p. 48).

Additionally, although Goffman's perspective undoubtedly has the capability to illustrate the capacity of an individual to influence and direct the activities of others, Goffman openly admitted that it is 'a heuristic device, which will not necessarily fit all the features of the subject matter to which it is applied' (Williams, 1980, p. 235). He was acutely aware of the limitations of his own approach and that of the dramaturgical metaphor in particular (Hepworth, 1980). Hence, he urged those who used the 'model' to drop it once the analysis was complete, as it has served its purpose. In his own words, 'And so here, the language and mask of the stage [should] be dropped. Scaffolds, after all, are to build other things with, and should be erected with an eye to taking them down' (Goffman, 1959, p. 254).

In taking away the dramaturgical metaphor we see that the interviewed coaches consciously tried to engineer their athletes' impressions of themselves in a variety of ways. They were involved in a number of impression 'games' to gain and maintain the respect of their athletes, as they all considered this crucial to success in the coaching endeavour. These games, which constituted the presentation of an idealised coaching self, ranged from always maintaining an image of being in control of events, to trying as best they could to relate to their athletes through occasionally presenting a 'human face', whilst generally maintaining a certain distance between the parties. The partial exceptions to this last strategy were those coaches of individual sports, **Di Bass** and **Peter Stanley. Stanley**, in particular, dispensed with the maintenance of a social distance, and aspired instead to become a trusted friend to his athletes, because this is what he thought the particular nature of his sport and his situation demanded. Also crucial in this regard for all the coaches was the necessity to bend to circumstances, thus being able to read and react flexibly to the dynamic coaching context. Finally, although an element of deception was readily admitted, often in the form of 'white lies', overriding this was the belief that to inspire and hold the respect of their athletes, coaches had to be perceived as sincere and honest in their actions. **Ian McGeechan** spoke for many of them as he emphasised this point: 'I tell them [the players] that I'm honest with myself and I'm honest with the players. I put my hand up when things go wrong and try to compliment them when things go right. I think they really appreciate that.'

CHAPTER 13

▼ **COACHES' POWER**

BY PAUL POTRAC

INTRODUCTION

Power is widely recognised as the ability of one individual to influence another person or persons (Lukes, 1993; Raven, 1986; Stahelski & Payton, 1995). It is considered to be an omnipresent feature of social life, which not only impacts upon our thoughts and ambitions but also our interactions with others (Kipnis, 2001; Lee Chai & Bargh, 2001; Tomlinson, 1998). In this respect, Kipnis (2001) contends that, as individuals are dependent upon others in the quest to fulfil their needs and desires, whether it is material goods, information or to dominate, they are subsequently impelled to exercise power and influence on a daily basis. It is perhaps therefore unsurprising that Snyder and Kiviniemi (2001) recently concluded that even the most basic social interaction is 'indelibly tinged by the issues of power and power differences' (p. 133). While research into the concept of power is presently enjoying a period of considerable growth in fields such as organisational, industrial and social psychology (Bruins, 1999), its centrality to the coaching process has, to date, been largely ignored (Jones *et al.*, 2002; Lyle, 1999). The paucity of such work is surprising taking into account the recent affirmations of other authors as well as ourselves (Tomlinson, 1998; Lyle, 1999; Jones, 2000; Jones & Armour, 2000) that power is an inherent feature of social relationships and hence of understanding social interaction within sports settings. Given that we have argued in the preceding chapters of this book that social interaction lies at the heart of the coaching process, it would appear that an understanding of the dynamic power relationship that exists between coach and

athlete is necessary for effective coach education and effective coaching practice to occur (Jones *et al.*, 2002; Potrac *et al.*, 2002).

In order to address this neglect, the broad purpose of this chapter is to explore how social power (i.e., power wielded in a social context) influences the dynamics of the interpersonal interactions that take place between coach and athlete within the context of top-level sport. In borrowing from the work of Kipnis (2001) in social psychology, we contend that a critical question for researchers and educators in coaching science to examine is not *whether* coaches and athletes exercise power but, alternatively, *how* they exercise power. Hence, an attempt is made to unravel the complex and dynamic concept of power in terms of constraints and opportunities associated with the various forms of its use in the coaching context. It is based on the premise that practitioners and educators not only require a detailed understanding of the various tactics that coaches use to influence athletes, but also how such approaches impact upon and are understood by athletes, whilst also acknowledging the potential for athletes to wield power over coaches (Jones *et al.*, 2002).

In keeping with this book's general philosophy, the aim is not to provide prescriptions as to what coaches ought to do but, instead, it is to become increasingly discursive about the complex power-dominated nature of the coaching process. Hence, following an introductory discussion, we use the analytical framework of social power and its component parts (French & Raven, 1959; Raven, 1992; Hardy, 1995; Kidman, 2001) to explore how the coaches, both individually and collectively, attempt to create, maintain and advance constructive and positive working relationships with their particular athletes. In addition, the concept of empowerment (Kidman, 2001) is employed, as we seek to not only analyse how social power is used by, and influences, the coaches' practice, but also to chart the relationships that exist between the various forms of social power. Hence, it is worth noting that, while the concepts of pedagogy, social role, interaction, and power are dealt with separately in this book to clarify the analysis, as we have previously suggested (Jones *et al.*, 2002; Potrac *et al.*, 2002), when attempting to understand and explain coaching behaviour, these concepts are inextricably interlinked. Consequently, as this chapter unfolds we make connections from and between preceding discussions on coaches' pedagogy, roles and interactions.

WHAT IS SOCIAL POWER?

According to Thompson (1998, p. 42), 'power is used in different senses within different paradigms or theoretical frameworks'. Indeed, there are a wide range of definitions, conceptualisations and models of social power. However, despite these differences, power has typically been viewed as the 'ability to get others to do what you want them to do' (Weber, 1978), or 'to get them to do something they otherwise would not do' (Hardy, 1995, p. xiii).

In taking a broader view of the nature of power, however, Tomlinson (1998, p. 235) described it as a 'central dynamic of human societies', thus suggesting that it is an essential component of any social activity. Hargreaves' (1986, p. 3) definition of power as a relationship between agents (i.e., individuals), 'the outcome of which is determined by [their] access to relevant resources and their use of appropriate strategies in specific conditions of struggle with other agents', seems to further support the argument that power is omnipresent in social life. Similarly, for Foucault, power was seen as diffuse, permeating every aspect of social life, in ways that could be productive as well as repressive (McDonald & Birrell, 1999). The need to embrace a complex definition of power, therefore, is essential if we are to go beyond a superficial examination of its workings to explore the hidden ways in which it operates and shapes the lives of those who exercise it and those who are subject to it (Hardy, 1995). Thus, any examination of power would be incomplete without recognition of the way it remains hidden and mobilised in apparently apolitical structures (such as coaching). Furthermore, as Locke (1985) has concluded, power, is not merely imposed from above but 'involve[s] the active consent of subordinate groups and the taming of resistance through accommodation' (McDonald & Birrell, 1999). Hence, a comprehensive investigation of power necessitates an understanding of resistance against it. Indeed, resistance itself can be considered as an expression of power, which adds to the complexity of understanding interactions between social agents. It can also be argued that as long as a participant in a social encounter has a function, and a value, then they are not entirely powerless (Dunning, 1986).

Lukes' (1993, p. 504) description of power as 'the capacity to produce or contribute to outcomes by significantly affecting another or others' can be applied to coaching. Indeed, the coaching process of guiding athletes to fulfil their potentialities, by its very nature, necessitates the use of complex forms of power (Bell, 1989). Within this context, Borrie (1996) has suggested that the level of power and control that the coach can exert over many aspects of the athletes' environment will affect the nature of coach–athlete interaction on the practice field. However, power in this context is still subject to resistance, and a coach must be sensitive to the various forms through which this can be expressed if effective coaching is to be achieved. In emphasising the value of such awareness and inquiry to teacher and coach education provision, Locke (1985) has advocated that any improvement in teaching and coaching practice must include the recognition of the unique power structure of each situation, including the varying and constantly changing measures of cooperation and compliance from charges (i.e., students or athletes). In what we consider to be a tentative step towards achieving this goal, the remainder of this chapter seeks to address the following questions: How does a coach get his or her athletes to do what he or she wants? What are the sources of a coach's power? How could a coach further cultivate that power?

SPORTS COACHING CULTURES

OBTAINING, MAINTAINING AND ADVANCING SOCIAL POWER

All of the coaches in this book highlighted the importance for a coach to command the 'respect' and 'trust' of his or her athletes. The consensus viewpoint which emerged was that the quality of the interpersonal relationship that existed between coach and athlete (defined by many as 'respect') directly impacted upon the receptiveness of the athlete to the coach's pedagogical strategies, athlete learning, and, ultimately, competitive performance. In order to understand how such athlete respect was obtained, this section explores the differing forms and varieties of coaches' power from the basis of the refined and extended version (Raven, 1965; 1992) of French and Raven's (1959) classic typology of social power in human relations. In particular, it aims to examine how the coaches in this book attempted to obtain, maintain and advance their social relations with, and influence over, their athletes using the concepts of legitimate, expert, informational, referent, reward and coercive power. Here, each base of social power is examined within the coaching context, as are the potential consequences, both positive and negative, of their use and the interaction between them. Like all typologies, it must be treated with caution as the 'types' are rarely as easily divided in reality as they are in theory, but it does have the virtue of highlighting some of the different dimensions of a complex, multilayered, multifaceted concept. Finally, the issue of the empowerment of athletes within the coaching process is explored and debated.

'Legitimate power', also known as 'positional power' (Erchul & Raven, 1997), is defined as the power that derives solely from a person's position within a particular social structure or organisation and not because of any other special qualities a person may posses (Slack, 1997). In the context of coaching, it can be speculated that simply occupying the role of the coach affords the incumbent a degree of legitimate power. In drawing upon the work of Erchul and Raven (1997) in education, a coach who relies upon legitimate power is essentially projecting an image that suggests, 'After all I am the coach, and I am doing what my job requires – helping you to become better performers. As an athlete, you should feel obliged to accept what I have to offer.' However, this source of power in itself is insufficient for a coach to gain and hold the full confidence and respect of athletes (Potrac et al., 2000). Indeed, while most coaches are granted this form of power upon entering the coaching environment, it is their future actions that dictate whether such power is enhanced or eroded. In this respect, Thompson (1998, p. 45) suggests that 'power is a feature of everyday actions and interactions in so far as it involves individuals making decisions and living with the consequences of those decisions'. He further suggests that while such actions can be used to enhance the power an individual holds, they can, alternatively, be used to give power away. Consequently, it can be argued that the power a coach exercises over his or her athletes is not a fixed quality that he or she has or does not have but, instead, depends upon the choices he or she makes (Thompson, 1998). The coaches in this book would appear to agree with this particular viewpoint. Indeed, when talking about the coaches that they had worked with and for, many identified several

features that they considered to be affecting the levels of 'trust' and 'respect' afforded to a coach by athletes. For example, **Graham Taylor** recalled how inappropriate training methods and the unrealistic expectations of one of his former coaches had a negative impact on credibility: 'What it taught me was that the training sessions were for his benefit, and I thought "that can't be right".' Similarly, **Hope Powell** described how the mannerisms and the language of some of the coaches that she played under served only to 'turn players off', while in a more positive light, **Lois Muir** discussed the ways in which Dixie Cochran's motivational and interpersonal skills had served to inspire her as a player. The critical point that arises here is that the respect afforded to coaches by players is largely determined by how coaches go about enacting and fulfilling the coaching role. In keeping with the preceding chapter on coaches' roles, it seems clear that simply occupying the role without serious reflective consideration upon its wider contextual demands (i.e. relying only on legitimate power) is insufficient for a coach to secure the full co-operation, confidence and respect of athletes.

Following on from this, early research on the maintenance and enhancement of a coach's power (Potrac *et al.*, 2000) suggests that the acquisition and demonstration of expert power (French & Raven, 1959) is essential to gain and hold the respect of athletes. Slack (1997, p. 181) defined expert power as that which 'accrues to a person because of the special knowledge or skill she [*sic*] possesses'. Tauber (1985) however has suggested that the expert power of a teacher (or coach in this case) is not solely based upon his or her knowledge but upon the perceptions of the students (or athletes) regarding that knowledge. In short, 'the greater the student perception, the greater the expert power' that is afforded (Tauber, 1985, p. 6). Echoing the point made in the earlier chapters on coaches' roles and interactions, the issue within coaching then, becomes that of athlete perception and the image portrayed by the coach in creating that perception. As Bell (1989, p. 16) reminds us: '[As a coach] the greater your perceived knowledge and competence, the greater your power'. The expert power of a coach therefore would depend upon his or her expertise as demonstrated on the training ground, and the athletes' perception of it. Hence, it can be argued that coaches are continuously involved in trying to maintain or enhance their legitimate power through the use and further development of expert power. Such a concept is consistent with Shetty's (1978, p. 177) argument that types of power are not discrete and may overlap, thus 'the possession of one type of power can affect the extent and effectiveness of other types'.

The need to maintain and develop the power of the coach over the athletes, often through demonstrated expertise, was in keeping with the outlook of the coaches in this book. For example, **Bob Dwyer** suggested that if a coach 'can't understand the game or communicate that knowledge' then he or she 'is going to have problems'. Similarly, **Ian McGeechan** believes that a coach needs an in-depth technical and tactical knowledge of his or her sport and needs to demonstrate this in conversations with athletes, as if 'you cannot be a full part of that [the technical and tactical discussions], you would lose the respect of the players'. Additionally,

Peter Stanley described how it was essential for the coach to convey a knowledge-able and credible persona. Indeed, he believes that the information and feedback that is provided to the athletes must be seen explicitly and repeatedly to contribute to improved performances; otherwise, athletes would begin to question their value and his or her credibility as a coach. In addition, he also outlined how, for similar reasons, he refrains from actively demonstrating techniques because, due to his self-confessed limited ability as an athlete, he feels that providing his athletes with poor demonstrations would also result in a loss of respect for him as a coach. Such findings are in keeping with those from the previous chapter on coaches' interactions, where it was suggested that coaching practitioners are required to give convincing impressions of their roles to others. It appears that it is not enough for a coach to possess a detailed knowledge of their sport, but he or she must convey this knowledge in a manner that his deemed appropriate by his or her athletes for credibility and power to be maintained (Potrac, 2000).

Although expert power can be used to reinforce the legitimate power that coaches have as a consequence of their social role, expert power used in isolation can result in a very limited power base (Benfari *et al.*, 1986). Indeed, Benfari *et al.* (1986) have suggested that its continued or overuse could result in barriers arising between a coach and others, including athletes and administrators, that may be difficult to remove. In this respect, they note that the method and style of the transmission of knowledge is critical in forming perceptions about the coach. Specifically, they concluded that 'advice given in an authoritarian manner will be seen as a put down' (Benfari *et al.*, 1986, p. 14), thus emphasising the importance of understanding some of the nuances of social processes. This sentiment was shared by a number of the coaches in this book. For example, **Graham Taylor** emphasised the need for coaching practitioners not to take themselves too seriously or be viewed as pompous, as such behaviour can serve to alienate the coach from the players. **Steve Harrison** also considered that he needed to be seen to be on a par with his players if he was to get the best from them in terms of performance. Here he noted:

> I've recognised that you've got to be on a level with the players to get a response at the coaching level. I've got to be seen to be on their wave-length. If I'm on their wavelength, I'll be all right. If not, then things get harder and harder.

Harrison thus firmly believes that in addition to having 'knowledge of the game', 'it's how and when you express that knowledge that is important'. Such statements highlight the value placed by the coaches on their social competences and what might be described as their personal repertoires, as they were aware of the need to be contextually sensitive when imparting expert knowledge if their athletes were to make best use of the advice on offer.

Closely allied to expert power is the notion of informational power, also known as persuasion. This power base is determined by the quality of the information, or strength of an argument, that a coach can present to an athlete or athletes in order

to influence a change in their behaviour (Raven, 1992). Unlike expert power, where an athlete's thinking is 'I don't really understand exactly why, but the coach really knows this topic so he (or she) must be right', the strength of informational power lies in the recognition by the athlete that 'I listened carefully to the coach and I can now see for myself that this is clearly the best way to deal with the problem' (Erchul & Raven, 1997). In discussing the benefits of informational power, Erchul and Raven (1997) suggested that in comparison to the other bases of power, it can be maintained without social dependence upon the influencing agent, the coach in the case of this book. Simply put, the athlete believes 'I am doing this differently because *I really believe* for myself that this is now the best way' (Erchul & Raven, 1997, p. 139). The significance of informational power was echoed in all the coaches' stories in this book. In particular, they considered that it was essential for a coach to persuade his or her athletes to 'buy into' their particular programme if the coaching process was to be a productive and successful one. A strategy implemented by many to achieve this goal was to highlight the connections between the benefits obtained from the various training exercises, activities and drills undertaken, and competitive performance. For example, **Graham Taylor**, **Steve Harrison** and **Peter Stanley** all insist that the instruction and learning that takes place on the training field must not only be directly transferable to competitive situations but, importantly, that the coach should ensure that the athletes are fully aware of how what they are being asked to do actually contributes towards enhancing their performance. **Ian McGeechan** also attaches great importance to explaining to players why they are asked to do things in a certain way, as he considers it necessary for players to believe in what the coach is asking them to do if on-the-field success is to become a reality: 'I try and tell them what we are doing and why. I give them reasons for the things that I do.' Similarly, **Bob Dwyer** outlined how a player's understanding of a particular task or role and their subsequent performance of it, is greatly enhanced if the coach clearly outlines the rationale behind it. Hence, he suggested that a coach should not only clarify 'how to do things' to athletes but also 'why we should do them' in a clear and logical manner. Finally here, **Lois Muir** was equally critical of 'warm fuzzy drills' and advocated that 'no one should do an activity [in practice] not knowing how they can use it on the court'. Like the others, she believes in delivering sessions relevant to the game, with the players' understanding of that being paramount.

A further consideration in this context is the use of reward power (French & Raven, 1959; Raven, 1965), which has been defined as 'the power that comes from one person's control over another's rewards' (Slack, 1997, p. 181). As with other aspects of power, the effective use of reward power is dependent upon the meanings recipients attach to it (Benfari *et al.*, 1986). Thus, 'the key to effective use of "reward power" is to be able to tell how much of which reward, delivered how frequently and for how long a time is best for each student' (Tauber, 1985, p. 5). Such an analysis of coaching delivery could be insightful when trying to understand how and why coaches create climates of incentives, what impact they have on

coach–athlete relationships, and why they are sometimes successful. Of particular interest here is Raven's (1993) discussion of the concept of the personal form of reward power, which goes beyond tangible incentives. Here, he suggests that personal approval from someone who we like can result in a powerful form of reward power. **Steve Harrison** in particular was very aware of this notion, as he believed that players are more likely to respond to coaches 'who tell them positive things rather than [giving] them negatives all the time'. The concept also resonates with the coaches' general belief in establishing positive learning and working environments in their sessions, although, within them, any praise given had to be genuinely earned.

In addition to reward power, coaching behaviour can, at times, be explained in terms of coercive power (French & Raven, 1959), which derives from the ability of one person to punish another (Slack, 1997). Although the use of coercion is generally regarded as 'dysfunctional because it alienates people and builds up resentment' (Slack, 1997, p. 181), it nevertheless remains at the disposal of the coach. Indeed, the combined use of reward power and coercive power could affect the extent and effectiveness of other types of power (Shetty, 1978). Specifically, 'the judicious use of reward power and coercive power can increase the effectiveness of legitimate power; inappropriate use, however, will decrease legitimate power' (Shetty, 1978, p. 177). Again, the emphasis appears to be on the delivery, or the athletes' perception of delivery, rather than on the message alone. From the perspective of the coaches in this book, the practice of publicly berating poor performance or 'bawling-out' a player was seen as totally unproductive, as it was considered to result in a decline in the respect of the players for the coach. For example, **Steve Harrison** noted that 'if you hit people with negatives all the time, then they think "bollocks to you"' and so will be less receptive to the coach's advice and instruction. In a similar vein, **Hope Powell** asserted that aggressive and abusive behaviour is highly unlikely to have any positive impact on the coach–athlete relationship in top-level sport. Instead, **Steve Harrison** suggested that a quiet word with a particular player or players was the best way to deal with the issues of poor discipline and lack of application. Such a belief is in keeping with the outlook of **Ian McGeeghan**, who generally prefers to deal with players in private, often with video evidence, to explain their shortcomings in detail so as to ensure player understanding. Indeed, the lesson that seems to emanate from the coaches' stories in this context is that if problems are sorted out in a supportive framework, athletes are more likely to respect both the coach and his or her advice, and so be more willing to play for him or her. As **Steve Harrison** highlighted, 'why damage your relationship with a player when you're going to need him [or her] tomorrow!'

The final element of French and Raven's (1959) typology is that of referent power, which is based on the 'student's identification with the teacher and his/her desire to be like him/her' (Tauber, 1985, p. 4). Consequently, unlike legitimate power, which is based on position, referent power is personal as it is the person, not the position, who is respected. Such power wielders are seen to possess desirable

personal characteristics, with many willing to accept their power in order to become more like them (Tauber, 1985). This type of power is often referred to in everyday parlance as 'charisma'; an elusive quality that only the lucky few are allegedly born with. Thus, similar to the earlier discussed concept of 'self in role' (see Chapter 11), an examination of how a referent power base is established and developed could provide a very fruitful area of inquiry into how coaches inspire athletes to transcend what were previously considered to be limitations.

The coaches in this book attached great store to the development and maintenance of their respective referent power bases and, accordingly, highlighted several strategies that they employed to achieve them. Chief among these, echoing the earlier discussion of 'self in role' and 'charismatic leadership' (see Chapter 11), was the need to demonstrate an ethic of social care for their players both inside and outside the sporting environment. For example, **Bob Dwyer** suggested that it was necessary for a coach to establish relationships with his or her players whereby they firmly consider him or her to be working towards their best interests: 'If we can lead them into thinking that they're all part of the plans of the club, then they'll perform better, so I have to get them to believe in me.' In order to achieve this, he attempts to create a positive training environment where all the players are led to believe that they are valued. Hence, he tries to enter into a partnership with the players in terms of working towards achieving performance goals, an approach he considers to be particularly effective. Of significance in establishing this partnership was the considered use of humour to break down social barriers and, more importantly, taking a sincere interest in his players' well-being outside of the sporting context. Indeed, this latter function was considered by **Dwyer** to be one of the most crucial for a coach. He believes that his players will only respond to him and his coaching methods wholeheartedly if they consider the rugby club to be 'part of the family'. Consequently, he strives to include his players' partners and children in the life of the club. This involves many and various tasks such as helping new players and their families to find and settle into new accommodation, arranging social functions, and securing extra tickets for matches. For **Bob Dwyer**, an effective coaching practitioner is someone who is not only concerned about developing the playing abilities of players, but who also cares about the general well-being of those players and their families; a facet that he believes is fully appreciated by his players.

Graham Taylor echoed similar sentiments. Like **Bob Dwyer**, he emphasised the importance of being seen to care for athletes holistically in order to facilitate maximal athlete performance. He even commented that he remembers the birthdays of his players and their families, as he considers that such gestures serve to reinforce his players' respect for him as a person, rather than just as a competent and knowledgeable professional: 'You're actually showing them that you care, and whilst you show that you think about them and the other side of life, you stand to gain a great deal in terms of your working relationship with them.' Similarly, he also believed that the use of humour can also contribute to this process of establishing a coach's referent power by presenting the coach in a 'human light'

which he thinks is appreciated by players: 'It's no different to any other walk of life. You can't be too pompous . . . it's very important that the players can see that you like a laugh.' Indeed, for a coach to be successful, he contends that it is essential for him or her to be 'liked' by players: 'I think the best coaches will be respected but, to a great degree, they will also be liked.' The connection here with the earlier discussion on the concept of 'role distance' (see Chapter 11) is clear with the coach attempting to boost his referent power in order to strengthen the 'working consensus' with his players. Similarly, **Peter Stanley**, **Steve Harrison**, **Ian McGeeghan**, **Lois Muir**, **Di Bass** and **Hope Powell** all attribute their successes, in part, to the establishment of good relationships with their respective players and treating them in a manner that engenders respect.

A final and interesting concept to be brought into the framework is that of 'nutrient' power (May, 1972) or empowerment (Kidman, 2001). Such power is defined as that 'for (to help) another person' (Kleiber, 1980, p. 35). The term 'empowerment' is derived from sociological theory and is generally regarded as the process by which individuals acquire greater control over the decisions that affect their lives (Kidman, 2001; Thompson, 1998). Simply put, it is where the individual has a voice (Thompson, 1998). In the context of sports coaching, an empowered athlete is one that has some choice over what happens in his or her sporting life (Kidman, 2001). It is where the performers and team have the opportunity to actively engage in shaping and determining their own direction (Arai, 1997; Kidman, 2001). In implementing an empowering approach, a coach could involve athletes in challenging an agreed playing style or game plan in the interest of improving it and also their wider knowledge of the sport. A philosophy of empowerment also aims to make athletes increasingly responsible for their own performances by giving them a degree of ownership over them. In this way, athletes can, theoretically, become knowledgeable about the options available to them and take greater control over their own development (Arai, 1997). Indeed, unlike the traditional autocratic approach to coaching, the role of the coach within an empowering framework is to provide support, to be a mentor, and to act as a source of knowledge and information (Kidman, 2001). Such a situation does not, of course, signify the elimination of power; rather it is a 'rational acceptance of all de facto powers' (Crozier, 1973, p. 224). Within sports coaching, such an approach could lead to increased commitment from athletes because they are making a greater investment of self in the process (Kidman, 2001).

The value of utilising an empowering philosophy was voiced by several of the coaches in this book. Perhaps the leading advocate here was **Peter Stanley**, who believes that such an approach is especially suited to him and his athletes due to the nature of track and field athletics. In this respect, the athletes often have to compete without him being present as they take part in different competitions at various locations on the same day. Additionally, the rules of track and field athletics forbid the coach from advising athletes once the competition has started. Consequently, Peter was particularly keen for his athletes to develop the ability to solve problems for themselves: 'They have to have the awareness to perceive what

is happening and make the necessary adjustments themselves.' In order to develop this quality in his athletes, he outlined how, as an athlete gains more experience, the power differential between him and the performer changes so that, eventually, the coach becomes an advisor to the athlete: 'For me, coaching is about guidance rather than control.' Furthermore, he indicated that, for his athletes to be able to take full responsibility for their actions, it was necessary for him to explain why he wants them to engage in a certain activity or programme of training and to be open to subsequent feedback and questions from them. In this way, he considers that he is providing athletes with the opportunity to develop a deep and full understanding of their particular event. In a similar vein, **Di Bass** expects her swimmers to be fully committed, thinking and involved performers who share responsibility with the coach for their self-improvement. Her goal is to create an environment where the athletes would undertake a training session even if the coach were not present. Her approach is a democratic one that emphasises talking *with* her swimmers rather than *at* them. **Hope Powell** also emphasised her desire to develop players who can accept responsibility for their performances, and are capable of thinking independently to solve their own problems on the pitch. She laments the traditional coach-centred approach in football, which she considers to have resulted in mechanistic reactions on behalf of players: 'Players just don't think for themselves.' **Graham Taylor**, **Bob Dwyer**, **Lois Muir**, **Ian McGeeghan** and **Steve Harrison** all expressed comparable sentiments in this regard. Hence, while they voiced their belief in developing and using structured training programmes, they also emphasised the importance of 'growing' players because of the need to prepare players for on-field responsibility, decision-making, and game understanding. The image given was one of 'a facilitator that gives players their team understanding' (**Lois Muir**).

A subsequent issue raised here concerns the depth and impact of athlete input following consultation; that is, how democratic in reality is the procedure and what are the constraints on 'full and free' participation in the sporting decision making process? (Hardy, 1995). Early work by Bachrach and Baratz (1963; 1970) developed the concept of a second phase of power in this regard – 'a process whereby issues are excluded from decision making, confining the agenda to "safe" questions [as it] allows the more powerful actors to determine outcomes from behind the scenes' (Hardy, 1995, p. xvi). Perhaps, therefore, coaches only allow their athletes to have an illusion of empowerment, as they continue to control the 'agenda' items (Jones, 2001). Similarly, Lukes (1974, p. 24) has argued that power can be used to prevent conflict if it is employed to shape 'perceptions, cognitions and preferences in such a way' that those subject to it can imagine no alternative and thus just 'accept their role in the existing order of things'. Hence, athletes, or anyone subject to power, may be 'duped, hoodwinked, coerced, cajoled, or manipulated into political inactivity' (Saunders, 1980, p. 22), if they perceive their lot to be a satisfactory one. Such an outlook is in keeping with the practice of several of the coaches in this book and echoes the discussion in Chapter 12 on 'presenting the self' and 'coaching front'. In this regard, **Ian McGeeghan**, in an

effort to ensure that his players 'buy into his game plan', involves them in discussions about the team's direction. However, far from being a 'free for all', the discussions are limited to a fixed agenda set by him. As a consequence, he believes that the players value having an input into team affairs, while he is, in effect, able to maintain and exercise firm control over major issues relating to the coaching process. In keeping with such a strategy, both **Bob Dwyer** and **Lois Muir** outlined that while they are willing to listen to the ideas and feedback of their respective players, the onus was very much on the players to convince them of the value and workability of their suggestions, something that **Dwyer** considered to be a very difficult task in his case. Similarly, **Lois Muir** noted that there were times when she appeared to listen patiently to players to give them the desired impression, whilst in reality she was just 'waiting for them to finish because I was going to do my own thing anyway'. It seems therefore, that the coaches, with the possible exceptions of **Peter Stanley** and **Di Bass**, although willing to voice support for athlete empowerment concepts, were more concerned with athlete 'buy in' to their programmes than the real thing. Again, the connections with issues raised in previous chapters are apparent, particularly so with the 'white lies' the coaches told, and the 'illusion of inclusion' (Chapter 12) they gave to their athletes. What appears to bind these intermingling strands of thought and theory together into a common thread however is the use of a form of power to manage the athletes' perception of the coach.

CONCLUSION

All of the coaches in this book consistently and passionately regarded the ability to secure the 'trust' and 'respect' of their athletes as an essential ingredient of effective coaching practice. Hence, they stressed the need to establish a working climate whereby athletes not only respect the coach as a competent professional, but also as a person. For these coaches, the desire to have athletes 'believe in' them as social beings, trusting in their knowledge, decisions and advice can never be overstated and, more importantly, should never be ignored. Some of the lessons that resonate from the coaches' stories are, that for a coach to obtain and retain power, he or she must (among other things) understand athletes, care for them inside and outside of the sporting environment, and possess a set of technical and tactical ideals that they can clearly understand and implement in competition (Hamilton, 1997; Potrac, 2000). This involves the reflective use of numerous specific power strategies.

Finally, it is apparent that the relationship between coach and athlete is ingrained with aspects of social power. Indeed, in many ways the coaches in this book consider elements of power and their discretionary exercise to be at the heart of the coaching process. In drawing upon the bases of social power (French & Raven, 1959; Raven, 1965; 1992) and recent research on empowerment (Kidman, 2001), it is hoped that this chapter has illustrated the importance for coaching practitioners to be able to 'recognise and accept the ubiquity of power, to understand the bases of power, and to assess their effectiveness and the side effects of the use of power, which can sometimes be beneficial, and sometimes harmful' (Raven, 1986, p. 63).

CHAPTER 14

▼ CONCLUSION

SUMMARY

The purpose of this book was to study the social process that is coaching through the eyes of top-level coaches. We have focused on elements of interplay between 'structure' and 'agency', thus presenting a complex account of being an elite coach. Actions and events have been examined from a broadly sociological perspective that has, so far, received little attention in coaching theory. Hence, this book represents an attempt to 'make clear what was previously unclear, [to point to] the significance of things which had been regarded as of little or no consequence and [to disentangle] what was previously an indiscriminate muddle' (Burns, 1992, p. 6). Whereas we are not claiming to have totally 'disentangled' the complexities of a social process, perhaps we can claim to have made that tangle more transparent. The principal objective then, in addition to providing detailed descriptions of elite coaches' beliefs and philosophies, was to illustrate the potential for personal freedom (but not unfettered freedom) in coaching. It was demonstrated that social order is constructed and therefore can be dealt with (modified, evolved, adapted, improved) like other constructions, and that coaching resides somewhere in the dynamic space between the constraints on coaches' actions and the opportunities that coaches can construct for themselves.

From the stories and analyses, a picture emerges of coaching as a diverse and demanding occupation that requires a high level of physical and mental vigour on the part of practitioners. As the roles in which coaches need to engage are multiple, dynamic and complex, generalisations regarding coaches and their practices are not easily forthcoming. However, although the coaching role is certainly 'broad

and ill-defined', elements of sociological inquiry which attempt to understand the connections between people and society, and biography and history, can provide an in-depth analysis of this most human of jobs (O'Brien & Kollock, 1991). Indeed, it is in the ability of sociology to illuminate patterns of social life and to clarify the opportunities and constraints that exist within them, that its strength lies.

Recognising the nature of coaching as a social construction has wide-ranging implications for coaches. Once we come to understand the origins of patterned behaviour that constitute social structures, we come to recognise our place in contributing to such patterns (O'Brien & Kollock, 1991). Indeed, if individuals can

> envision all the parts, they can imagine different combinations and different outcomes, and therefore can envision possibilities for change. The result is that [they can] increase their repertoire of behavioural options across settings by understanding the constraints and the potential outcomes of their anticipated behaviour in a given situation.
>
> (O'Brien & Kollock, 1991, p. 144)

Such awareness could provide coaches with a greater understanding of the range of their possible roles, particularly in relation to others within the sporting context.

The coaches' stories told within this book provide a detailed and contextualised illustration of some important issues within coaching. For example, one of the most clearly illustrated themes to emerge is the belief in working *with* players and athletes to get the best out of them. This relates to the need to know athletes as individuals and to view the world from their perspective if their capabilities are to be realised. Such empathy is indicative of how the coaches interviewed here were influenced by their own experience as athletes, and echoes the findings of earlier work (Saury & Durand, 1998). This type of implicit knowledge, which could be defined as professional 'know-how', might also be linked to the sensitivity and flexibility expert coaches need to adjust to unexpected and problematic tasks (Saury & Durand, 1998; Coté *et al.*, 1995). Indeed, all of the coaches interviewed in this book were very aware of the need to adapt to changing circumstances if they were to be successful in their practice. In explaining such knowledge, Saury and Durand (1998, p. 264) conclude: 'The practical experience of coaches may be stored in the form of contextualised directories of diagnostics and operational acts. These directories help make complex situations meaningful and permit appropriate actions following the immediate recognition of situations by analogy with past experiences.' Taking account of their experiential knowledge and the influence of past mentors, the stories of the coaches included here illustrate some of the ways in which this process occurs in practice.

Although desiring a 'special' positive relationship with their athletes, many of the coaches also believed in the requirement to remain 'one step away' from them; thus respecting and using the authoritative coaching role as a resource to direct and organise. Such a strategy of 'maintaining arms' length relationships' echoes the findings of Sedgewick *et al.,* (1997, p. 87) whose coaches, although agreeing on the value of positive rapport with athletes, emphasised the need to establish and maintain appropriate boundaries, particularly in relation to role and associated types of behaviour. On the other hand, **Peter Stanley** perhaps due to the nature of his circumstances and (individual) sport, believed in the need to develop stronger bonds with his athletes. To a certain extent therefore, the coaches' professional knowledge reflected a socialisation process of 'how a coach should act' whereby they had clear ideas of how the coaching role should be fulfilled, based on knowledge gleaned from mentors and their own personal experiences.

Examining the stories at another analytical level, it can be argued that the dialectic of the coach's role and player expectation, and the need to be flexible within that framework, characterised the influence of both structure and agency on the coaches' working philosophies. It appears that they do indeed behave both how they choose and how they are influenced to choose (Lemert, 1997). This is a dialectic that is clearly illustrated in the coaches' stories, and has implications for coach educators in two principal ways. First, more attention needs to be paid to the structural constraints on coaches, on role fulfilment and consequent knowledge generation. Coaches need to become aware of the socialisation processes acting upon them, so that they can become increasingly active in 'role-making' or 'role-using' as opposed to merely 'role-playing' (Callero, 1994). Additionally, in raising awareness of social influences on beliefs and behaviour which 'construct the person of the coach', coaches could further become aware of the value-laden nature of their practice leading to increased awareness of alternatives (Jones, 2000, p. 39). Second, the coaches' belief in the need to be highly adaptive calls into question the current rationality of coach education programmes. This deduction echoes that of Saury and Durand (1998), who concluded that the cognitive functioning of expert coaches was neither founded on reason nor planning. Rather, it was 'very flexible, and based on continuous step-by-step tuning to the context' (p. 264), albeit embedded in a deep knowledge of their sport and an already established general framework of behaviour. In this respect, the coaching process and coaching practice can be considered as 'regulated improvisation' (Bourdieu, 1977, p. 79). Such coaches, to which the stories presented here relate well, are described as: 'A "cognitive alchemy" consisting of a flexible application of (social) rules, using deeply integrated past experiences, resolving (never total or optimal) contradictions or dilemmas at the moment they emerge, recognising typical scenarios, and so forth' (Saury & Durand, 1998, p. 265).

It was generally agreed among the coaches interviewed, that there was no 'one best way' of coaching, as different circumstances required different qualities if they wished to be effective. Although the need for 'flexibility' was a recurrent theme for the coaches, it was also apparent that their ability to handle complex decisions remained subject to certain cognitive and social limitations. Hence, some aspects of their working context already appeared to be established thus limiting the possibilities open to them. The point to remember here, however, is that the coaches seemed aware of such limitations and were in a constant process of exploring and redefining them. Through such consciousness, they demonstrated their commitment to the coaching process and their role within it in a way that transcended both. Hence, the sincere, caring, focused and reflective individual was seen to emerge from behind the coach's mask. Such a commitment was discussed as expressing the 'self in role', and concurs with Noel's (1989) concept of occupational 'magnificent obsession'.

With regard to the book's organisation, we believe that at one level the coaches' stories speak for themselves and hence need little comment for us. However, issues that emerged from the stories, for us, were the themes that we considered worthy of further discussion and thus were expanded into separate chapters. Clearly, these are personal selections and it would be possible to identify others. However, in addition to their descriptive purposes, the constructs employed within these chapters (role, interaction, pedagogy and power) are valuable heuristic tools, in and of themselves, for understanding the coaching process. Hence, by using these tools we attempted to interpret the raw data of experiences and feelings to help readers make sense of, and understand, both the coaches' stories and their own experiences in relation to coaching practice.

Although the analysis has been presented in linear chapters, perhaps the most significant issue to evolve from this investigation is the apparent interdependent relationship that exists between the concepts discussed. For example, the stories and analytical chapters suggest that the pedagogical processes of a practitioner are built from experiential knowledge and are linked to strong beliefs about a coach's 'role'. In this respect, it appears that a top-level coaching practitioner needs to fulfil the expectations of his or her athletes as a first step in gaining that all-important 'respect'. In order to fulfil these demands, the coach consciously attempts to present an idealised image (Goffman, 1959) of himself or herself to the athletes. Hence, it could be contended that the power afforded to a coach is determined by the audiences' (in this case the athletes') perceptions of the quality of his or her performance within the practice environment. In this way, pedagogy, role, power and interaction are all combined in the coach's persona and working modes of behaviour.

POSSIBLE DIRECTIONS FOR FUTURE RESEARCH

A number of potentially fruitful avenues of research have emerged from the findings of this project. The respondents' criticisms of existing coach education provision provides an area for such inquiry. In this respect, an investigation into the surveying of top-level coaches' views to generate an understanding of their educational needs and wants could provide valuable information for those involved in the design and implementation of coach education schemes. In addition to identifying desired content, this line of inquiry could also address issues about the mode of course delivery and assessment. Such research could be useful in formulating coach education courses that more fully meet the demands and expectations of top-level coaches (Graber, 1989).

In a similar vein, the value ascribed by respondents to the significant influence of mentors in the development of their respective pedagogical strategies, further reinforces Bloom et al.'s (1998) plea for coach educators to more fully consider the possible benefits of mentoring schemes. However, before such schemes can become a reality it is necessary to investigate mentoring from the perspectives of athletes and coaches in order to develop a greater understanding of the types and quality of relationships that develop (Perna, et al., 1996). In this respect, Bloom et al. (1998) recommend the utilisation of qualitative methods of inquiry, which enable both athletes and coaches to express personal views on the importance of mentoring in the development of their respective athletic and coaching careers.

While recent academic discourse has pointed to the need to examine the impact of situational factors on coaching behaviour (e.g., Jones, 2000; Potrac et al., 2000; Lyle, 1999; Coté et al., 1995), more needs to be done. Furthermore, the limited existing research (e.g., Coté et al., 1995), while acknowledging that contextual factors are a central part of coaching, has tended not only to fail to fully describe these factors, but has also ascribed them a peripheral position within the conceptualisation of coaching and coach effectiveness. While the findings of this study provide some insight into the impact of contextual and situational factors on the coaching behaviour of elite coaches, it is contended that much more extensive research is required if a fuller understanding of the impact of contextual workplace conditions on coaching behaviour is to evolve. Additionally, in keeping with the work of Kahan (1999), future studies of coaching behaviour could utilise longitudinal approaches to analyse how practitioners' pedagogical strategies evolve or remain constant in relation to selected contextual variables over several seasons.

In the quest to gain a broader understanding of the coaching process, it also appears necessary to probe the meanings and varieties of the shared experiences of the coach and athlete (Brewer et al., 1999). Specifically, in the quest to develop a contextual understanding of the instructional process in sports coaching, it is necessary to investigate the impact of the pedagogical practices of a coach upon the performer. If coaches are to be successful, it is essential that they acquire knowledge of what types of coaching behaviour are desired by, and most effective for, their athletes (Brewer et al., 1999; Laughlin & Laughlin, 1994). Research to date (e.g., Hanson & Gould, 1988) has shown that coaching practitioners do not generally read their athletes well, thus Strean (1998) contends that the posing of the right open-ended questions will provide key information about how performers are experiencing their own learning and coach interventions. Similarly, Langley (1997) asserts that, in order to develop a comprehensive understanding of the instructional process in sport, it is necessary to include the athlete's perspective of skill learning as 'research on a student's [athlete's] subjective experience may result in a more contextual and unified picture of student [athlete] learning and offers the teacher [coach] an expanded knowledge base on student [athlete] learning processes' (p. 142). In particular, Langley (1997) suggests that the interpretive paradigm can be utilised to investigate how the athlete's subjective experience of skill learning impacts upon his or her interpretation of coach feedback. Specifically, in echoing the work of Lee *et al.*, (1993), he notes that

> gaining access to these interpretations would be immensely valuable for understanding why teacher [coach] feedback appears to have differential effects on student [athlete] learning. Thus, an important focus involves determining how students [athletes], who differ along particular variables (e.g., goal orientation, skill level, perceived competence), interpret the meaning of teacher [coach] feedback during skill learning.
>
> (Langley, pp. 152–153)

The emphasis on performer perspectives has great potential to inform practice, as, 'because athletes are recognisable to themselves in research findings, they can relate to the analyses and results in a way that allow them to transfer across settings and make connections to their own performance conditions and practices' (Strean, 1998, p. 342). Given that it is generally agreed that the job of a coach is to help athletes achieve their best level of performance (Coakley, 1994; Douge & Hastie, 1993; Lyle, 1986), the performers' perceptions of how the coach seeks to impart knowledge and develop their skills to the maximum should be central to any conceptual model of effective coaching (Langley, 1997).

Finally, in echoing the work of Nyberg (1981) in education, the dynamic power relationship that appears to exist between coaches and athletes is worthy of future research. In recognising that the coaching process is characterised by complex power relations which, in turn, are subject to the 'ebb and flow of influences, illustrative of the reflexive and generative capacities of human actors to confirm, adapt, negotiate and at times re-make their institutions and cultures' (Tomlinson, 1998, p. 238), it seems that a broad agenda for research is identified. Indeed, numerous research questions and study opportunities exist in this sphere. For example: to what extent do coaches wield power only to the degree that athletes perceive them to have such power? And why do athletes consent to power being wielded over them? (Tauber, 1985). In further borrowing from the work of Tauber (1985) future investigations could address such issues as: Are some power bases, such as coercive and reward powers, overused or ineffectively used? With coaching practitioners being increasingly held accountable for the outcome of their efforts (Coakley, 1994), coaches must effectively exercise power, hence they need a grasp of the 'power bases available and the potential limits of each' (Tauber, 1985, p. 16). Finally, it is worth restating that while the coaching process does not preclude personal philosophy, or the effects of social interaction, coaching theory has been hindered by the reluctance of coaches to develop a language for describing and explaining personal practices. As coaching is a human activity with all the accompanying problems and possibilities, future coach research and consequent education should more nearly reflect such realities (Jones, 2000; Potrac *et al.*, 2000).

CONCLUDING THOUGHTS

Without wishing to embark on a paradigmatic justification for the method used within this project, there is a need here to recognise both the strengths and weaknesses of the limited subject design and what it brings to coaching research. On the one hand, if the experiences of an expert are taken as the subject of wider critical reflection, then this study provides valuable insights into the types of knowledge that such coaches might need to possess to survive in a highly competitive environment. It also provides tentative evidence that coach education programmes should include components which reflect on the influences of structure and agency on role fulfilment, practical experience, interaction with mentors and developing within coaches an integrated knowledge base structured around the cues presented by real-life coaching problems. By incorporating such components, coach educators could find receptive audiences. On the other hand, it must be recognised that there are elements of the coaches' stories that are unique. Also, although these are stories told by the coaches and written from data that were approved by them they are, in the final event, stories constructed by us, the writers. The multilayered process of analysing and writing the stories is difficult to retell in full. There are undoubtedly places where our own experiences and lenses have caused us to emphasise some aspects rather than others. Nonetheless, we would maintain that as the basis for beginning a process of coach critical reflection, it could serve very well. They are, as was noted before, stories to be shared and it is the sharing process that, ultimately, will result in the project achieving wider goals.

▼ REFERENCES

Abraham, A., & Collins, D. (1998). Examining and extending research in coach development. *Quest, 50,* 59–79.

Arai, S.M. (1997). Empowerment: from the theoretical to the personal. *Journal of Leisurability, 23*(1), 3–11.

Arends, R.I. (1988). *Learning to Teach.* New York: Random House.

Armour, K.M., & Jones, R.L. (1998). *Physical Education Teachers' Lives and Careers: P.E., Sport and Educational Status.* London: Falmer Press.

Armour, K.M., & Jones, R.L. (2000). The practical heart within: the value of the sociology of sport. In R.L. Jones, & K.M. Armour (eds), *Sociology of Sport: Theory and Practice,* London: Addison Wesley Longman, 1–10.

Ayers, B. (1989). *The Good Preschool Teacher: Six Teachers Reflect on Their Lives.* New York: Teachers College Press.

Bachrach, P., & Baratz, M.S. (1963). Decisions and nondecisions: an analytical framework. *American Political Science Review, 57,* 641–651.

Bachrach, P., & Baratz, M.S. (1970). *Power and Poverty.* London: Oxford University Press.

Bandura, A. (1977). *Social Learning Theory.* Englewood Cliffs, NJ: Prentice-Hall.

Bass, B. (1981). *Stogdill's Handbook of Leadership.* New York: Free Press.

Belbin, R.M. (1981). *Management Teams: Why They Succeed or Fail.* Portsmouth, NH: Heinemann Educational Books.

Bell, K. (1989). *Coaching Excellence.* Austin, TX: Keel.

Benfari, R.C., Wilkinson, H.E., & Orth, C.D. (1986). The effective use of power. *Business Horizons, 29,* 12–16.

Bloom, G.A., Durand-Bush, N., Schinke, R.J., & Salmella, J.H. (1998). The importance of mentoring in the development of coaches and athletes. *International Journal of Sport Psychology, 29,* 267–281.

Blum, L. (1994). *Moral Judgement and Particularity.* Cambridge: Cambridge University Press.

Blum, A., & McHugh, P. (1984). *Self-Reflection in the Arts and Sciences.* Atlantic Highlands, NJ: Humanities Press.

Borrie, A. (1996). Coaching science. In T. Reilly (ed.), *Science and Soccer,* London: E & FN Spon, 243–258

Bourdieu, P. (1977). *Outline of a Theory of Practice.* Cambridge: Cambridge University Press.

Bourdieu, P. (1989). Social space and symbolic power. *Sociological Theory, 7,* 14–25.

Bourdieu, P. (1990). *The Logic of Practice.* Stanford, CA: Stanford Unversity Press.

Bourdieu, P. (1993). *The Field of Cultural Production: Essays in Art and Leisure*. New York: Columbia University Press.

Branaman, A. (2000). Goffman's social theory. In C. Lemert, & A. Branaman, (eds), *The Goffman Reader*, Oxford: Blackwell Publishers, xlv–lxxxii.

Branhart, A. (1994). Erving Goffman: the presentation of the self in everyday life. Available at <http://www.cfmc.com/adamb/writings/goffman.htm>.

Brewer, C.J., & Jones, R.L. (2002). A five-stage process for establishing contextually valid systematic observation instruments: the case of rugby union. *The Sport Psychologist*, *16*(2), 138–159.

Brewer, C., Jones, R.L., Potrac, P., & Armour, K. (1999). *Players' perceptions of coaching behaviour in elite level rugby union: a qualitative analysis*. Paper presented at the AIESEP '99 World Conference, 7–9 April, Besançon, France.

Broderick, A. (1999). Role theory and the management of service encounters. *The Service Industry Journal*, *2*, 117–131.

Brookfield, S. (1998). On the certainty of public shaming: working with students who just don't get it. In C. Rust (ed.), *Improving Students as Learners*, Oxford: OCSD, 17–31.

Bruins, J. (1999). Social power and influence tactics: a theoretical introduction. *Journal of Social Issues*, *55*(1), 7–14.

Bruner, J. (1999). Folk pedagogies. In J. Leach & B. Moon (eds). *Learners and Pedagogy*, London: Paul Chapman Publishers, 4–20.

Burns, T. (1992). *Erving Goffman*. London: Routledge.

Callero, P. (1994). From role-playing to role using: understanding role as a resource. *Social Psychology Quarterly*, *57*(3), 228–243.

Carron, A.V. (1980). Role behaviour and the coach–athlete interaction. *International Review of Sport Sociology*, *13*, 51–65.

Carron, A.V. (1988). *Group Dynamics in Sport: Theoretical and Practical Issues*. London, ON: Sports Dynamics.

Carron, A.V., & Widmeyer, W.N. (1996). Team building in sport. Paper presented at the Association for the Advancement of Applied Sport Psychology. Williamsburg, VA.

Clandinin, D.J., & Connelly, F.M. (1994). Personal experience methods. In N. Denzin and Y. Lincoln (eds), *Handbook of Qualitative Research*, Newbury Park, CA: Sage, 413–427.

Coakley, J.J. (1994). *Sport and Society: Issues and Controversies* (5th edn). St. Louis, MI: C.V. Mosby.

Connell, R. (1985). *Teachers' Work*. London: Allen & Unwin.

Cote, J., Salmela, J.H., Trudel, P., Baria, A., & Russell, S. (1995). The coaching model: a grounded assessment of expert gymnastic coaches' knowledge. *Journal of Sport and Exercise Psychology*, *17*(1), 1–17.

Crozier, M. (1973). The problem of power. In C. Hardy (1995) (ed.), *Power and Politics in Organisations*, Aldershot, UK: Dartmouth Publishing, 3–20.

Cuban, L. (1993). The lure of curriculum reform and its pitiful history. *Phi Delta Kappan*, *75*, 182–185.

Cushion, C. (2001) The coaching process in professional youth football: an ethnography of practice. Unpublished Ph.D. thesis. Brunel University, UK.

Danziger, R.C. (1982). Coaching humanistically: an alternative experience. *The Physical Educator*, *39*, 121–125.

Day, C. (1999). *Developing Teachers: The Challenge of Lifelong Learning*. London: Falmer Press.

Denton, D. (1972). *Existential Reflections on Teaching*. North Quincy, MA: Christopher.

Ditton, J. (ed.) (1980) *The view from Goffman*. London: Macmillan.

Douge, B., & Hastie, P. (1993). Coach effectiveness. *Sport Science Review, 2*(2), 14–29.

Dowling Naess, F.J. (1996). Life events and curriculum change: the life history of a Norwegian educator. *European Physical Education Review, 2*(1), 41–53.

Dunning, E. (1986). The sociology of sport in Europe and the United States: critical observations from an 'Eliasian' perspective. In R. Rees & A. Miracle (eds), *Sport and Social Theory*, Champaign, IL: Human Kinetics, 29–56.

Ely, M., Vinz, R., Downing, M., & Anzul, M. (1997). *On Writing Qualitative Research: Living by Words*. London: Falmer Press.

Erben, M. (ed.) (1998). *Biography and Education: A Reader*. London: Falmer Press.

Erchul, W.P., & Raven, B.H. (1997). Social power in school consultation: a contemporary view of French and Raven's bases of power model. *Journal of School Psychology, 35*(2), 137–171.

Fernández-Balboa, J.M. (1998a). Transcending masculinities: linking personhood and pedagogy. In C. Hickey, L. Fitzclarence, & R. Mathews (eds), *Where the Boys Are: Masculinity, Sport and Education*, Geelong, Victoria: Deakin University Press, 121–139.

Fernández-Balboa, J.M. (1998b). Poisonous pedagogy in physical education. AIESEP/Adelphi Conference Proceedings, July 1998, Garden City, NY, 83–87.

Fiol, C.E., Harris, D., & House, R. (1999). *Leadership Quarterly, 10*(3), 449–482.

French, J.R.P., Jr., & Raven, B. (1959). The bases of social power. In D. Cartwright (ed.), *Studies in Social Power*, Ann Arbor, MI: University of Michigan Press, 150–167.

Garet, S.M., Porter, C.A., Desimone, L., Birman, B.F., & Yoon, K.S. (2001). What makes professional development effective? Results from a national sample of teachers. *American Educational Research Journal, 38*(4), 915–945.

Gensemer, R.E. (1980). *Humanism and Behaviorism in Physical Education*. Washington DC: National Education Association.

Goffman, E. (1959). *The Presentation of Self in Everyday life*. Garden City, NY: Doubleday.

Goffman, E. (1969a). *Where the Action Is*. London: Penguin Press.

Goffman, E. (1969b). *Strategic Interaction*. Philadelphia: University of Pennsylvania Press.

Goodson, I.F. (1992). Sponsoring the teacher's voice: teachers' lives and teacher development. In A. Hargreaves & M.G. Fullan (eds), *Understanding Teacher Development*, London: Cassell, 110–121.

Gouws, D.J. (1995) The role concept in career development. In D. Super, B. Sverko & C. Super (eds), *Life Roles, Values and Careers: International Findings of the Work Importance Study*, San Francisco: Jossey-Bass, 22–53.

Graber, K. (1989). Teaching tomorrow's teachers: Professional preparation as an agent of socialisation. In T. Templin, & P. Schempp (eds), *Socialisation into Physical Education: Learning to Teach*, Indianapolis, IN: Benchmark Press, 59–80.

Hallam, S., & Ireson, J (1999). Pedagogy in the secondary school. In P. Mortimore (ed.), *Understanding Pedagogy and its Impact on Learning*, London: Paul Chapman Publishing, 68–97.

Hamilton, G. (1997). The rise and fall of Arrigo Sacchi: Is a manager's playing background little more than an anecdote? In J. King & J. King (eds), *The Cult of the Manager*, London: Virgin Publishing, 104–116.

Hammersley, M., & Atkinson, P. (1983). *Ethnography: Principles in Practice*. London: Tavistock.

Hanson, T., & Gould, D. (1988). Factors affecting the ability of coaches to estimate their trait and state anxiety levels. *The Sport Psychologist, 2*, 298–313.

Hardy, C. (1995). Introduction. In C. Hardy (ed.), *Power and Politics in Organisations*, Aldershot: Dartmouth, xiii–xxv.

Hargreaves, D. (2001). A future for the school curriculum. Available at <http://www.qca.org.uk/ca/14–19/dh_speech.asp>.

Hargreaves, J. (1986). *Sport, Power and Culture*. Polity Press: Cambridge.

Hargreaves, A., & Fullan, M.G. (eds) (1992). *Understanding Teacher Development*. London: Cassell.

Heise, D.R. (1977). Social action as the control of affect. *Behavioural Science, 22*, 163–167.

Heise, D.R. (1979). *Understanding Events: Affect and the Construction of Social Action*. New York: Cambridge University Press.

Hellison, D. (1973). *Humanistic Physical Education*. Englewood Cliffs, NJ: Princeton Press.

Hellison, D. (1995). *Teaching Responsibility Through Physical Education*. Champaign, IL: Human Kinetics.

Hendry, L.B. (1969). A personality study of highly successful and 'ideal' swimming coaches. *Research Quarterly, 40*, 299–305.

Hepworth, M. (1980). Deviance and control in everyday life: The contribution of Erving Goffman. In J. Ditton (ed.), *The View from Goffman*, London: Macmillan, 80–99.

Jarvie, G., & Maguire, J. (1994). *Sport and Leisure in Social Thought*. London: Routledge.

Jones, R.L. (2000). Toward a sociology of coaching. In R.L. Jones & K.M. Armour (eds), *The Sociology of Sport in Practice*, London: Addison Wesley Longman, 33–43.

Jones, R.L. (2001). Applying empowerment in coaching: Some thoughts and considerations. In L. Kidman (ed.), *Innovative Coaching: Empowering your Athletes*, Christchurch, NZ: Innovative Communications, 83–94.

Jones, R.L., & Armour, K. (2000). *The Sociology of Sport: Theory and Practice*. London: Addison Wesley Longman.

Jones, R.L., Armour, K., & Potrac, P. (2002). Understanding coaching practice: a suggested framework for social analysis. *Quest, 54*(1), 34–48.

Kahan, D. (1999). Coaching behaviour: a review of the systematic observation research literature. *Applied Research in Coaching and Athletics Annual, 14*, 17–58.

Kekale, J. (1998). Academic leaders and the field of possibilities. *International Leadership in Education, 1*(3), 237–255.

Kidman, L. (2001). *Developing Decision Makers: An Empowerment Approach to Coaching*. Christchurch, NZ: Innovative Print Communications.

Kipnis, D. (2001). Using power: Newton's second law. In A. Lee-Chai & J. Bargh (eds), *The Use and Abuse of Power: Multiple Perspectives on the Causes of Corruption*, Philadelphia: Taylor & Francis, 3–17.

Kleiber, D.A. (1980). The meaning of power in sport. *International Journal of Sport Psychology, 11*, 34–41.

Kossek, E.E., Noe, R.A., & DeMarr, B.J. (1999). Work–family role synthesis: individual and organizational determinants. *International Journal of Conflict Management, 2*, 102–129.

Langley, D. (1997). Exploring student skill learning: a case for investigating subjective experience, *Quest, 49*, 142–160.

Laughlin, N., & Laughlin, S. (1994). The relationship between similarity in perceptions of teacher/coach leader behaviour and evaluations of their effectiveness. *International Journal of Sport Psychology, 22*, 396–410.

Lave, J., & Wenger, E. (1999). Learning and pedagogy in communities of practice. In J. Leach & B. Moon (eds), *Learners and Pedagogy*. London: Paul Chapman Publishers, 21–33.

Leach, J., & Moon, B. (eds), (1999). *Learners and Pedagogy*. London: Paul Chapman Publishers.

Lee, M. (1993). Growing up in sport. In M. Lee (ed.), *Coaching Children in Sport: Principles and Practice*, London: E & FN Spon, 91–105.

Lee, A., Keh, N., & Magill, R. (1993). Instructional effects of teacher feedback in physical education. *Journal of Teaching in Physical Education, 12*, 228–243.

Lee-Chai, A.Y. & Bargh, J.A. (2001). *The Use and Abuse of Power: Multiple Perspectives on the Causes of Corruption*. Philadelphia: Taylor & Francis.

Leifer, E.M. (1988). Interaction preludes to role setting: exploratory local action. *American Sociological Review, 53*, 865–878.

Lemert, C. (1997). *Social Things: An Introduction to the Sociological Life*. New York: Rowman & Littlefield.

Lemert, C. & Branaman, A. (2000). *The Goffman Reader*. Oxford: Blackwell Publishers.

Locke, L.F. (1985). Research and the improvement of teaching: the professor as the problem. In G. Barrette, R. Feingold, R. Rees & M. Pieron (eds), *Myths, Models and Methods in Sport Pedagogy*, Champaign, IL: Human Kinetics, 1–26.

Lofland, J. (1980). Early Goffman: Style, structure, substance, soul. In J. Ditton (ed.), *The View from Goffman*, London: Macmillan, 24–51.

Lombardo, B.J. (1987). *The Humanistic Coach: From Theory to Practice*. Springfield, IL: C.C. Thomas.

Lopata, H.Z. (1991). Role theory. In J. Blau & N. Goodman (eds), *Social Roles and Social Institutions: Essays in Honour of Rose Laub Coser*, Boulder CO: Westview Press, 1–11.

Loughran, J., & Gunstone, R. (1997). Professional development in residence: developing reflection on science teaching and learning. *Journal of Education for Teaching, 23*(2), 159–178.

Lukes, S. (1974). *Power: A Radical View*. London: Macmillan.

Lukes, S. (1993). Three distinctive views of power compared. In M. Hill (ed.), *The Policy Process: A Reader*, London: Harvester Wheatsheaf, 50–58.

Lyle, J. (1986). Coach education: preparation for a profession. In *Proceedings of the VIII Commonwealth and International Conference on Sport, Physical Education, Dance, Recreation and Health*, London: FN Spon, 1–25.

Lyle, J. (1999). The coaching process: an overview. In N. Cross & J. Lyle (eds), *The Coaching Process: Principles and Practice for Sport*, Oxford: Butterworth-Heinemann, 3–24.

McCrimmon, M. (1995). Teams without roles: empowering teams for greater creativity. *Journal of Management Development, 14*(6), 35–41.

McDonald, M.G. & Birrell, S. (1999). Reading sport critically: a methodology for interrogating power. *Sociology of Sport Journal, 16*, 283–300.

Mack, D., & Gammage, K.L. (1998). Attention to group factors: coach considerations to building an effective team. *Avante, 4*(3), 118–129.

Marsh, I., Keating, M., Eyre, A., Campbell, R., & McKenzie, J. (1996). *Making Sense of Society: an Introduction to Sociology*. London: Longman.

Martens, R. (1987). Science, knowledge and sport psychology. *The Sport Psychologist, 1*, 29–55.

May, R. (1972). *Power and Innocence*. W.W. Norton: New York.

Mead, G.H. (1952). *Mind, Self and Society*. Chicago: University of Chicago Press.

Mumma, F.S. (1994). *What Makes Your Team Tick? Team-Work and Team Roles*. King of Prussia, PA: HDRQ.

NFER (National Foundation for Educational Research) (2001). *Continuing Professional Development: LEA and School Support for Teachers*. Berkshire, UK: NFER.

NPEAT (National Partnership for Excellence and Accountability in Teaching) (1998). Improving professional development: eight research-based principles. Available at: <http://www.npeat.org>.

Noel, A. (1989). Strategic cores and magnificent obsessions: discovering strategy formation through daily activities of CEO's. *Strategic Management Journal, 10*, 33–49.

Noddings, N. (1992). *The Challenge to Care in Schools*. New York: Teachers College Press

Nyberg, D. (1981). *Power over Power*. Ithaca, NY: Cornell University Press.

Oakes, J. (1989). What educational indicators? The case for assessing school context. *Educational Evaluation and Policy Analysis, 11*, 182–199.

O'Brien, J.A., & Kollock, P. (1991). Social exchange theory as a conceptual framework for teaching the sociological perspective. *Teaching Sociology, 19*, 140–153.

O'Conner, A., & Macdonald, D. (2002). Up close and personal on physical education teachers' identity: is conflict an issue? *Sport Education and Society, 7*(1), 37–54.

Ollhoff, J., & Ollhoff, L. (1996). *School-age Care from the Perspective of Social Role Theory*. Report by the Minnesota State Department of Children, Families and Learning. St. Paul, MN.

Pajak, E.F., Cramer, S.E., & Konke, K. (1984). Role set determinants of teacher reports of classroom behavior. Paper presented at the Annual Conference of the Eastern Educational Research Association, West Palm Beach, Florida, February 9–12.

Penney, D., & Waring, M. (2000). The absent agenda and physical education. *Journal of Sport Pedagogy, 6*(1), 4–37.

Perna, F.M., Zaichkowsky, L., & Bocknek, G. (1996). The association of mentoring with psycho-social development among male athletes at termination of college career. *Journal of Applied Sport Psychology, 8*, 76–88.

Pope, W. (1998). Emile Durkheim. In R. Stones (ed.), *Key Sociological Thinkers*, Basingstoke, UK: Macmillan, 46–58.

Potrac, P. (2000). A comparative analysis of the working behaviours of top-level English and Norwegian football coaches. Unpublished Ph.D. dissertation, Brunel University, London.

Potrac, P., Jones, R.L., Armour, K.M., & Brewer, C. (2000). Towards an holistic under-standing of the instructional process: a case study of an expert English soccer coach. Paper presented at the Pre-Olympic Congress, 7–13 September, Brisbane, Australia.

Potrac, P., Jones, R.L., & Armour, K.M. (2002). 'It's all about getting respect': the coaching behaviours of an expert English soccer coach. *Sport, Education and Society, 7*(2), 183–202.

Putnam, R.T., & Borko, H. (2000). What do new views of knowledge and thinking have to say about research on teacher learning? *Educational Researcher, 29*(1), 4–15.

Raffel, S. (1998). Revisiting role theory: roles and the problem of the self. *Sociological Research Online, 4*(2). Available at: <http://www.socresonline.org.uk/4/2/raffel.html>.

Raven, B.H. (1965). Social influence and power. In I.D. Steiner & M. Fishbein (eds), *Current Studies in Social Psychology*, New York: Holt, Reinhart, & Winston, 371–381.

Raven, B.H. (1986). A taxonomy of power in human relations. *Psychiatric Annals, 16*(11), 633–636.

Raven, B.H. (1992). A power interaction-model of interpersonal influence: French and Raven 30 years later. *Journal of Social Behaviour and Personality, 7*(2), 217–244.

Raven, B.H. (1993). The bases of power: origins and recent developments. *Journal of Social Issues, 49*(4), 227–251.

Richardson, L. (2000). New writing practices in qualitative research. *Sociology of Sport Journal, 17*(1), 5–20.

Ritzer, G. (1996). *Sociological Theory.* Singapore: McGraw-Hill.

Roberts, D., & Treasure, D. (1993). The importance of the study of children in sport: an overview. In M. Lee (ed.) *Coaching Children in Sport: Principles and Practice,* London, England: E & FN Spon, 3–16.

Rodham, K. (2000). Role theory and the analysis of the managerial work: the case of occupational health. *Journal of Applied Management Studies, 9*(1), 71–81.

Sage, G. (1989). Becoming a high school coach: from playing sport to coaching. *Research Quarterly for Exercise and Sport, 60*(1), 81–92.

Sarbin, T.R. (1995). Emotional life, rhetoric and roles. *Journal of Narrative and Life History, 5*(3), 213–220.

Saunders, P. (1980). *Urban Politics: a Sociological Interpretation.* Harmondsworth, UK: Penguin.

Saury, J., & Durand, M. (1998). Practical knowledge in expert coaches: on-site study of coaching in sailing. *Research Quarterly for Exercise and Sport, 69*(3), 254–266.

Savater, F. (1997). *El Valor de Educar.* Barcelona: Ariel.

Scheibe, K.E. (1979). *Mirrors, Masks, Lies and Secrets.* New York: Praeger.

Schempp, P.G., & Graber, K.C. (1992). Teacher socialisation from a dialectic perspective: pre-training through induction. *Journal of Teaching in Physical Education, 11,* 329–348.

Schempp, P.G. (1993). Constructing professional knowledge: a case study of an experienced high school teacher. *Journal of Teaching in Physical Education, 13,* 2–23.

Schwalbe, M.L. (1987). Mead among the cognitivists: roles as performance imagery. *Journal for the Theory of Social Behaviour, 17,* 113–133.

Seale, C. (1998). Qualitiative interviewing. In C. Seale (ed.), *Researching Society and Culture,* London: Sage, 202–216.

Secord, P.F., & Backman, C.W. (1974). *Social Psychology* (2nd edn). New York: McGraw-Hill.

Sedgewick, W.A., Cote, J., & Dowd, J. (1997). Confidence building strategies used by Canadian high-level rowing coaches. *Avanate, 3*(3), 80–92.

Shamir, B., House, R.J., & Arthur, M. (1993). The motivational effects of charismatic leadership: a self concept based on theory. *Organizational Science, 4*(4), 577–594.

Shaw, B. (1981). *Educational Practice and Sociology: An Introduction.* Oxford: Oxford University Press.

Shetty, Y.K. (1978). Managerial power and organisational effectiveness: a contingency analysis. *Journal of Management Studies, 15,* 176–186.

Shulman, L.S. (1999). Knowledge and teaching: foundations of the new reform. In J. Leach & B. Moon (eds). *Learners and Pedagogy,* London: Paul Chapman Publishers, 61–77.

Slack, T. (1997). *Understanding Sport Organisations: the Application of Organisation Theory.* Champaign IL: Human Kinetics Publishers.

Snyder, M., & Kiviniemi, M. (2001). Getting what they came for: how power influences the dynamics and outcomes of interpersonal interaction. In A. Lee-Chai & J. Bargh (eds), *The Use and Abuse of Power: Multiple Perspectives on the Causes of Corruption,* Philadelphia: Taylor & Francis, 133–155.

Sparkes, A.C. (1987). Strategic rhetoric: a constraint in changing the practice of teachers. *British Journal of Sociology of Education, 8,* 37–54.

Sparkes, A., & Templin, T. (1992). Life histories and physical education teachers: exploring the meanings of marginality. In A. Sparkes (ed.), *Research in Physical Education and Sport: Exploring Alternative Visions*, London: Falmer Press, 118–145.

Squires, G. (1999). *Teaching as a Professional Discipline*. London: Falmer Press.

Stahelski, A., & Payton, C. (1995). The effects of status cues on choices of social power and influence strategies. *Journal of Social Psychology, 135*(5), 553–560.

Stake, R. (1995). *The Art of Case Study Research*. Thousand Oaks, CA: Sage.

Stein, M.K., Schwan Smith, M., & Silver, E.A. (1999). The development of professional developers: learning to assist teachers in new settings in new ways. *Harvard Educational Review, 69*(3), 237–269.

Stone, E. (2000). Iconoclastes: poor pedagogy. *Journal of Teaching for Education. 26*(1), 93–95.

Strean, W. (1998). Possibilities for qualitative research in sports psychology. *The Sport Psychologist, 12*, 333–345.

Tauber, R.T. (1985). French and Raven's power bases: an appropriate focus for educational researchers and practitioners. Paper presented at the Educational Research Association Craft Knowledge seminar, 12 April, Stirling, UK.

Taylor, C. (1989). *Sources of the Self*. Cambridge: Cambridge University Press.

Thompson, N. (1998). *Promoting Equality: Challenging Discrimination and Oppression in the Human Services*. Basingstoke, UK: Palgrave.

Tomlinson, A. (1998). Power: domination, negotiation and resistance in sports cultures. *Journal of Sport and Social Issues, 22*(3), 235–240.

Troyer, L., Mueller, C.W., & Osinsky, P.I. (2000). Who's the boss? A role-theoretic analysis of customer work. *Work and Occupations, 27*(3), 406–427.

Troyer, L., & Younts, C.W. (1997). Whose expectations matter? The relative power of first- and second-order expectations in determining social influence. *American Journal of Sociology, 103*(3), 692–732.

Ulrich, C., & Walker, L.T. (1982). Sanity in sport. In C. Ulrich (ed.), *Education for the 80's: Physical Education*, Washington, DC: National Educational Association, 70–78.

Van Dyne, L., Cummings, L., & Parks, J. (1995). Extra role behaviours: in pursuit of construct and definitional clarity (a bridge over muddied waters). In B.M. Staw & L.L. Cummings (eds), *Research in Organizational Behaviour*, Greenwich, CT: JAI Press, 215–285.

van Manan, M. (1999). The language of pedagogy and primacy of student experience. In J. Loughran (ed.), *Researching Teaching: Methodologies and Practices for Understanding Pedagogy*, London: Falmer Press, 13–27.

Watkins, C., & Mortimore, P. (1999). Pedagogy: what do we know. In P. Mortimore (ed.), *Understanding Pedagogy*, London: Paul Chapman Publishing, 1–19.

Weber, M. (1978). *The Protestant Ethic and the Spirit of Capitalism*. London: Allen & Unwin.

Williams, R. (1980). Goffman's sociology of talk. In J. Ditton (ed.), *The View from Goffman*, London: Macmillan, 210–232.

Williams, R. (1998). Erving Goffman. In R. Stones (ed.), *Key Sociological Thinkers*, Basingstoke, UK: Macmillan, 151–162.

Wilson, M. (1996). Asking questions. In R. Sapsford & V. Jupp (eds), *Data Collection and Analyses*, London: Sage, 94–120.

Wragg, E.C., Haynes, G.S., Wragg, C.M., & Chamberlin, R.P. (2000). *Failing Teachers?* London: Routledge.

Zimmerman, D. (1970). The practicalities of rule use. In J. Douglas (ed.), *Understanding Everyday Life*, Chicago: Aldine Press, 221–238.

Znaniecki, F.W. (1954). Basic problems of contemporary sociology. *American Sociological Review, 19,* 519–524.

▼ INDEX